>*BASIC*<
HORSEMANSHIP

English · and · Western

>*BASIC*<
HORSEMANSHIP

English · and · Western

ELEANOR F. PRINCE
AND
GAYDELL M. COLLIER

Foreword by William Steinkraus

Drawings by E. F. Prince,
unless otherwise credited
Photographs by the authors,
unless otherwise credited

DOUBLEDAY
NEW YORK   LONDON   TORONTO   SYDNEY   AUCKLAND

To Our Parents and Families

PUBLISHED BY DOUBLEDAY
a division of Bantam Doubleday Dell Publishing Group, Inc.
1540 Broadway, New York, New York 10036

DOUBLEDAY, and the portrayal of an anchor
with a dolphin are trademarks of Doubleday, a division
of Bantam Doubleday Dell Publishing Group, Inc.

Book design by Tasha Hall

Library of Congress Cataloging-in-Publication Data
Prince, Eleanor F.
Basic horsemanship: English and western / by Eleanor F. Prince
and Gaydell M. Collier ; foreword by William Steinkraus ;
drawings by E. F. Prince ; photographs by the authors.
p.   cm.
Includes bibliographical references and index.
1. Horsemanship.   2. Western riding.   I. Collier, Gaydell M.
II. Title.
SF309.P843   1993
798.2—dc20   92-17834
CIP
Library of Congress Catalog Card Number 71-144289
ISBN 0-385-42264-4
Copyright © 1974, 1993 by Gaydell Collier and Eleanor Prince
All Rights Reserved
Printed in the United States of America

5   7   9   10   8   6   4

> F O R E W O R D <

William Steinkraus

It is a common fault among riders, especially novice riders, to be too "seat-conscious." The victims of this preoccupation become so interested in riding a particular seat that they forget to ride the horse, and sacrifice most of the pleasures of riding to the futile search for the perfect seat.

The search is futile because there is, of course, no such thing. The only perfect seat is a perfectly adaptable one, capable of readily assuming the particular attitude and balance that is most appropriate to the situation at hand. In this sense, anyone who is interested in riding well must seek to acquire not so much a perfect seat as a useful collection of seats, one large enough to include something appropriate for most ordinary types of horses and riding problems.

In the days when the great cavalry schools of the world were the main fonts of equestrian wisdom, major emphasis used to be placed on the benefits to be derived from sampling a variety of riding experiences. Young officers were urged if not obliged to supplement their "duty" riding with fox hunting, 'chasing, polo, and eventing, and the best of them emerged with an ability to ride just about anything on four legs and make a pretty decent job of it.

I think they proved the point. In my own case, I happen to have spent most of my riding career in some form of what is customarily termed the hunter seat, but I've spent a lot of time in other ones, too. I've galloped race horses, shown saddle horses, "ponied" horses from a Western saddle, and dropped my stirrups down to ride dressage, and I'm certain that each of these experiences has contributed something to my overall technique.

Hence, I could hardly be more sympathetic to the basic approach of this fine newly revised book. I agree with Eleanor Prince and Gay Collier that it is not only possible but advantageous to learn and teach both English and Western riding more or less together, and I am certain that the rider who learns early in life to appreciate the broad common ground they share will already be much closer to understanding what riding is really all about. The authors are to be congratulated for presenting this sound yet novel thesis so sensibly and persuasively.

> A C K N O W L E D G M E N T S <

Our very special thanks . . .

  to A. R. Gaydell for reviewing the early manuscript and offering suggestions,

  to William Steinkraus for his help with preliminary organization and focus, and for contributing his comments on the final manuscript,

  to Richard Beck for reviewing the final manuscript and writing comments,

  to Jenny Collier, Leslie Turner, and other Sodergreen Horsemanship School girls who posed endlessly for "just one more photo,"

  to Jean L. Maier, Margaret Everett, and Frank H. Collier for their help in preparing the manuscript,

  to Herb Pownall, John Henberg, and the University of Wyoming Photo Service for their assistance and special care in preparing our photographs,

  to Ellin K. Roberts, our editor, for her help, encouragement, and endless patience, and

  to all our friends—both human and equine—who have made this book possible.

ELEANOR F. PRINCE
GAYDELL M. COLLIER

> ACKNOWLEDGMENTS <

For the Second Edition

Special thanks also . . .

- to Lisa Puraty and Kirsten Springer Ingebrigtsen for setting up and posing for photographs,
- to the 1991 Sodergreen Horsemanship School students for "time out" from lessons for photographs,
- to Teri Hallman for providing a dressage photo,
- to Linda Nelson for information on therapeutic riding,
- to the American Quarter Horse Association and the American Horse Shows Association, for permission to reprint tests and patterns,
- to Dr. Conrad J. Kercher, professor of animal science, University of Wyoming, for information on nutrition, and
- to Carol Altaffer and Wyoming Photo Express, Devils Tower, Wyoming, for their special efforts and fine work in preparing our photographs.

EFP—GMC
March 1992

>CONTENTS<

CHAPTER II   BEGINNING HORSEMANSHIP— THE FIRST LESSON   18

CHAPTER IX   JUMPING

>INTRODUCTION<

Understanding is the essence of harmonious horsemanship. Anyone may climb on a horse and with a little practice manage to stay there; but without understanding, harmonious horsemanship is almost impossible.

Understanding is a distillation of knowledge and experience. It is the comprehension of how and why a horse behaves or reacts, and what you should do to motivate the behavior or counteract the reaction. With understanding as a basis, you will work consistently with kindness, confidence, and ability.

Learn about horses, and you will learn more about riding. In *Basic Horsemanship: English and Western* we are trying to establish, from your very first lesson in riding, a basis for continuing on to a full and intelligent understanding of horses. This is the book's primary purpose—to offer the reader a solid foundation for continuing on to advanced or specialized equitation, whether it be dressage, hunting, cutting contests, or just plain enjoyment.

It is written for the adult student who is teaching himself or his children to ride, or for the teenager who rides alone or with friends. With this in mind, we have tried to present the step-by-step instructions as clearly as possible.

The book is also written as a guide for riding instructors. It will be useful for the accomplished rider who would like to instruct but doesn't quite know how to begin, and also for the experienced instructor who may wish to check his own qualifications or expose himself to new ideas and to the latest in safety rules and devices.

Finally, it is our purpose in this book to present the whole of the American riding scene as it is today. We emphasize the similarity of English and Western horsemanship, give both styles in detail, and underscore the advantages of each for various purposes. The fact that Western horsemanship has become popular in the East, especially for casual riding, and that English horsemanship is now frequently seen throughout the West, especially at horse shows, emphasizes the point that for modern American horsemen there is something to gain from each style.

Fig. 1   "Looking at you as though he has plans for you. . . ."

If You Are a Beginning Student

Beginning to ride, like the beginning of any endeavor, is a special moment in your life. Perhaps you have looked forward to this moment for a long time, and envision yourself accepting a blue ribbon in the show ring, or flying over fences at a hunt, or meeting with ease any obstacle along a trail.

Then perhaps you take another look at the large animal in front of you and you unconsciously wonder if you're really strong enough to manage such a beast. Right now he's looking at you as though he has plans for you—or if his eyes are half closed, maybe he's just trying to lull you into complacency so that he can dump you with style.

In short, perhaps you are a bit apprehensive, as with any new adventure. That's why your first few riding experiences can be so important: either you will be thrilled and elated, looking forward to the next ride with enthusiasm; or you will be discouraged and throw up your hands at the whole business.

And so we start at the very beginning—by taking the time to get to know your horse. Horsemanship consists of much more than merely perching in the saddle. You should understand your horse and realize that it is not your strength that controls him. You should know *why* you are learning to ride in this particular way.

The lessons beginning in Chapter II have been carefully integrated to get you off to a good start. You will learn the first basic steps in horsemanship, building confidence in yourself and in your horse. And you will begin your groundwork in reading as a basis for all-around knowledge and understanding.

Take your time and keep at it constantly and consistently. If you have your own horse, you are able to ride a little every day. But even if you can ride only once a week, work consistently and without rushing. You should feel confident in all phases of one lesson before going on to the next.

You should have a steady, reliable horse. And by all means have a helper for the first lessons. Even if the helper has never seen a horse before, you can read through the pertinent part of the lesson together and go on from there. Remember that good horsemanship is based on a solid foundation of basic skills and an understanding of basic safety rules for both yourself and your horse. You can't do algebra before you can add 2 and 2. So don't hurry, do keep at it, do check constantly with the book, and above all, enjoy yourself!

If You Are an Intermediate or Advanced Student

You know how to ride well, you have developed a good seat, and you have light hands. What can this basic course in riding hold for you?

This basic approach may improve your understanding of the principles behind riding: the reasons for doing things as you have learned to do them. Or, in comparing these methods with your own, you will broaden your concept of good horsemanship. Perhaps you are thinking of training a horse yourself. It will be easier for you and better for your horse if you understand coordinated methods of riding and training.

Perhaps most important to today's American horseman is the opportunity to broaden his versatility and riding experience by becoming proficient in both English and Western equitation.

In any case, your horse as a pleasure animal will benefit from his increased versatility and become a better companion—more interested and more interesting—as new horizons are opened. Increased understanding between you and your horse unfolds as you work and train together. And through understanding, your goal of harmonious horsemanship is more readily attainable.

If You Are an Instructor

After each part of a lesson, there is a note to the instructor, indicating ways to clarify points, problems to watch for, safety rules, and teaching methods. If you are an experienced instructor, you may find some helpful new ideas; the diagrams and study suggestions in the appendixes may be useful in your teaching program.

If you are a new instructor, using this book as your text, you will want to understand the entire lesson from your student's viewpoint. This arrangement of material gives you the entire first lessons in a coordinated, detailed, and easily understood way.

Most important, you may wish to broaden your present riding program by adding Western (or English) equitation. These lessons will help if you are not thoroughly familiar with the other system of riding. Because responsibility will promote good behavior in your student, do not do everything for him. After demonstrating, let him try for himself.

If You Want to Be an Instructor

Not everyone can be an instructor, nor should everyone be. Instructing is not easy. How do you know whether or not *you* can instruct?

You should like people, especially children, and you should enjoy teaching them. Further, you should love horses and be able to impart this love to others.

You must be a good horseman and a confident example to your students. It will help to have a natural, calm authority that inspires their confidence in you and in themselves. Your voice, by its tone and emphasis, will command, calm, reassure, or reprimand rider or horse.

You should be able to adapt your timing and teaching methods to each individual pupil, to evaluate him accurately, and to give him just the right horse at each stage of development. It will be helpful to have the ability to organize effectively, to make decisions quickly and accurately, to anticipate trouble and prepare for it, to make clear, concise explanations, and to mete out impartial criticism.

A sense of humor is vital, and of course you must have patience and self-control in heroic proportions. There is never any excuse (though there are a million provocations) for losing your temper when working with students or horses.

If You Are Looking for an Instructor

As a student, you should be concerned with the credentials of your instructor. Answering the following questions will help you choose and evaluate an instructor.

1. Does your instructor demonstrate a sense of security by showing professionalism in demeanor and apparel? Is he organized and safety-conscious?
2. Is your instructor mature, responsible, and sensitive? Is he experienced in all aspects of stable management and able to teach the discipline you choose to learn? Does he demonstrate as he teaches, thus inspiring the students to make progress?
3. Is the stable where your instructor works safe and clean? Do the horses look well fed and well cared for? Is tack safe and clean? Is it properly and conveniently stored?
4. Is the instructor trained in first aid (with a first aid kit available)? Does he require his students to wear safety helmets and riding boots?
5. Does the instructor teach a structured lesson with short- and long-term goals? Does he use lesson plans?
6. Are release slips for students required? (See sample release forms in Appendix C.)
7. Most important of all, is your instructor understanding and patient with his students? Does he seem flexible and sensitive to their needs as well as to the needs of his horses?

Reading About Riding

Riding is one of the most satisfying of all sports. It can be even more enjoyable when you know something about horses and the world of horsemen. Horse lore encompasses many different fields of knowledge, and there are books covering every phase of the subject.

By reading, you will learn about horses and you gain a bit of vicarious experience. The better your understanding, the better rider you are apt to be.

Second, you broaden your knowledge by reading, and may develop an interest in a particular phase of advanced horsemanship. This will encourage you to think more deeply about why you ride in a particular way and how you can communicate most effectively with your horse.

Finally, by reading you learn about other schools of riding and about the different methods and ideas of horsemen. There are dramatic contradictions in the theory of horsemanship, even more in practice. Different schools of riding may even employ opposite methods to attain the same result. Each is backed by sound reasoning, or at least by what someone has considered sound. Tolerance and understanding of another person's methods help you to be a better and more complete horseman.

The list of recommended books we have included may be used to follow an organized reading plan, or might help you to find the practical information you may need on selecting a horse, management, feeding, breeding, foaling, or other relevant problems.

Instructors may wish to suggest weekly reading or home-study assignments for older students who are interested and will benefit from it. Intensified programs at summer camps and horsemanship schools should make full use of resource material (see Appendix D).

Please remember that the methods we present are not the only methods of teaching riding—far from it. In the all-encompassing field of horses there are many differing schools of thought; we have tried to point out some of these in the selected references. We are presenting here those methods that, for over forty years of experience, have proved *for us* to be the most effective, practical, and conducive to an intelligent understanding of horses, *most of the time*. Different horses, different students, different conditions all have their effect, and this is why no one can ever learn all there is to know about riding. It's what makes riding a continuing challenge.

>*BASIC*<
*H*ORSEMANSHIP

English · and · Western

The Gaits and the Seat

Part 1 · The Gaits

When a horse trots, exactly what is he doing with his legs and feet? Why do the walk, the trot, and the canter or lope *feel* so different to a rider? Why is a horse less apt to slip on slick ground when he is trotting than when he is cantering?

A thorough technical knowledge of the action of each gait will help you to improve your position in the saddle and to learn your best application of the aids. You will have a better understanding of the usefulness and limitations of each gait, and you will see how each one affects the stabilization of the horse.

The Walk

The walk is a four-beat gait in which each hoofbeat is heard separately. Listen to the sound of the gait: da-DUM, da-DUM, da-DUM, da-DUM. Each movement is performed in a definite order: the first beat is made by the right hind foot, followed by the right fore, then left hind, and the fourth beat is by the left fore.

The walk should be cadenced, brisk, and relaxed. The rider's position during the walk is essentially the same as at the halt; however, in responding

The walk. (Kirsten Ingebrigtsen riding Reveille, owned by Bob Doherty)

to the motion, his body will be more elastic. When riding the Western seat, the walk should be brisk, free-moving, and rhythmical. A little less contact with the horse's mouth is customary, but there should not be a "sloppy" rein.

The walk calls for less muscular and nervous tension than do the other gaits, and therefore is less important than the trot or canter in developing the muscles of both horse and rider. Because of this, the walk is relaxing and of a rewarding nature for both horse and rider. In training the horse, the walk calms and reenergizes. The instructor uses the walk while explaining some new concept, allowing both horse and rider to recover wind and enthusiasm for the next maneuver. On the trail, the effect of the walk is to quiet and reassure the horse—especially if he is inexperienced—when encountering strange objects or noises.

The walk is a very stable gait because the horse is always supported by at least two legs; that is, at no time does he lose contact with the ground. Therefore, it is the safest gait to use when the footing is bad. When the horse is walking, there is little danger of him slipping on ice, mud, or wet leaves. At the walk, the horse is balanced and can turn easily, while the rider can easily stay balanced and confident.

The head and neck of the horse at the walk and canter are of particular interest to the rider. Watch a horse walk (or canter) and you will see his head and neck move rhythmically, forward and back. When riding, your hands should give and take with this movement and not restrict this freedom of the head.

The Trot, Slow Trot, and Jog

The trot is an even, two-beat gait and sounds like this: DUM, DUM, DUM, DUM. The horse alternately places the two diagonal pairs of feet on the ground. After each pair strikes the ground, there is a moment of suspension during which there is no contact with the ground. But in spite of the moment of suspension, the trot is a stable gait. It is the most regular and rhythmical, and the most easily balanced for both horse and rider.

The normal trot develops muscles throughout the body of the horse and especially in his legs. Trotting up and down hills helps to strengthen the hindquarters of young horses. The trot will exercise a high-spirited and/or insecure horse, when he may be too excitable for control at a faster gait, or when the walk may quiet him but does not give enough exercise to work him out. If the riding ring or trail is slightly muddy, the slow trot may be used because the horse is well balanced and there is not as much danger of him slipping. The horse will tend to stay more alert than at a walk. This is especially true at the posting trot, and he will also naturally carry himself in his best manner.

The trot.

Since there is little motion in the horse's upper body at the trot, the rider tends to stiffen his back. This is in contrast to the walk and lope, both of which contribute to suppleness of the back. Riders often sit the slow trot and rise (post) to the normal trot. The reason for posting is to make the faster trot more enjoyable to both horse and rider. It is customary to post to the outside diagonal when riding in a ring; that is, to rise as the horse's outside shoulder and leg move forward. For example, when trotting to the left (or posting to the right diagonal), the rider rises as the horse's right (outside) shoulder and leg move forward and sits again as the right shoulder and leg come back.

Why should you post to a given diagonal? When trotting in a circle, the outside legs of the horse are describing a larger circle than the inside legs. By posting we tend to relieve the outside muscles, helping the horse to improve his balance and to develop his muscles an equal amount on both sides. If you were to ride a horse whose previous riders had posted to only one diagonal, you would notice one diagonal to be distinctly more rough and uneven than the other. (Riding experts do not all agree that it is best to post on the outside diagonal—some say it helps the horse more to post on the inside diagonal. This is a matter of debate, however. In English equitation classes in the United States, it is customary and correct to post on the outside diagonal.)

On the trail or when traveling in a straight line, it does not matter which diagonal you take, but change it often so as not to tire your horse.

In Western riding the term "jog" or "jog trot" is used instead of "slow trot" or "trot." The jog is usually a bit slower than the slow trot. Some horse-show judges prefer a "collected" jog; some, a faster jog. (These terms are defined in the glossary.) The faster jog would normally be used on the trail because it is a more relaxed gait, and because the horse's head is lower and therefore in a better position to see irregularities of the ground. As a rule, the collected jog would be better used in the show ring, where impulsion, presence, and carriage of the horse are more important.

The Canter, Gallop, and Lope

The canter is a natural three-beat gait. It sounds this way: ba-da-DUM, ba-da-DUM. When on the right lead, the sequence of hoofbeats is: near-hind, off-hind and near-fore together, off-fore, and period of suspension. Because the three beats of the gait are not executed equally by the right and left legs, it is possible to have the opposite pattern of hoofbeats. In this case the horse is on the left lead, and the sequence is: off-hind, near-hind and off-fore together, near-fore, and suspension.

Although the gallop is essentially the same gait, it has four beats: ba-da-la-DUM, ba-da-la-DUM. The sequence of the beats on a right lead is: (first beat) near-hind, near-hind and (second beat) off-hind, off-hind and (third beat) near-fore, near-fore alone, near-fore and (fourth beat) off-fore, off-fore alone, and period of suspension.

The canter should be balanced and collected; that is, the horse's weight should be supported about equally by the hindquarters and the forehand. To accomplish this, his hind legs must be well under him, not trailing behind. At the canter the horse is not truly straight. His spine, from head to tail, is flexed to one side or the other (depending on direction), so as to be slightly and evenly arched.

As at the trot, the horse when cantering should develop his muscles equally on both sides. Most horses have a natural preference for either the left or the right lead. If they are given no specific direction, many horses will almost always canter on the preferred lead. This tends to develop muscles on one side only, allowing the horse to become stiff on the other side. It is important for this tendency to be corrected early in their training by giving extra practice on the unfavored lead, thereby developing all-around suppleness.

To recognize which lead the horse is taking, watch the forefeet (if you are watching the horse from the ground), or glance down at the shoulders if you are mounted. In the recurring pattern of the canter, the left foot (and

The canter or lope, right lead. (Kirsten Ingebrigtsen riding Reveille.)

The canter or lope, left lead.

shoulder) always reaches farther ahead than the right when on the left lead. (This may appear as though the left foreleg has started the pattern of the canter. Actually the canter begins with a hind leg and this in turn initiates the takeoff of the opposite foreleg. On a left lead, it is the right hind leg that initiates the three-beat pattern.)

Do not confuse leads and diagonals. Remember to keep in mind that at the canter to the left, the horse is on the left lead. At the trot to the left, the rider posts on the outside, or right, diagonal.

Work at the canter will supple the young horse's back and loins. And this, of course, will also help to improve his trot. He will also develop in balance, control (responsiveness to the aids), and confidence in his rider.

The lope is the Western term for the canter. It should be a "rocking chair" gait. In Western equitation classes, horse and rider tend to appear more relaxed than in English equitation. There is usually not as much emphasis on collection.

Under Western working conditions, a fast lope may be called for suddenly to check bolting calves or for other reasons. Working cowhorses are usually ridden with a more severe bit and loose rein. Here form often takes second place to getting the job done. A good cowhorse will have developed balance (he'll use the correct lead naturally), timing, and "cow sense." He can think like a cow, anticipate her moves, and be prepared for them with little help from the rider. In fact, the rider uses a loose rein so as not to interfere with his horse.

Fig. 2 "Rein-pulling and leg-thumping. . . ."

Part 2 · The Seat

Before actually beginning our lessons, it is important to have in mind, as a kind of thought picture, the ideal position that you will want to achieve, or have your students achieve. When you are sitting on a horse correctly, how will you look? Exactly how will you carry your body or hold your hands or place your feet?

The rider's position, as he sits on a horse, is called the "seat." You will see several different recognized seats used in horse shows, and a number of entirely original (and horrendous) seats on dude trail rides, public bridle paths, and wherever the climb-on-and-ride amateurs take off for a Sunday afternoon of rein-pulling and leg-thumping.

We use the Basic Seat (also known as the Balanced Seat) and its variation, the modern Western Seat. The Basic Seat is widely used today because it is fundamental and all-purpose. Other seats, such as the Classic Seat, the

Forward Seat, and the Saddle Seat, are used for specific reasons by American horsemen, and may be studied when a rider chooses to specialize in that style of riding.

The Basic Seat

The Basic Seat may be considered a fundamental seat for all forms of riding. Master the Basic Seat and you may then go on to other seats as you desire. When speaking of the Basic Seat, we are usually referring to the seat as used in English-style equitation. However, the Western Seat as we teach it, and as it is judged in Western equitation classes today, is simply a modification of the Basic Seat. Although we will discuss it separately later, the same set of principles applies equally to English and to modern Western riding.

When riding the Basic Seat, you remain in balance with your horse. Your position changes so as to maintain equilibrium with your horse. Or, to put it another way, you adapt your position either to the extension or collection of your horse. In collected gaits, the center of gravity of the horse shifts toward his hindquarters, and the rider holds his body upright in the saddle. As the horse turns, the rider maintains balance over the horse's center of gravity by pressure of the inside seat bone in accordance with the degree of turn. When the horse breaks into an extended gallop, his center of gravity moves forward, and the rider leans forward to maintain equilibrium.

Why is this desirable? Because this is the easiest way to achieve harmony between horse and rider. The rider is in balance; he is "with" his horse; therefore, he is secure. He is relaxed (a stiff seat is insecure), but ready for any change in gait or unexpected movement of the horse. Security leads to control. Because the rider is balanced, he is best able to make use of the aids—in short, to communicate with his horse.

This harmony of balance is desirable for the horse as well as for the rider. Because the horse is in balance himself, and because he is not hampered by an off-balance weight on his back, he is best able to do the job you want him to do. He is immediately ready to respond to the aids, to carry out his part in the harmony of communication. And finally, the Basic Seat is a very flexible seat, adaptable for any type of riding.

An Overall View of the Basic Seat—English Equitation

First, let's look at the overall picture of the Basic Seat while at the halt. The horse is balanced—his weight is evenly distributed on all four feet; his neck and head are naturally alert and in line with his body.

The rider's weight is also evenly distributed and does not hinder the horse: the rider is sitting on the strongest and deepest part of the horse's back (directly behind the withers). The saddle, whether English or Western, must be a type that puts the rider into the correct position over the horse's center of gravity. (Most cut-back saddles, for instance, tend to place the rider behind the center of gravity; many Western saddles, because of the slope of the seat, also tend to throw the rider's weight back.) The seat of the saddle should fit the rider; one that is too long or too short may not make you uncomfortable, but either one will keep you from taking the proper position in the saddle. The correct adjustment (length) of the stirrups is also important.

The rider looks alert, relaxed, supple, with a strong and secure seat. In short, he and the horse look comfortable and unified. This makes it possible for the rider to use his aids efficiently.

Good horsemanship entails understanding, patience, and love; in short, mental equilibrium as well as physical equilibrium.

The Basic Seat in Detail

Breaking down the overall picture of the Basic Seat, let's start from the top down, using the position with the horse at the halt.

Your head should be up with your eyes looking ahead. Not only will your whole body be better balanced, but you can see what is ahead of your horse and be ready.

Your shoulders should be square and comfortable, and your arms should hang naturally to your elbow. Your elbow acts as a fulcrum—you want to have a direct, straight line from the horse's bit along the reins to the elbow. Your upper body should be erect, supple, and balanced over your feet, adjusting to the speed and direction of your horse.

Your hands should be quiet, separated about two inches evenly across the withers, with equal contact on the reins. Keep wrists straight and flexible. Your hands may form a "roof" over the horse's withers—that is, be parallel to the withers (see page 12).* The height of the hands depends somewhat on the horse's head carriage, but should be as low as possible. The reins go up through the hands and across the palms.

The buttocks, with muscles relaxed, rest in the middle of the saddle. You are chiefly supported by the two seat bones. Your thighs should point toward

---

*Experienced horsemen prefer to keep their hands vertical, the thumbs on top and the wrists straight. However, beginners using this method are often apt to hold their hands too high, use their hands too strongly, and stiffen their wrists. The "roof" method, in which the hands are kept parallel to the withers, usually encourages flexibility and gentleness in the beginning student.

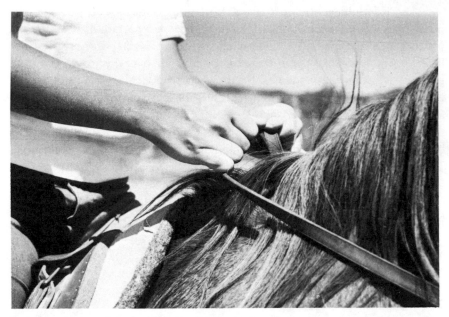

Beginner position of the hands in English equitation: the hands form a "roof" over the withers. After the first lessons, the rein should pass between the fourth and fifth fingers; at first, however, this method gives more control, especially with young, small-handed students.

Correct position of the legs and feet.

the horse's shoulder and be in close, light contact with your horse. Your knees should be turned in against your horse so that there is no space showing between knee and saddle (when looking from the front or rear)—in other words, there should be contact from the lower calf of the leg up through the thigh. The ankle and side of the knee are in line with your horse's center of gravity. Carry the lower leg back so that the knee and toe are in line. The heel is pushed well down and the ball of the foot rests on the inside of the stirrup iron (so that part of the underside of the foot can be seen by someone standing on the ground). Avoid driving the foot "home" (middle or arch of foot rests on stirrup), although some riders do this in jumping. Much more flexibility is obtained from a stirrup placed under the ball of the foot.

The toes should be turned at approximately a 45-degree angle out from the center line of the horse. A 90-degree angle destroys the knee contact; toes parallel to the horse minimize the calf contact and tend to stiffen the ankle. When the correct seat is achieved, an imaginary line can be drawn vertically from ear through shoulder, hip, and ankle.

The Western Seat

The modern Western Seat may be considered a modification of the Basic Seat. It should *not* be confused with the TV Western Seat, where the rider sits back on the cantle, legs straight and feet forward, slouched with rounded shoulders and dangling reins at a slow gait, hunched forward with elbows flapping at a gallop.

Again, let's start by taking an overall view of the Western Seat.

Tall in the saddle! An often-used phrase describing Western riding, it's nevertheless a good one. Your head is held high and proud; your heels are down. You tend to look more relaxed than in the English saddle, but you must maintain an alert manner. The same principles follow for Western and English equitation. (Be sure, therefore, to read and study English as well as Western.) Your weight placement and balance should be the same and your body will adjust to the horse's gaits just as in English. Of course, there are some changes in style, so again we'll start from the top down in describing the Western position.

Head should be up; chin in a normal position, eyes straight ahead, shoulders square. The trunk of your body should be straight but relaxed. Keep your shoulders and body balanced and straight (at a 90-degree angle to the center line of the horse). Your arms should hang naturally from the shoulder as in English. Your left arm is bent at the elbow, and your left hand (if you are right-handed) holds the reins as low as possible. However, because of the saddle horn, it may be necessary to hold the reins somewhat higher

Fig. 3   The Western Basic Seat.

than in English. (Some Western riders maintain that the rein hand should not be carried in front of the horn; however, much depends on how the horse carries his head and on the rider's build.) The reins should be held so as to maintain light contact with the horse's mouth.

Your right elbow is slightly bent in order to rest the right hand on the right thigh. It is important to keep this hand in continual contact with your thigh; a hand flopping up and down does nothing for your general appearance. It also will tend to throw you off balance, and make your body lopsided in the saddle. This is a serious fault which may cause your rein hand to move too far forward.

There are other right-hand positions. In one, the elbow is bent and the right hand is held close to (but not touching) the belt buckle; only experienced Western riders should consider this method, because the hand can move around (out of position) too easily. Another position is with the right arm straight down at the side; this method has the same problems as above if the rider's seat is insecure. If you are left-handed, you may use your right hand on the reins and keep your left hand on your thigh. (You must also keep your rope on the left side of the saddle in the show ring, instead of on the right where it normally goes.) You should not switch hands on the reins.

Keep your feet under you with your heels low and your feet close to the horse. The stirrups will be somewhat longer than in English, but you want a flexed knee rather than a straight leg. Although a Western saddle does

Fig. 4 Standard method of holding the reins.

Fig. 5 California style—the romal is held in the right hand.

somewhat hamper the flexibility of the legs, still the legs are used actively in the same way as in English.

There are two generally accepted ways of holding the reins. In the Rocky Mountain area the "standard" method is usually used. The reins are held as shown in Figure 4. You may keep one finger between the reins when using the standard method. This is a natural position that allows for full flexibility of the wrist.

In the California method the reins come up through the fist position from the bottom, with romal hanging down on the off side of the horse. It is customary to use braided reins while riding California style (see Figure 5), and the free hand may hold the romal (at least sixteen inches from the rein hand).

Since judges are influenced somewhat by the traditional practice in that locality, it is usually best to adopt the method that is most common in your area.

There are fads in the show ring as well as in the fashion field. From time to time the California method is popular. Used with braided headstall and reins, romal, rope, and hobbles, it is considered showy and neat. Fads can change quickly, and what might be "in" one year may well be "out" the next. It is wise to check with the current *AHSA* or *American Quarter Horse Rule Book* (or other authority, depending on the show) before entering a class.

As we discuss the Basic Seat in the pages that follow, remember that what is said may be applied to either English or Western equitation. You are essentially concentrating on the Basic Seat, whichever method you prefer to use. For a complete understanding of basic riding, be sure to read *both* the English and Western presentations.

Unsaying What's Been Said

Proper position is important. Usually the best results are achieved when your position conforms to the standard. This is because position serves as a foundation for harmonious horsemanship. But harmonious horsemanship sometimes exceeds the bounds of technical perfection. Occasionally there's a square hole into which you'll have to pound your round peg.

What if the placid animal you're riding is suddenly startled by a jackrabbit, rears up a little, takes the bit in his teeth, and then comes down in an all-out gallop? Your flexible, gentle hands are helpless because this is an abnormal situation requiring a pulley-rein or other strong method of control.

Or, if your horse unexpectedly takes off early into a five-foot jump, the beauty of your classic form may be blown to the winds. Your flying feet and unorthodox seat are of little importance so long as you are not interfering with the horse in his efforts to clear the jump.

Usually what is theoretically correct and what is the best thing to do at the time are one and the same. But be alert to extenuating circumstances. The fact that horses are not computerized machines is one of their greatest glories.

Fig. 6 "An abnormal situation. . . ."

Part 3 · Resources to Aid the Instructor

Creative instructors use varied teaching tools to help the progress of their students. Prepare thoroughly for each demonstration: the resource must fit the lesson and further the goal and purpose of the class. Using the following resources alone or in combination will make your lessons exciting and innovative. Encourage your students to contribute and participate.

Handouts encourage the students and help tie in specific information with the practical aspect of the class—a good reinforcement.

Chalkboards are easily seen by a group, and can be prepared before class or used during a lecture to illustrate points.

Charts, posters, calendars, and pictures—hung in strategic places such as the tack room or lecture area—are not only decorative but will teach and reinforce your lessons. The horse's anatomy, gaits (footfalls), and parts of tack are some examples. Future events and competition results can be marked on large, colorful calendars.

Videos and slides can be selected to reinforce previous lessons or to introduce new ones. They are educational as well as entertaining. Using a video camera to record a student's performance during a series of lessons—beginning, middle, and end—will show progress and pinpoint areas that need further work.

Books and periodicals should be available for students to browse through or study. If possible, a library of horse books should be available for reference (at the stable complex) to help with assigned reports, for information, or for comparing techniques. Include works representative of all aspects and schools of horsemanship as well as current popular horse magazines. Other up-to-date reference works, such as rule books of the American Horse Shows Association and American Quarter Horse Association, should be available at all times. Encourage students to become familiar with them, especially when preparing for competition.

Visiting professionals inspire students, give current and specialized information, and add an element of interest and variety to your instruction. These might include veterinarians, farriers, trainers, successful exhibitors, authors, or other authorities.

Actual stable tools, grooming aids, tack, training and safety devices, and other "show-and-tell" items can be used to coordinate with handouts.

The appendixes in the back of this book give resources and references that can be copied to use as handouts or in any way desired by the instructor.

CHAPTER TWO

Beginning Horsemanship

The First Lesson

Now we are ready to begin the actual lessons. The first lesson is divided into three parts—in the stall, at the crosstie, and in the corral—with time out to discuss tack and equipment. Remember, a good beginning is like a promise made; the accomplishment and joy of riding, a promise kept.

Part 1 · In the Stall

Knowing Your Horse

Your horse is in a large box stall in the barn or stable. You have selected him with the help of an experienced horseman as a steady, reliable, and knowledgeable mount. He will, in effect, teach you to ride. But first you must make the proper beginning. You want to get to know him, and you want to give him the opportunity to get used to you and your voice.

Speak to your horse, and pat him as he comes over to the stall door or gate.

INSTRUCTOR: *Introduce the horse to your student, and encourage the child to pet him. (In a class situation, make sure that each child has a chance to pet the horse and to perform the succeeding directions individ-*

ually.) The importance of a good beginning cannot be overemphasized. By first introducing the horse, by encouraging the student to become acquainted with him, handle him, and understand him, any fears or anxieties the child may feel are quieted. Often a student may be especially apprehensive because of a previous unfortunate experience. But with this gradual introduction to the horse, the student is in the right frame of mind when the time comes to mount. He is ready and eager to learn. His attention is on this horse now, not on what happened once upon a time.

This introduction is equally important for the exuberant child who is overeager to get on and go. It will help him to understand that a horse has personality and feelings, and that he cannot be treated as an inanimate machine.

Introducing the horse to the child—a good beginning.

Haltering Your Horse

Hold the halter in your left hand with the lead shank over your right shoulder. This leaves your right hand free to open the stall gate. Open the gate, enter (making sure you have the horse's attention), and close the gate behind you. Stand at the horse's near side and put on the halter. In horseman's terminology, the left side of the horse is always the "near" side and the right is the "off" side.

Holding the halter correctly (lead rope over shoulder) leaves a hand free to open a gate. It also leaves you prepared to halter the horse. In your left hand, hold the halter by its nosepiece and crownpiece (part placed behind the ears), as shown. Reach under the horse's throat with your left hand (holding the halter), and at the same time reach over his neck with your right hand (thus encircling his neck). Take the end of the crownpiece with your right hand. Lower the nosepiece (left hand) and place it up over the horse's nose. Raise the halter into position (approximately 2 inches below the cheekbone) and fasten the crownpiece. If this student intends to ride, she should be dressed appropriately with helmet and boots.

INSTRUCTOR: *For this lesson choose your steadiest and most reliable beginner horse. He is absolutely gentle and nothing in the world would induce him to kick, shy, or otherwise put your student in a dangerous position. Nevertheless, the child should learn safety measures from the first. If he understands that a horse is easily frightened, he will remember to speak to him when approaching, and to approach from the near side—never directly from behind.*

Show both rope and leather halters to your student and let him handle them. Select the one you plan to use and show him how to fasten it. Have him fasten and unfasten it several times. Then ask him to watch

A leather halter (left) and a rope halter. Web halters are constructed like the leather halter.

carefully while you demonstrate: enter the stall, halter the horse, lead him out of the stall, turn him around, and lead him back into the stall. Then remove the halter and have the student repeat your actions. Help him to hold the halter correctly and to put it on the horse properly. If the child is too young to reach, hold him up so that he can buckle the halter. Doing everything himself that he can do will help to give him confidence in himself and his horse.

Leading Your Horse

Hold the leadrope in your right hand a foot or so from the halter. The bight of the lead rope should be folded so as to form a figure-eight and held in your left hand (see page 22). When the rope is held in this way, it combines a maximum of control with a maximum of safety. If the horse should bolt and you are unable to hold him, there are no loops to entangle your hands or feet, which might drag you or otherwise injure you.

You are standing on the horse's near side. Now lead him out of the stall and down the aisle. Keep well to his left—don't get in front of him. He should move along with you, his shoulder about even with, or slightly behind, your shoulder.

The length of lead shank you use depends upon your height, the horse's

Leading the horse correctly.

height, where you are leading the horse, and the temperament of the horse himself. The length should give you maximum control, and yet be natural and comfortable for you and the horse.

INSTRUCTOR: *Explain to the child why you lead the horse in this way. He should understand that this is safe, sensible conduct and also that it is correct showmanship.*

Turning Your Horse

If you have enough room, you can lead your horse in a circle to the right to turn him. In this way, you walk a larger circle around the horse, and there is no danger of being stepped on. More often, though, you will find space limited, and you'll have to turn the horse around in his stall, or in a narrow aisle.

Stand facing the horse's side. Turn him around by pulling on the halter shank with your left hand as you push his hindquarters away from you with your right hand.

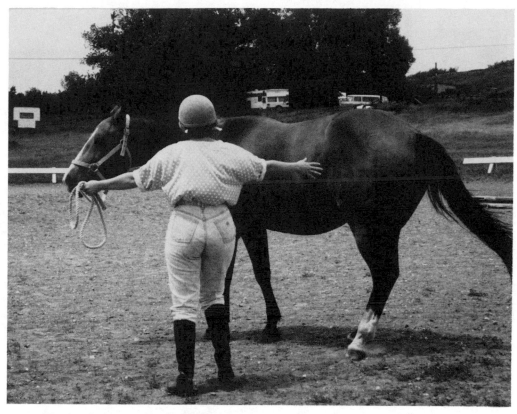

Turning the horse around safely.

INSTRUCTOR: *This method is the best we've found for keeping little feet from under the horse's hoofs. Emphasize to youngsters the importance of keeping out of the way. "The horse would not step on you on purpose, but look—when turning like this he can't see where he's putting his feet."*

Remind your student to watch out for the horse's hindquarters and not bang them by turning too sharply when going through a narrow opening.

Help your student to turn the horse, to return him to his stall so that he is facing the gate, and to remove the halter. Then have him repeat the whole process again, alone if he is able, giving help or correcting faults only where necessary. If it seems necessary, let him do this several times until he has mastered the technique and proceeds with confidence. Then have him lead the horse to the crosstie.

Part 2 · At the Crosstie

Using the Crosstie

The crosstie consists of two ropes (or sometimes chains), each with a snap in one end and the other end attached to opposite walls or posts. When both clips are snapped into the ring of the halter, the two ropes run as one line between the two walls, with the horse's head at the center.

Lead the horse to the crosstie and fasten the snaps.

INSTRUCTOR: *Explain the reasons for using the crosstie:*

1. *It keeps the horse in one position—he can not move forward, back, or to the side, yet he is not unduly restricted or uncomfortable.*
2. *It allows the handler to move around the horse easily to groom him, care for his feet, and saddle him.*

At an outdoor crosstie.

The Grooming Shelf and the Grooming Tools

Grooming removes the dirt from the horse's hair, stimulates his skin, and aids in general circulation. The grooming tools are kept together on a shelf convenient to the crosstie. When grooming your horse, use the tools always in the same order, so that he will come to expect each phase of the grooming. Clean the tools briefly before returning them to the shelf.

A horse usually enjoys grooming. If he does not, chances are that he has been groomed very little or that he has been handled roughly. Establish a regular time for grooming and always do it in exactly the same way. Talk to him pleasantly while you are grooming him.

INSTRUCTOR: *Give your student a "grooming tools instruction sheet" (see Appendix A) and show him the grooming shelf. Point out each tool on the shelf and the corresponding drawing on the paper. With small children, we call this shelf the horse's dresser, corresponding to their own dresser or bureau. Here the horse's tools are kept neatly, "just as you should keep your comb and brush at home."*

Demonstrate how each tool is used and explain the purpose of grooming: to contribute to the horse's well-being. "Just as we brush our hair, file our nails, and so on, the horse is helped to look and feel his best."

Currycomb

The purpose of the currycomb is to bring the dirt and old hair to the surface and to stimulate circulation. Metal currycombs are used on caked mud and when the horse is shedding. They are not recommended for general use because they may cut the skin.

Use a rubber or plastic currycomb on the fleshy parts of the horse—not on his legs except when caked with mud, and never on his head. Work the comb vigorously, with a circular motion. Start up on the neck on the near side, work downward and back, covering chest, shoulder, and so on back to the hindquarters. Then repeat on the other side.

Often a currycomb can be used on one hand and the dandy brush in the other. However, a beginner usually does better when he works with one thing at a time and does one complete job.

Clean the currycomb by tapping it against the wall or a post or on your boot heel to loosen any hair or dirt particles. Then return it to the grooming shelf.

Using the currycomb.

INSTRUCTOR: *Explain to your student that some horses are ticklish under the barrel (around the stomach). A strange horse may be touchy there and around the loin area—he may even kick. Teach the child to be alert for signs of discomfort in the horse.*

All-Purpose (Dandy) Brush

The purpose of brushing the horse is to lift out and sweep away all the dirt that has been left on the surface by the currycomb. In doing so, it also smooths and conditions the hair.

Use the brush vigorously, with long, sweeping strokes. Flick the brush outward at the end of the stroke to send the dirt out and away instead of merely rearranging it on the horse.

Again, work from front to back and from top to bottom, but brush in the direction in which the hair grows. Remember that the horse is a three-dimensional animal—don't forget to brush his face and head, chest, the inside of his legs, under the barrel, and his feet.

Be very careful around the eyes. Careless brush strokes could make a horse head-shy as well as damage the eye.

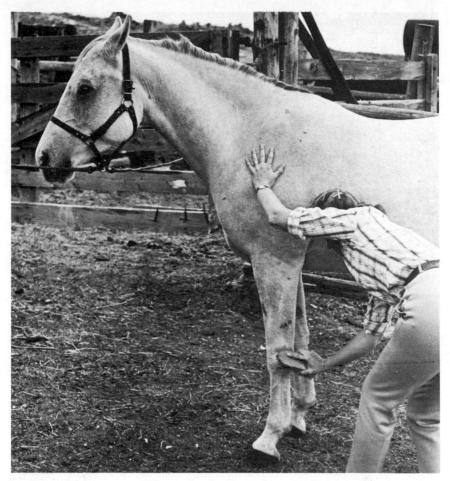

Brushing the leg.

INSTRUCTOR: *Point out the different kinds of brushes, and explain the purpose for which each is used. Show as many as you have. Point out how the hair grows on a horse—show with your hand the different directions in which the hair lies on the flank. Give special attention to the head, showing that the hair grows in one direction on one side of the face, the other way on the opposite side.*

Point out how the horse's eyes protrude and emphasize the importance of not touching the eye with the brush.

Brushing the Mane and Tail

There are metal combs for the mane and tail, but they can pull out the live hairs. It is usually better to use your hand and the brush.

Combing the mane with your fingers.

Brush the mane straight down with the dandy brush, and brush it all to one side of the neck. If it is a little matted, use one hand as a comb. Claw your fingers and run them through the hair—this parts the hair but doesn't pull.

When brushing the tail, stand to one side of the horse instead of directly behind him. Pull *part* of the tail over to you and brush straight down. The tail fans out as you do this and makes brushing easy. Separate the hairs as you did the mane, using your hand as a comb.

Clean the brush by rubbing the bristles over a sharp corner, or along a rope of the crosstie—most of the dirt and hair will flick away from the brush.

Brushing the tail.

A good tool for finishing the mane and tail is a dog-grooming brush. The little metal tines are set in rubber so that they are flexible and don't pull out the hair.

INSTRUCTOR: *Demonstrate the combing action with your hand and show how to stand when brushing the tail. Caution the student that it is never wise to stand directly behind a horse. He may not kick, but if he were frightened he might lunge back suddenly.*

Hoof Pick

The purpose of the hoof pick is to clean out the hoof, removing any stones, accumulated dirt, or other foreign matter that may be lodged around the frog (see Appendix A). If not cleaned away, these could cause the horse to become sore and lame, or may lead to worse difficulties such as thrush.

Stand at the horse's near shoulder, facing the rear of the horse. Run your left hand down the inside of the horse's leg to his pastern—he will probably pick up his foot himself. If he does not, lift the foot by placing your hand under the fetlock joint. You may push your elbow against the back of his knee to encourage him to bend his leg. As he bends his knee, slide your hand around the pastern and hold the hoof so that you can see the sole clearly.

If the horse doesn't pick up his foot, lean against his shoulder to shift his weight to the other leg. You can also pinch the tendon with index finger and thumb, as shown below.

Pinching the tendon to encourage the horse to lift his foot.

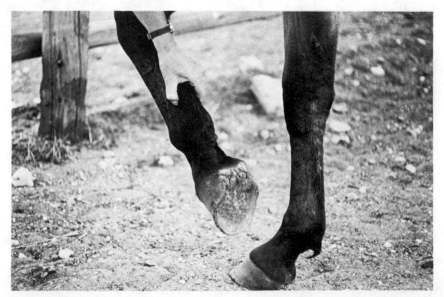

Use the hoof pick firmly, to pry loose foreign material. Clean around the frog and around the wall. Although the hoof is hard here, it is not insensitive. Be firm, but not rough. Start out gently rather than overzealously.

Wipe any foreign material off the pick before returning it to the shelf.

INSTRUCTOR: *As you demonstrate use of the hoof pick, explain that when a horse is groomed regularly, always in the same way, he will learn to*

Cleaning around the frog.

Cleaning around the hoof wall.

anticipate your movements. He will have his weight off of each foot in turn, ready for you to pick it up, or he will even pick it up by himself. When you pick up a hind foot, the horse may stretch out his leg. This might startle a beginner into dropping the hoof. We raise a hind leg (always facing the hindquarters) by first bringing it forward gently, then taking it back into cleaning position.

With young children, you will have to pick up and hold the foot for them. Emphasize, especially to children, that they must keep their own feet out of the way. And never drop the horse's hoof! Let it down easily.

Hoof Dressing

If necessary—that is, if the hoof appears very dry or has cracks—apply a hoof dressing at the coronet band and on down the hoof. Do not brush dressing over the nails of the shod hoof, as the dressing will soften the hoof wall and the shoe may become loose. You may purchase a prepared hoof dressing, or make your own using the following formula: one-third bacon fat, one-third pine tar, and one-third neatsfoot oil. (You may go heavy on the bacon fat, using somewhat smaller proportions of the other ingredients. The bacon fat need not be strained; use it straight as it comes from the frypan.) Use a one-and-a-half or two-inch paintbrush to apply the dressing easily, evenly, and cleanly. (The dressing may solidify in cold weather and be difficult to apply. Set the can in warm water or in the sun and it will liquefy quickly.)

The condition of your horse's feet is very important. See Chapter X, Part 4, on how to care for your horse's feet.

Soft Cloth

Use a clean, soft cloth to wipe around the eyes and to wipe out the nostrils. While doing this also check to see that the ears are clean. Rubbing the horse with the cloth gives a final smooth polish.

Insect Repellent

In the summer, wipe safe insect repellent on sensitive areas (neck, lower legs, under stomach), and use spray on the body if the horse will allow it. Do not apply insect spray where the saddle and girth will be placed. You may apply insect-repellent roll-ons to sensitive areas such as around nose, eyes, ears, and mouth, and around wounds or lesions.

INSTRUCTOR: *Some horses will not allow spraying. Be sure to find out before allowing a student to spray, as the horse may react violently. In such cases, all insect repellents should be applied with a cloth.*

Part 3 · Tack and Other Equipment

Leave the horse at the crosstie and go to your tack room. The specific bit and bridle used for any particular horse are designed to obtain the best performance from the horse while being the most comfortable for him. It is very important for the bit and bridle to fit the horse, and this is why each horse has his own.

Saddles are designed mainly to fit the rider: you will find a tremendous difference in the comfort of various saddles if you try them out. However, the tree (see glossary) must be of the proper size to fit the horse comfortably.

The best way to become familiar with tack and equipment is to study horse catalogs, visit tack shops, and observe trainers and other professional horsemen.

Bits and Bridles

The purpose of the bridle is to hold the bit, and the purpose of the bit is to communicate with the horse. When the rider considers the reins and bit to be part of an extremely delicate and intercoordinated communications system requiring refined controls, rather than a combination of steering column and hand brake, he has graduated from the beginner classification. Remember that any bit is worthless without the rider's proper use of all the aids.

The following important bits are discussed briefly; each has many variations with specific uses. (See the illustrations of bits in Appendix A.)

The Snaffle

The snaffle bit is one of the most popular and widely used bits because of its mild and gentle action on the horse's mouth. It is the bit most often used for early training of the green horse. The dressage rider uses the snaffle almost exclusively until the higher dressage test levels are reached. A horse with a spoiled mouth can benefit from thorough fundamental work with a snaffle bit. The Western horse may be started in a hackamore or in a snaffle bit. (Often, the horse started in a hackamore is switched to the snaffle bit after a certain level of training is reached.) Generally, a beginner rider should use a snaffle bit to avoid hurting the horse's mouth and to learn control of the single rein before attempting to use the double rein.

The snaffle bit is usually jointed at the center, and there is a ring at each end to which the single reins are attached. The bit gives a pinching type of action. According to the hand action, it bears on the corners of the mouth, on the outside of the bars of the mouth, or on the lips, allowing the tongue to move freely.

The thicker the bit, the milder its action. Because a rider is less likely to hurt the horse's mouth when using a thick, heavy bit, this type is usually best for the beginner horse or beginner rider. Narrow, thin snaffle bits are more powerful and lose the mild effect of the heavier snaffle. The German egg butt bit (a heavy snaffle often used with rubber bit guards) is especially popular. The bit guards keep the bit rings from rubbing on the corners of the lips, and keep the bit from pulling through the mouth.

Other types of snaffle bits, designed for specific purposes, include the hunting snaffle and racing snaffle.

The cowboy snaffle is popular with Western riders. With long shanks and a curb strap, it is more severe than the ordinary snaffle. However, if used correctly, it obtains good flexion and refined control.

INSTRUCTOR: *Warn your student that sharp pulls on* one *snaffle rein can be more severe than the rough use of the curb. A horse should never be punished in the mouth.*

The Curb

There are also many different kinds of curb bits. They differ from the snaffle mainly in the fact that they are not jointed, they have shanks of varying lengths to which the reins are attached, they use a curb chain or strap, and they are more severe than the snaffle. The action of the curb works on the lever principle, with the curb chain acting as a fulcrum. The curb works directly on the tongue and on the bars of the mouth. Since it is a solid mouthpiece, it acts upon both sides of the lower jaw at once and makes no provision for one-sided action as does the snaffle. Curb bits may be straight or arched, or they may have a high or low port (U-shaped bend in the center of the bit). The purpose of the port is to give more room to the tongue. An extremely high port will bear into the roof of a horse's mouth. This is a very severe type of curb and should be used only by experienced riders and for horses with special problems.

One of the bridles most often used in advanced English equitation is the double bridle. It is actually two bridles in one—a complete snaffle (called the bridoon) and a complete curb (called the Weymouth), each with its own set of reins. The two bits can be used separately or in conjunction with each other. Although the double bridle is capable of powerful action, it should not be thought of as a safety brake. It is actually a delicately refined signaling device. When properly used in conjunction with other refined aids, it helps the rider to attain unified control of the horse's whole body.

The English Pelham bridle has a single bit with rings for upper reins and shanks with rings for curb reins. It also uses a curb chain. The Pelham makes one bit perform the task of two. Most horsemen do not find it as capable of refined control as the double bridle, nor as relaxing as the snaffle; however, some horses prefer it to anything else. This is an excellent bit to teach the rider the use of double reins and is helpful to the horse as a transitional bit to the double bridle.

The Western curb differs from the English curb in its higher port, longer shanks, and leather curb strap (instead of chain). There are some acceptable Western curb straps currently on the market with a chain in the center part of the strap. More severe than the cowboy snaffle, the Western curb is an effective bit where greater control is needed, and it is widely used.

Other Bits and the Hackamore

Grazing bits are widely used in the West. They usually have a slight port or a straight bit with long, backward-sloping shanks. The English-type Walking Horse bit is similar.

The Kimberwicke combines snaffle rings with a curb bit.

Spade bits are extremely severe. Through them the expert rider can obtain refined control. They should never be used by an inexpert rider.

There are several different types of hackamores, some capable of more delicate control than others. Often, a Western horse may be started in a hackamore, then later switched to a snaffle bit, and finally to a curb. Some Western horses, however, are trained exclusively in a hackamore. When skillfully used, the hackamore can produce a very polished, refined control.

Various other bits, hackamore bits, and bitless bridles may be used effectively by knowledgeable riders, depending upon the individual horse.

Saddles

All saddles are built along the same general principles of construction. The framework, called the tree, must be strong enough to withstand the pressure, high enough to clear the horse's withers and backbone, and wide enough to fit the horse's back comfortably.

There are many variations of the English saddle, designed for specific functions such as jumping, dressage, hunting, or all-purpose. Until the advanced rider is sure of his area of specialization, it is usually best to avoid extremes in design and to use an all-purpose saddle. No matter what type of saddle, it should be shaped to help the rider sit in the center of the seat, allowing him to maintain the Basic Seat properly. Avoid saddles that are constructed with their lowest point behind the center, a fault particularly common in Western saddles.

Western saddles also have varieties in design, depending upon their use for roping, parade, barrel racing, and so on. Be sure that there is room in the gullet for the withers. Should the gullet sit right down on the withers, it would soon gall and even injure the horse (fistula of the withers). The Western saddle that has a free swing in the stirrups is desirable. Stiff stirrup leathers inhibit leg aids and cramp the rider's legs.

It is sometimes necessary to fix the stirrups on a new Western saddle so that they are turned properly. Soak the stirrup leathers in water and place the saddle on a stand or fence rail. Run a crowbar or heavy iron pipe through both stirrups so that they are turned properly. Leave for a day or longer if possible.

Try to avoid carved leather in an everyday saddle. Plain leather, either smooth or roughout, is more comfortable on trail rides and in the training arena. A roughout saddle holds moisture and can be uncomfortable on a wet day. The carved saddle has its place in the show ring or in a parade.

See Chapter 4 ("Stable Management and Tack") of our book *Basic Horse Care* for the proper fitting of English and Western saddles.

Artificial Aids

Spurs, Whips, Crops, and Bats

The more patience and insight you have, the less you will need to use artificial aids. When training a young horse with patience and quiet handling, it is rarely necessary to use whip, crop, or spurs. These aids, in the hands of a knowledgeable horseman, can help the advancing horse to understand what is required. As such they are devices of communication, not punishment.

When an older horse has soured, fallen into bad habits, or become lazy, an artificial aid may be needed to wake him up or enforce discipline. Since horses are individuals, they will respond to these aids in different ways. A spoken reprimand may be shattering to a sensitive horse; another horse may be unmoved by anything less than a good swat.

Riding a lazy horse on a long trail ride would not be a pleasure; the constant kicking and swatting would be frustrating and tiring. On such a horse, the occasional active use of spurs might work wonders. Simply wearing spurs or carrying a crop or bat is enough to perk up some lazy horses. This is why some spurs are made to jingle-jangle; the noise reminds the horse that he had better be on his toes.

The less you spur a high-spirited or spooky horse the better. Spurs are for communication, but they must be used with understanding. Spurs should not be used by the inexperienced rider because he is not yet able to control his legs in all situations. The spur must prick at the correct moment and with the proper amount of lightness or severity to be quietly effective. Improper use will irritate the horse. It may actually numb his sides or injure them, and it may induce the horse to cowkick, wring his tail, or develop other bad habits. Except for rodeo bronc riding, spurs should never be used in front of the cinch.

Never use spurs or whip when your temper is short. You'll do far more harm than good, and many times irreparable damage will result, not so much physically, but to the mental balance and confidence of your horse.

The intelligent use of the whip to induce impulsion or to teach the driving influence of your legs and back muscles is sometimes necessary and helpful.

Martingales, Dropped Noseband, Draw Reins

The standing martingale, or tiedown, runs from the noseband of the bridle to the girth. Its purpose is to limit the upward movement of the head without restricting the forward movement. The horse must be able to extend his neck but be prevented from stargazing, rearing, or throwing his head back. Correct use of the martingale depends upon its proper adjustment.

The standing martingale will not cure a horse of head throwing and related problems, but it will save the rider from a nasty bump when the horse throws his head up and will improve the rider's control of his mount. It is usually not recommended for jumping because the adjustment might not be correct for the needed stretch of the neck.

The dropped noseband.

Adjustment of the martingale is correct if, when the horse's head is up in natural position for movement, you can push the martingale up from underneath to reach into the horse's throat.

The running martingale is Y-shaped, with a ring at each tip of the Y and a loop at its base to slip over the girth. The snaffle reins run through the rings. Adjustment is correct if both rings, brought up on one side of the neck, reach the withers. (The martingale should be attached to the girth when measuring.) The running martingale is usually used with a snaffle bit.

The neck straps of the standing and running martingales should fit so as to admit the width of your hand at the withers.

The running martingale has the same uses as the tiedown, but it is a much more flexible aid with more uses. It is excellent as a training aid for a horse with an unmade mouth. Further, it acts as a safety device; if an inexperienced horse were to bolt with a snaffle, the rider would have little control because the horse could seize the bit in his teeth. The running martingale would hold the bit against the bars, thereby giving the needed control. It can be used when jumping since it allows the horse to stretch his neck as much as necessary when the rider gives with his hands.

The Irish martingale connects the two reins by means of a short leather strap with rings at both ends. This has no other use than to keep the horse from throwing both reins over on one side of his neck when he throws his head.

The dropped noseband is generally used in conjunction with the snaffle bit. Since many horses evade the action of the snaffle, the dropped noseband is very effective in keeping the horse's mouth closed and his snaffle in place. When the dropped noseband is correctly fitted, it gives control without resorting to a stronger bit. We find it very effective in the dressage tests when riding a stallion.

Draw reins are occasionally used by both English and Western trainers. These reins pass from the girth through the large rings of the snaffle to the hands. The rider has a great deal of leverage with draw reins. If not used judiciously, they can make a horse sore-necked and rebellious, if not "broken-necked." (The horse is overbent with an unpleasing arch in his neck.) Injudicious use can produce forced, artificial collection. Sometimes draw reins are substituted for side reins in longe training.

Part 4 · Getting Ready to Ride

Suggested Safety Rules for the Student

INSTRUCTOR: *A good beginning should certainly include safety, courtesy, and good work ethics. Posted rules and regulations help students, parents, and staff learn their limits and be aware of problems that might arise while around horses. You may wish to use the following rules, or include others adapted to your situation.*

1. *Do not run, play, or climb on hay in the barn or stable area. Riding double is not allowed.*
2. *Do not ride or handle someone else's horses without permission (except in an emergency).*
3. *Consider your horse's comfort—use proper and well-fitting tack, groom regularly, consider nutrition and quality in feeding, keep stall clean. When feeding your own horse, feed at the same time as the stable feeds, and keep your area clean and neat.*
4. *Follow safety rules when approaching, haltering, leading, tying, grooming, saddling, and bridling.*
5. *Use courtesy and good manners at all times.*
6. *Wear approved riding apparel, including an approved hard hat,*

*especially when jumping. Wear boots with some heel—do not ride
in moccasins, sneakers, loafers, sandals, or barefoot.*

7. *Open gates wide enough when bringing horses through, but watch
loose horses.*
8. *Walk your horse before tightening girth or cinch.*
9. *Warm bits on cold days; wash or wipe clean after use. Close halters
and hang bridles correctly in tack room. Clean out grooming tools
after use.*
10. *Leave saddle blankets with wet-side or dirty-side up on Western
saddles.*

But now back to our beginner, for whom we use a saddle pad, without
stirrups, for the early lessons. The saddle pad is shaped like an English
saddle, but has no tree; therefore, it molds to the horse's back. It is made of
three-quarter-inch felt and is reinforced with leather at pressure points. The
girth is strong and guards against chafing. It is attached to the saddle so as to
go completely around the horse like a surcingle; thus no stitching can pull out
and the pad cannot come loose. The pad comes equipped with safety stirrup
bars enabling the stirrups to be attached or removed easily. We'll explain
more about why we use the saddle pad a little further on.

This felt saddle pad, reinforced with leather, has no tree but has safety stirrup bars.

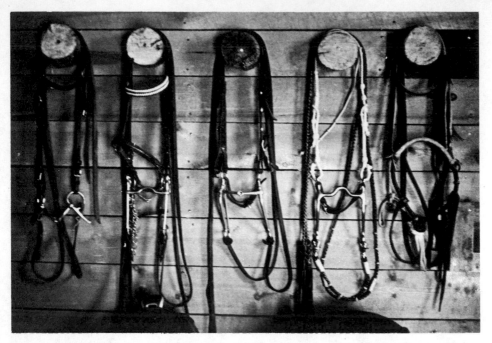

Bridles: from left to right, the snaffle (with half cheeks), full bridle (the Weymouth), cowboy snaffle, Western curb bridle (showing medium port curb bit), bosal-type hackamore.

Take the bridle, a saddle pad, and a blanket, and return to the horse. Set the bridle on a peg, and the saddle pad over a stall partition or other appropriate place.

INSTRUCTOR: *Show how the bridles are hung and briefly explain the uses of different bits and bridles. (The snaffle, curb, and Pelham or full bridle are enough to discuss at this stage.) Point out the different saddles and how they are set on the saddle racks. If you have English, Western, and/or Army (McClellan) saddles, briefly point out the differences and explain their uses. Show and explain also the uses of saddle pads and blankets. Of course, if the child is quite young, all of this may be skipped over for now.*

You will demonstrate tacking up during this first lesson, but from here on, the student will do it under your direction.

Saddling Your Horse

Set the blanket gently on the horse's back about three or four inches in front of the withers. Then slide it back an inch or two to keep the hair smooth. Set the saddle pad or saddle gently on the blanket, in the correct position, leaving about three or four inches of the blanket showing in front of the saddle pad. Blankets tend to work back somewhat as the horse moves. This arrangement allows some working to take place without necessitating a rearrangement of the tack.

Bareback pads are available, but generally the stirrups are permanently attached and do not have safety stirrup bars as shown on page 72. Such pads are dangerous and should not be used unless equipped with stirrup covers so that the child's foot cannot go through the stirrup. If you do not have the proper kind of pad, the student may ride bareback. If you use a saddle, see Chapter IV, "Tacking Up."

Move around to the off side of the horse. Take down the girth, and check that the blanket and pad are smooth and even. Then return to the near side, reach under the horse for the girth, and make sure that it is straight. Then tighten the girth, slowly and gently, until it is snug but not tight. Lead your horse about forty feet and again tighten the girth, this time very snugly. Some horses may need this repeated more than once.

INSTRUCTOR: *Explain the importance of keeping the hair smooth under the blanket as you demonstrate saddling. Pull away any mane that may be caught under the saddle near the withers.*

After the girth has been tightened sufficiently, show your student

Saddles: the McClellan, English, and Western.

how to pull each foreleg forward so that the horse's skin under the girth is smooth (free of wrinkles that could chafe behind the horse's elbow). Explain also that a horse may "blow up," that is, hold his breath while the girth is being tightened. When he lets out his breath, the girth is loose. Tell the child to walk the horse for several feet and then check the girth before mounting.

Bridling Your Horse

Now bridle the horse, leaving the halter on underneath; this enables the horse to be led easily either by the student or by the instructor. Although some horses have specific problems or vices that make them difficult to bridle (see Chapter X), generally the best way to bridle the horse is as illustrated and explained in the pictures.

In cold weather remember that a metal bit in the horse's mouth will be uncomfortable and, if cold enough, injurious. Warm the bit first by holding it a moment or two in your hand, by breathing on it, or by dipping it in warm water.

If you avoid hurting your horse when bridling him, you are not likely to develop any trouble. It is worthwhile to be very careful of his teeth, eyes, and ears.

INSTRUCTOR: *Don't expect the student to bridle the horse this first lesson. A very small or young child will not be able to bridle his horse for some time; however, perhaps he can fasten the throatlatch. He then feels he has contributed.*

Explain the reasons for each step (leave on the halter, warm the bit in winter, avoid hitting the horse's teeth, be careful of his ears). For unbridling, see "Finishing the Lesson."

Leading the Horse to the Corral

Unfasten the crosstie and lead your horse out into the ring or corral. Practice leading him around the ring, using the leadrope. Be sure to turn and walk in both directions.

The reins should remain over the horse's neck. Split reins may be knotted or, better yet, a slip loop may be used. Knots will eventually crack the leather and may make reins hard to handle because of the bends they leave.

Bridling over the halter. When you hold the bridle in this way, you are ready to pull the bridle up with your right hand as soon as the horse opens his mouth to take the bit.

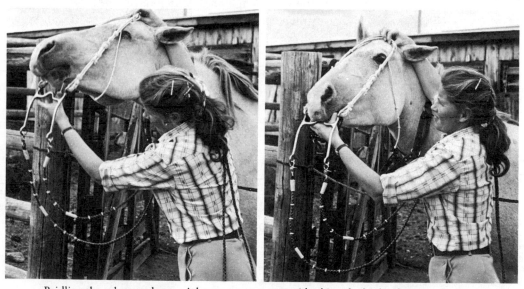

Bridling the reluctant horse. A horse may try to avoid taking the bit by throwing up his head and pressing his lips together. Your right hand holds the crown piece as your left hand uses thumb and fingers to open the horse's mouth at the bars.

INSTRUCTOR: *The time taken for leading the horse gives the student another few minutes to become acquainted with his mount. It is relaxing for him, especially if he is somewhat nervous. Remind him to keep his feet out of the way.*

Part 5 · In the Corral

The Corral or Ring

A medium-sized corral next to your barn or stable is ideal; during the first lessons it is handy to be near the sources of equipment.

INSTRUCTOR: *Let's take another quick look at the horse while the student is leading him around. This is a typical beginner's horse. He may not look like much but he's been around and knows the ropes. He is aged to the point where he won't be afraid of anything, either foreign objects or sounds, or the rider clinging or poking in the wrong places. He is willing (this is important), easily managed, and patient with beginning riders— he doesn't take advantage of them.*

As always, it is difficult to achieve the ideal. If your beginner horse falls short in some respect, know the horse well enough so that you can forestall any problems that might arise.

Mounting the Horse

It is both traditional and correct to mount from the near side of your horse. (In training a horse, it is wise to teach him to stand for mounting and dismounting from the off side as well as the near side. It improves his balance and there may be unforeseen emergencies on the trail that would necessitate working from the off side. Most horses, however, would be scandalized at any attempt to mount from the right, and it is considered incorrect unless asked for by a judge, as in a trail class.)

Small riders can't begin to mount by themselves, and beginning adults often have a great deal of trouble mounting correctly until their muscles have limbered up. In some places, mounting blocks are available, but generally it is better to know how to mount without one. Because of this, and because, also, we are not using stirrups, we first learn the "leg up" method of mounting. You should, by all means, have someone to help you during your first three or four lessons. This is as important from the point of view of safety as it is from the standpoint of mechanics and common sense.

The Leg Up

Hold the reins and a lock of mane in your left hand, and put your right hand on the pommel area (or top forward part) of the saddle pad. Stand on your right leg and bend your left leg at the knee. Your helper should hold your left ankle and calf as illustrated, and count, "One, two, three, *hup!*" Bend your right knee just a bit on "three" and spring up on "hup." As you spring, your helper will boost your left leg.

Balance on your hands, and then swing your right leg over the horse's croup without kicking him. Settle lightly into the saddle pad.

Beginners are often surprised at how little effort it takes to give a leg up when the student springs correctly on the count of "hup." A small woman can effectively give a leg up to a heavy man without strain. Without proper coordination, however, you may try to lift a dead weight, and the results are sad—rather like hoisting a huge sack of grain into an overhead bin. There-

Giving a leg up.

Giving a leg up to a small child. (Your left hand may move up to steady the child around her waist.)

fore, especially with the heavier rider, it may be wise to practice coordinating "one, two, three, *hup!*" several times before actually going ahead with the leg up.

Incidentally, until you are familiar with giving a leg up, proceed with some caution. We've seen riders neatly boosted up and right on over the other side!

INSTRUCTOR: *It may take a child several lessons to learn to spring up at the right time; at first you will probably have to do all of the lifting.*

With the smaller child, have him hold the reins in the left hand, and reach with both hands as far up on the side of horse and saddle pad as he can reach; you have control of the leadrope. Hold his left calf in your right hand, and steady him around the waist with your left hand. Count "one, two, three, hup!" and give him a boost. The child will then slide his hands up until he can grasp a lock of mane with his left hand and put his right hand on the saddle pad, then continue with sliding his leg over. He is thus learning the correct method of taking a leg up right from the start.

In the Saddle

At last, you are sitting on the horse—on the saddle pad, with no stirrups. Sit as far forward as is comfortable and pick up the reins.

The saddle pad is perfect for learning to ride. As in bareback riding, you can feel the horse's muscles and get accustomed to his motion. There is more security in being close to the horse, and you have a better idea of what the horse is doing. Best of all, there is a personal feeling of relationship—here is a warm, honest-to-gosh animal. The saddle pad, however, is not as slippery as the horse's bare back, and thereby gives security.

Hold the reins evenly and lightly. As your assistant leads the horse around, don't try to do anything in particular. Just sit there and feel the horse—his warmth, his muscles, his movement.

All right, now try to assume the Basic Seat position. Remember that the proper seat begins with the horse. He should be alert, balanced, and standing on all four feet. Try to follow the lesson closely to assure yourself of a correct foundation at the beginning. From here on in, you will try to maintain the Basic Seat position, even without stirrups. Try to avoid stiffness. It may seem rough at first, but you will soon learn to relax in this position and be more comfortable than in any other.

Now try to maintain the Basic Seat position as your horse is led around for you.

INSTRUCTOR: *Lead the student, without giving any instruction, so that he can get the feel of the horse. Then explain the Basic Seat. (It would be helpful to have a more advanced student demonstrate how to sit properly.) He should try to assume the correct position, even though there are no stirrups. Correct his faults. Encourage him to maintain the Basic Seat at all times in the saddle, except, of course, when doing exercises.*

There are different ways of teaching bareback riding. Often the foot hangs naturally, the toes slightly down. In this case, beginning riders might lock their toes under the horse's elbows, supposedly for better grip, but thereby contracting the very muscles that should be elongated. Usually it is best for the rider to maintain the Basic Seat as though he had stirrups and full English tack, whether using the saddle pad or actually riding bareback. The Basic Seat is not dependent on tack, be it stirrups, saddle, or any other paraphernalia. It is an independent, common ground for the harmonious communication of rider and horse. (If you hold some reservations about this, notice in pictures the

The Basic Seat.

The Basic Seat from the front.

The student remembers to keep heels down and toes up by putting the English stirrups and leathers upside-down over the toes. Her torso should be more upright for good Basic Seat position.

many maneuvers of the Spanish Riding School of Vienna that are performed without stirrups.)

As the Horse Turns

The instructor or an assistant leads you in reverse by walking toward the center of the circle, and then back onto the same track in the opposite direction. During the reverses—and remember to work equally in both directions—maintain the Basic Seat by leaning into the turns *slightly*. Don't overemphasize this point. You are supposed to stay *with* the horse, not lean sideways. You do not want to collapse your hip, but push down with the seat bone toward the direction you wish to go. Naturally, on a slow turn at a walk, you will lean very little compared to the amount of lean required during a faster gait.

INSTRUCTOR: *The child is still getting the feel of the horse. Ask him to notice, as the horse is turning, how the horse's backbone, from poll to tail head, bends with the turn. (If your beginner horse does not flex too well on the turns, at least show how a well-trained horse should bend as he is turning. Emphasize that later on the rider will want to help him acquire flexibility and will be able to give the aids that will encourage this.) The horse's backbone should describe the arc of the circle on which he is turning.*

The easiest way to teach seat-bone pressure is to ask the student to look (turn the head) in the direction he wishes to go—not look down, but around. This helps the student to put pressure on the correct seat bone automatically.

Beginning Exercises

After holding, or trying to hold, the Basic position for the first time, you are apt to tire quickly. Your muscles are tense and you are probably rather stiff.

Now for relaxation, try some exercises. These beginning exercises will first be done while the horse is still. Later some of them may be done while the horse walks or trots.

There are several good reasons for exercises. They help a rider to improve his balance and coordination—he learns to move in a fluid way, moving one part of his body in coordination with other parts but without disturbing their independence or security. Exercises build muscles that are needed in riding, helping to speed the process of conditioning oneself to the best physical fitness possible. Most important, they relax the rider and help to give him a feeling of security.

INSTRUCTOR: *It is always wise to start an exercise while the horse is at the halt. Gradually work up to having the horse walk as the student gains confidence. You don't want anything to happen during the first few lessons that would frighten him. Your student's horse should be quiet, safe, and used to all kinds of exercises. Be sure he will accept riders who are uncoordinated and who perhaps will bang him in unexpected places inadvertently. You should be very safety-conscious in this aspect of your student's lessons.*

If reins are not used during the exercise, tie open reins together, open throatlatch of bridle and rebuckle around the reins to keep them up out of the way.

1. **Turning around in the saddle ("Around the World")**
   Start toward the right. Put your left foot over the horse's withers without kicking him in the head. You are now sitting sideways on the

off side of the horse. Swing your right foot over the croup and you are sitting on the saddle pad facing the hindquarters. Follow with the left leg and you're sideways again on the near side. Back over the withers with the right leg and you're again sitting properly in the saddle. Now repeat this exercise to the left. Your assistant will hold your horse and steady you for the first few times.

INSTRUCTOR: *Be sure, on these first two exercises, that there is a helper to steady the student, whether child or adult, and to hold the horse. It won't be long before the student is fairly comfortable at odd positions on the horse's back. But at first it seems like a long way up to be doing monkeyshines.*

2. Lying down

With your feet remaining in approximately the correct position, lie down on the horse's croup. Don't rush this, but once you manage to lie back on the horse, try to relax in this position. Later the horse will be led at a walk or even at a trot while you lie relaxed on his back.

Now try the exercise leaning forward on the horse's neck.

The lying-down exercise.

Leaning forward.

3. Forward-back

After the first lesson, this will be done at a walk. Swing your legs, from the knee, forward and back rhythmically. At first you are apt to move them only a few inches. Try to swing way forward and way back, of course without jabbing the horse.

INSTRUCTOR: *The main point of this exercise and the next one, beyond the other reasons mentioned above, is to develop the seat independently of the legs. The legs should be able to move radically without affecting the security of the seat.*

When calling for exercises, begin with "Prepare to" so that the student can think about what to do and how to do it. Your instruction should be rhythmical (forward, back, forward, back). Since many students do not have a sense of rhythm, you must help set the rhythm and pace (slow) of the exercise for them.

4. One-two

This is the same as the forward-back exercise, except that as the left foot goes forward, the right foot moves back. Again, try to move your legs forward and back as far as possible without disrupting your position.

5. Flexibility

While holding the reins very loosely, rotate your wrists and ankles.

6. Up-down

Sitting in the correct Basic Seat position, try to grip with your knees and lift yourself out of the saddle. Do this to the count of four, coming up on each count. Then relax.

The up-down exercise. (Student should wear helmet and boots, especially when using stirrups.)

INSTRUCTOR: *This is difficult to do at first but is an excellent exercise, laying the foundation for the posting trot and strengthening the muscles, especially in the thighs. To be correct, the upward motion comes from an opening of the knee angle, with little opening of the hip angle. At first the student will be inclined to jump out of the saddle, or may try to get by with hunching his shoulders and raising his elbows. (Tell him if he does this, "Don't flap your wings like a chicken." Such comparisons make it easier for a child to remember and to avoid the fault.) He should not rest his hands on the horse's withers. Help by motioning "up" with your hand on each count.*

7. **Accompanying mental exercise for the student**

Point out the parts of the horse which correspond to the parts of a human, such as head, neck, elbow, and so on. The student will learn all the parts of the horse in the next few lessons. Later he can touch on command the parts of the horse that can be reached easily.

Using the Aids

The aids are the signals, hopefully imperceptible, that a rider gives to his horse to tell him what to do. The natural aids are voice, weight (seat), hands, and legs (including your feet). Artificial aids (whip, spurs, etc.) were discussed on page 35. Remember that the horse is a very sensitive animal. When he has been correctly trained and handled, the slightest indication is enough to tell him what to do. Therefore, it is wise to start giving the aids very gently. If the horse doesn't respond, more pressure may be needed (called the "increasing aids"). For now, you will have to learn *how* to be gentle. You will be inclined to overuse the aids, since you must learn how to control your own hands, legs, and weight while on the horse. To protect the horse while you are learning, the reins should be kept long and the horse should be led.

INSTRUCTOR: *Make sure the student understands the reasons for giving the aids gently. In a class situation, it is best to have a helper for each horse. With only one student you will do well to lead the horse yourself.*

The Punishment-Reward Concept

An important concept to understand right here at the beginning is that pressure may be considered a form of punishment. Release is a form of reward. Through the leg or hand aids, you give the horse pressure. But as soon as he responds, the pressure is released—the horse is rewarded. Unreleased pressure may not only be uncomfortable to the horse, but it can also be dangerous because the horse will lose his sensitivity to the aids. This can best be explained if you will try it on yourself.

Pinch your forearm between thumb and index finger as hard as you can and keep the pressure steady. It hurts at first, but soon gets numb and no pain is felt at all. Now pinch your arm intermittently—and notice how much more sensitive it is to the pressure.

That's precisely how it would work on the horse's mouth and, to a lesser extent, wherever pressure is applied through the legs. Therefore, it is important to release the pressure when the horse responds to the desired direction or command.

INSTRUCTOR: *Explain this clearly and have your student try the pinching experiment. Emphasize especially the importance of being very gentle with the horse's mouth. Later on, when the student has increased his sensitivity and begins to develop good hands, you can explain that contact is maintained even when the pressure is released. For now there should be no attempt to maintain contact.*

Starting into a Walk

You have already used the weight aid, when you leaned slightly into the turn on the reverse. Now it is time to correlate your aids to give the horse a definite signal.

You are at the halt now. You are in the Basic Seat position, your reins rather long, and you want to start into a walk. Give the following aids simultaneously:

- Say "w-a-l-k," clearly and firmly but not roughly or noisily. Drag the word out a little, giving it a rising inflection.
- Give pressure with both legs on the girth—right where your legs should be. How much pressure you give depends upon the sensitivity of the horse. Press with the inside of your calves and increase gradually. With some horses you may have to kick slightly with your heels, but this should be a last resort. Give the pressure equally with both legs.
- Incline your body forward *slightly*. As the horse begins to walk, his center of gravity shifts forward slightly. To ask for the walk, the forward inclination of your body is a weight aid. Actually the inclination can be so slight as to be almost unnoticeable.
- Let your hands go forward a little, giving with the horse's mouth so that he can go forward.

You are now walking. As soon as the horse started forward, you released the pressure with your legs. But if the horse should slow down or offer to stop, you will have to give the aid again. Since the horse is being led, you should not have to worry about this.

INSTRUCTOR: *The beginner who learns to start a horse by clobbering him in the ribs is asking for trouble. This is why the ideal beginner horse should be calm but responsive. A complete deadhead will start the student into bad habits that he may have to learn the hard way to correct.*

Make sure that the student uses all the aids—voice, legs, weight, hands. Remind him, as you practice this, if he forgets one. Of course, now he is learning how *to control a horse—actually, you will be in control, starting the horse into a walk precisely as the student tries to coordinate the aids.*

Bringing Your Horse to a Halt

Even more important than moving out at the walk is learning how to stop the horse. Again, several aids must be given simultaneously:

- Say "Whoa!" This command should also be given firmly and clearly without shouting. But it should be a brisk word rather than drawn out.
- Take up with the reins. Eventually this will be only a slight movement with the fingers. Now, however, since the reins are loose to protect the horse, there will have to be a definite "take" to make any contact with the horse's mouth. Release, or give again, when the horse starts to halt. (Again, the "contact" concept will be used as the rider gains experience.)
- Your body reverts to the ideal Basic position at the standstill—weight moves back slightly.

INSTRUCTOR: *Watch carefully! Make sure that the student releases the pressure on the horse's mouth as the horse begins to stop.*

Practicing What You Have Learned

Now go around the ring a few more times—still being led—practicing the walk, halt, and a reverse or two.

Dismounting

To dismount, take the reins in your left hand and hold a lock of the mane as in mounting. Place your right hand on the front of the pad. Swing your right foot over the croup—without touching—and move your right hand to the back of the saddle pad. Balance on your hands before dropping lightly to the ground with knees bent. Your assistant should be on hand to steady you on dismounting.

INSTRUCTOR: *Stay near the child to steady him as he dismounts. This is even more important with a small child who has a long way to go to the ground. Don't abandon the student on this grand finale. When teaching children, always be on hand for any movement the child has to make that might scare him or involve a loss of his sense of security, or that may involve the horse's sense of security or balance. Remind the child to land with knees bent.*

During these first lessons, even if the child doesn't learn much, he should have fun and finish the lesson happily. In other words, don't take your instruction too seriously at this point. Whether or not the child coordinated his aids or leaned into the turns is not too important. Inject fun, without, of course, sacrificing the comfort of the horse or the safety of the child.

Finishing the Lesson

Lead the horse back to the crosstie. Fasten the halter loosely around his neck (retain control of the horse while unbridling and keep the halter handy). Carefully take off the bridle. Always remember to lower the bit gently and slowly from the horse's mouth at the same angle as the mouth, so that it does not bang on his teeth. Halter the horse and snap to the crossties. Sponge the bit and wipe it dry. Keeping the bit clean is important. A soiled, crusty bit can be uncomfortable and cause sores in the horse's mouth.

Unbuckle the girth, go around to the off side of the saddlepad, and put the girth over the top. Return to the near side, take off the pad, and set it on a rack or rail. Take off the blanket by pulling it back toward the croup—this keeps the hair smooth. Turn the blanket over and place it on top of the saddle pad so that it will air and any dampness can dry out. Replace the bridle and saddle pad in the tack room.

Brush the horse's back and around the girth area. If there is time, groom him again quickly. Pick up each foot to be sure that there are no foreign objects lodged in the hoof.

INSTRUCTOR: *Ask the student to watch carefully as you take off the saddle and bridle, clean the bit, and replace the tack. Make sure that he realizes the importance of replacing the tack where it belongs and of leaving it neat and clean. Now is the time to begin the formation of good habits.*

Also, expect the student to clean up any messes the horse makes in the barn. Show him, this time, how it should be done. This, too, is an important part of horsemanship.

Leaving Your Horse

Attach the leadrope, release the horse from the crosstie, and lead him to stall or pasture. Turn him to face the gate, pat him, unhalter him, bring back the rope and halter (which should be closed), and hang them in the appropriate spot.

Unless there is a specific reason, don't leave a halter on the horse when turning him out. Rope halters may shrink when wet. If it fits loosely, the horse may get a foot caught in it; and if this were to happen, he might either break a leg or become cast. He may also catch the halter over the top of a fence post and suffocate while struggling. There are safety halters which will release; however, our experience is that they are easily lost in the pasture. It is best to encourage your horse to come to you—or at least allow you to walk up to him to halter him.

INSTRUCTOR: *Ask the student to return the horse to stall or pasture. Give him a labeled grooming sheet and an unlabeled quiz sheet. His parents may give the quiz during the week. This is the time to talk with parents and to make any arrangements necessary for the next lesson.*

Encourage the child as he leaves. If he did well, tell him the horse must have really liked him since they got along so well (pleasing to a small child). You may not have accomplished everything, or even much of anything, but the child should leave enthused about riding. Encouragement is just as important for the older beginner.

Elementary Control at the Walk

Lessons 2 and 3

Part 1 · The Second Lesson

Preliminary Work

The first three lessons are designed to be given weekly; but if you are working at home with your own horse, you have the advantage of working slowly, doing a part of a lesson each day. The important thing is to feel confident as far as you have gone.

The fact that you are in the saddle every day, even if only for twenty or thirty minutes, will help you gain confidence more quickly and advance more rapidly. Be consistent, whether you repeat the last lesson or go on with the next.

The homework assignment for Lessons 2 and 3 is to learn the points of the horse. This week, study the forehand. Please turn to the labeled diagram in Appendix A. Find the withers. A horse is measured from the ground to the withers. His height is counted in hands—a hand equals four inches. A horse measuring fifty-eight inches from the ground to the withers would stand 14.2 (say "fourteen-two")—that is, 14 hands, two inches tall. When your horse is at the crosstie, identify all the points of the forehand and point them out.

Always thoroughly groom your horse before tacking up. Use the saddle pad without stirrups, and lead your horse to the corral.

INSTRUCTOR: *Give the student the same horse he had for the first lesson, provided they got along well. An experienced instructor will have little trouble in matching up the right horse with the right child. A new instructor will have to learn by experience. Usually common sense will keep him from making any seriously unsuitable matches.*

Tips for matching up horse and rider:

1. *The first consideration is temperament of horse and rider: A nervous rider should have a calm, patient horse.*
2. *Size should be compatible: It's best to have a small child on a small horse, and a large, heavy person should definitely have a horse that can carry him comfortably.*

Ask the student to halter the horse, lead him to the crosstie, and groom him. Repeat the terms so that the student will become familiar with them (such as hindquarters, forehand, near and off sides), and bring up new terms and information as they apply (such as withers, hand, and how to measure a horse). Mention and point out the hoof, frog, coronet, and pastern when cleaning the feet.

Now give the student his homework assignment for the week. There could be two diagrams of a horse, one labeled and one blank. He will have to learn only the points of the forehand this week. Point out the parts of the horse both at the crosstie and on the diagram. The student may test himself during the week on the blank sheet.

Show the student the proper way to carry the bridle: hold the crown piece in the left hand with the reins over his right shoulder. Make sure that the reins are off the ground.

Review saddling and bridling and let the child do as much as possible. As you work, point out and name those parts of bridle and saddle pad that must be handled, such as the throatlatch, crown piece, or girth.

Maintaining the Basic Seat

Your assistant or instructor will give you a leg up. Immediately assume the Basic Seat position and try for accuracy without tension. Although technically you are now learning English equitation, the seat serves as a sound basis for Western equitation as well.

Keep the entire position in mind constantly. You can't afford to let your legs flap around while you work on your hands. Concentrate on perfecting one thing at a time, but not at the expense of something else.

The proper way to carry a Western saddle (Lisa Puraty).

INSTRUCTOR: *You may find that some instructors prefer to work on a correct hand position one day, leg position another time, and back position still another, in the hope of avoiding confusion to the student. Generally, however, concentration on overall correctness is not confusing. It will be some time, of course, before the student can maintain the Basic Seat properly. But it is important to avoid allowing a bad habit to develop while concentrating on a good one. Naturally, you cannot demand immediate overall perfection, but you should hold it in mind as a goal. You may concentrate on improving, say, the position of the hands during one lesson, so long as you do so within the framework of the entire picture.*

Keeping Your Heels Down

It is often difficult for beginners to remember to keep their heels down. When a rider keeps his heels down, the effect is to bring his leg muscles into closer contact with the horse and to deepen his seat. Beginners can gain a proper understanding and feel of this effect only from experience. It is often easier, especially for young children, to approximate the proper position by remembering to keep their toes up.

If you have any difficulty keeping your heels down, use the stirrups that you removed from the saddle pad. Hang the stirrups upside-down, with leathers dangling, over your toes. You will have to keep your toes up in order to keep the stirrups on. (See Illustration on page 49.)

INSTRUCTOR: *You will find the loose-stirrup method a great aid in keeping the student's feet in the proper position. It is not necessary or advisable for the student to "jam" his heels down—just ensure that the heel should stay lower than the toe.*

In a class situation, make it a game. Anyone who loses a stirrup must replace the lost stirrup and go to the end of the line.

Reviewing the First Lesson

Review what you learned in the first lesson, except for the exercises. Start, halt, and make reverses. Remember to lean slightly into the turns and to use all the aids you learned in the first lesson when you start and stop.

INSTRUCTOR: *Review the first lesson, mentioning again the aids involved. Observe carefully to see if special attention should be given to any particular phase of the review. Of course the review will go much more quickly than the first lesson. If anything was not covered as stated in the first lesson, go into that now before going on.*

Emphasis of the Lesson—Using and Coordinating the Aids in Turning

Each riding lesson consists of review and new work. Emphasis is placed on the part of the lesson that involves the concentrated understanding of new concepts combined with the physical learning of new methods. Remember that harmonious horsemanship involves an understanding of *why* you do something as well as *how* to do it correctly.

The emphasis of this lesson is on using and coordinating the aids in turning your horse.

Learning to Use the Reins

Make sure you are holding your hands correctly, as shown in illustration on page 12.

When you turn, your hands give direction through the reins. At this stage in learning to ride, move your hands together. To turn left, the right hand follows the left hand several inches to the left. Always keep the same distance between your hands: approximately four inches.

Practice turning with the proper hand action as well as by leaning into the turns. You are still being led, and essentially, your horse is still being controlled by your assistant or the instructor while you are learning what to do.

INSTRUCTOR: *Show the student how to move his hands by moving them for him with the horse at a halt. Walk backward while leading the horse, and make right and left turns. Make sure that the student is moving his hands together, keeping an even distance between them. Watch for a tendency in beginning riders to lift their hands too high or to pull on the bearing (indirect) rein. This confuses the horse and also tends to unbalance the rider.*

The Action of the Legs

Now work on the leg aids. Review the punishment-reward concept: Pressure is a mild form of punishment and the horse will move away from the pressure. Your legs give and release pressure as do your hands.

What you are doing, in effect, is to hold your mount between your legs and hands. Your legs help to engage the horse's hindquarters and to turn and flex the horse. When you put pressure on both sides at the girth area, you are urging the horse to move ahead *into* the bit. If you release hand pressure at the same time, though maintaining contact, the horse moves forward.

Now, if you give pressure to the horse *behind* the girth, say with your right leg, you are pushing the horse's hindquarters slightly to the left, flexing him around your left leg, and therefore aiding the horse to turn left (when applied in combination with the rein). Your horse, in other words, does not move around a track like a railroad car, always stiff and straight, but rather like a dog curling around himself to lie down.

Therefore, when turning left, give pressure with your right leg behind the girth. When turning right, give pressure with your left leg behind the girth. Do not let the leg on the girth lose contact. Later, when you are more coordinated, this leg on the girth will exert pressure, helping to bend the horse around the inside leg.

INSTRUCTOR: *If your student is old enough, explain the reasons for the proper leg action on the turns. With small children, however, the use of the leg aids in turning will have to be repeated over and over until they become automatic. Lead the horse at a walk. (A good beginner horse may even follow you without benefit of a lead rope.) Turn to the left and to the right, pointing in the direction of the turn to give the student help and practice in coordinating the aids.*

There is a lot, now, for a young child to remember. Help him, if he has trouble, by "making like an airplane." Say "Now we're going left." Point to the left (his hands move left), lean to the left (he'll lean also), and hold your right arm up to show "this leg behind the girth." Practice

"Making like an airplane" to help the young student remember to lean into the turn, with his outside leg (right, in this case) behind the girth.

this several times in both directions, interspersing stops and starts. Beginning students do not understand the concept of weight displacement through seat-bone pressure, but the simple concept of "lean" left or right starts them on the right track. Later, when they have more experience, weight aids can be explained fully.

The Exercises

Go through your battery of exercises as learned in the first lesson. Except for turning-in-the-saddle and the lying-down exercises, do these at a walk. Always make sure an assistant is there to steady you and to control the horse.

INSTRUCTOR: *Variety in a lesson, especially for youngsters, keeps the lesson enjoyable. You will find too that keeping at one thing too long allows a child's attention to wander. If a student has trouble coordinating the aids, switch to an exercise or two to help him relax. If he is getting tired, stop altogether and go over the points of the horse.*

Managing Your Horse Alone

Now is the time to try managing your horse alone. (An assistant may help if you need it.) Remember to use all the aids, as gently as possible, increasing them if necessary. Walk around the ring in both directions. Try to stop at predetermined points, such as opposite the corral gate. Decide that you will touch, perhaps, a corral post or a spot on the barn. This may sound ridiculously easy, but accurate control of your mount is gained only by practice combined with intelligent thought.

INSTRUCTOR: *Stand nearby to give help if the student really needs it, but make sure he has the practice of working on his own. Younger children tend to allow the reins to get too long. If open reins are used, be sure that they are knotted together. Watch for such problems and correct them immediately. But as much as possible, allow the student to work out the problem of control without correction. Ask him to direct his horse to a corral post and other designated points and to touch them.*

If he has trouble managing his horse alone, review some part of the lesson he did especially well. Remember to end the lesson on a positive note, leaving the student encouraged and enthused.

Part 2 · The Third Lesson

Review and New Work

INSTRUCTOR: *It is important during the early lessons in horsemanship to give something new each lesson as well as to review the old material. It is better to accomplish only part of a lesson, if your student progresses slowly, than to take the whole lesson and repeat it, as is, for three weeks in a row. Even if it is only one exercise, or else a change of scene from one corral to another, you should add something new to maintain the interest of the beginning student. Variety helps to keep the horse from becoming bored and inattentive as well.*

Preliminaries to the Third Lesson

Last lesson you learned the parts of the forehand from the labeled diagram in Appendix A. For this week learn the points of the hindquarters.

Groom your horse and tack up (still without stirrups). Your assistant will give you a leg up and stand by while you review what you have learned so far. Work alone as much as possible.

INSTRUCTOR: *While the horse is at the crosstie, point out the parts of the forehand and ask the student to name them. Assign the parts of the hindquarters and go over them, referring both to the horse and the work sheet.*

Review the last two lessons, with the student managing his horse alone, if possible. After you review the exercises, introduce a new exercise: Have the student touch the parts of the horse that are not too difficult for him to reach, such as neck, withers, poll, point of hip, and so on. This exercise coincides with the written work by helping to instill the points of the horse (as well as improving the child's flexibility and confidence). The better able you are to complement your instruction with examples and instances, the more solid the instruction will be.

Emphasis of the Lesson—More Precise Control

Precise control of your mount must be acquired by practice. Beginning riders are apt to walk a very uneven line when attempting to move straight ahead, or to take up half the ring when turning their horse around. You know what to do, but you must acquire skill in the actual execution of the aids. Continue to practice starts, halts, and turns, working for smooth, coordinated control. Two figures that will help greatly to improve your precision are the reverse and the volte (vōl'-tay).

The Reverse

You have been making reverses all along, but now you should concentrate on executing the movement correctly.

A reverse is a simple change of direction. The rider leaves the rail and moves in a small circle (about twenty feet in diameter) toward the center of the ring. When half of the circle is completed, he returns to the rail, continuing on the same track but in the opposite direction. The pattern of the horse's tracks will make half a heart (see Figure 20 in Chapter XI).

This method of reverse is correct in horse shows throughout the West. (The identical figure in dressage riding is called the *half-volte and change.*) In some sections of the country, however, riders are supposed to reverse toward the rail rather than away from it. Make sure that you understand which direction of reverse is correct for your area before entering a horse show.

INSTRUCTOR: *Beginners tend to make their reverse pattern and voltes too large and uneven. Explain to them that at the faster gaits (trot and canter) the circle or half circle will probably be larger than at the slow trot or walk in these beginning stages. Dressage instructors require voltes and reverses of specific and exact size, but for now the most important thing to work for is roundness in the pattern and to avoid oversize patterns.*

The Volte

The volte is a complete, small circle made toward the inside of the ring (see Figure 21). The faster the gait, the larger will be the volte until the rider progresses beyond the beginning stages. At the walk, the diameter of the circle should be about twenty feet.

In a volte to the right, use the aids as when turning right. You will have to learn to give the horse the exact direction that keeps him on the circle. Try to avoid either too sharp a turn or drifting away from the circle. And you should try to straighten out properly when you return to the rail. The volte is *round*. It is easiest to achieve this, at first, by working in a corner of the ring, rather than along one side.

The volte is an important exercise which helps to develop your balance, control, and coordinative use of the aids.

INSTRUCTOR: *Lead the student for the first few times, emphasizing the importance of keeping the figure as close as possible to a perfect circle.*

The Stick Game

Again for relaxation and a change of pace, ride around the ring halting exactly at a predesignated spot, touching a gate or corral post.

The stick game is a variation of this practice in precision. Put a grain box, wide plastic pan, or other container in the center of the ring. Hold a stick in one hand along with the rein. Ride up close to the container, halt,

The stick game. Even though rider is not using stirrups, she should have safety helmet and boots.

take both reins in one hand, and try to drop the stick into the container. Approach the container from different angles. You will have to give your horse accurate aids to have him halt near enough to the box so that you can drop (not throw) the stick into it.

INSTRUCTOR: *Children enjoy this game. In a class, give the stick to the first rider. Have him walk around the ring and touch certain designated spots with the stick (one point each), then drop it into the container (five points).*

Introducing the Slow Trot

If all has gone well so far and if you feel ready for it, try a slow trot. The instructor or assistant should lead your horse to keep him from moving ahead too fast or from slowing up prematurely. Keep the reins loose—there is sometimes a tendency for beginners to "hang on with the reins." This is exactly what you don't want to do, for you must never jab at the horse's mouth.

Give the following aids:

- Squeeze equally with both legs (the amount of pressure depending on the sensitivity of your horse),
- say "Trot!" in a short, exclamatory manner,
- incline your body forward slightly, and
- move your hands slightly forward.

Then just sit, getting the feel of the gait. Once around the ring (or even less) is enough. Concentrate on trying to maintain the Basic Seat position without stiffening up. You will have to develop suppleness in your spine to sit the trot without bouncing.

INSTRUCTOR: *Usually children love to trot. They are eager to try it and will generally sit relaxed and enjoy it. Adults are liable to be much stiffer and more nervous about the faster, rougher gait.*

Make sure that all has gone well so far and that the student is ready for the slow trot. If you are in doubt, it will do no harm to wait another week before introducing it. Much depends on the student's individual progress.

First lead the horse at a slow trot while the student watches from the ground. He will see that the trot is a two-beat gait and get an idea of how it looks and sounds.

Leading at a slow trot—an assistant is ready to steady the child if necessary.

Help him mount up and give the aids as stated above, and lead the horse once around the ring at a slow trot. If the student is young, have an assistant walk beside the child to steady him. The assistant may hold the child's leg—not his back—if the youngster needs encouragement.

Except for teaching the aids for starting into the trot, there should be no instruction whatever at this time. This is purely an introductory exercise, allowing the student to feel the gait.

The Western Seat

If you wish to introduce Western riding now instead of several lessons farther on, turn to Chapter V before coming back to Chapter IV.

The Trot

Lesson Phases 4 and 5

Part 1 · Fourth Lesson Phase

Progress is an individual achievement. A student should feel that he is progressing according to his own ability, neither rushing ahead nor being held back. For this reason, the lessons will now be referred to as lesson *phases*. They are not intended to be taught or mastered in a week's time. How much time each lesson will take is an individual matter. Be sure to master one phase before going on to the next.

The home study assignments for these lessons are listed in Appendixes A and B. Instructors may wish to assign a new study sheet each week while the actual lesson phases themselves may take any number of weeks to master. If you are teaching yourself, do keep up with the written or study work on a weekly basis: It will greatly aid your all-round knowledge and understanding of horses and horsemanship.

Tacking Up

Groom your horse and tack up with bridle and saddle pad or English saddle. This time you will use stirrups. Slip the stirrup leather over the bar as shown in the illustration on page 72. This type of fastening is a safety device

The safety stirrup bar.

enabling the stirrup to release in case of an emergency. If you were to fall from the horse with your foot caught in the stirrup, the leather would slide off the bar and you would not be dragged.

When the saddle pad or any English saddle is not actually in use, the stirrups are run up on the leathers, and the girth is laid over the seat of the saddle.

Be sure, as always, that you check the off side of the saddle before tightening the girth. The girth may be turned or the saddle flap folded under.

INSTRUCTOR: *Show the student how to run the stirrups up on the leathers and ask him to do it. Students often have a tendency to run the stirrups up on the outside leather rather than the inside. Remind him to run up the stirrups before unsaddling. When the near stirrup is run up, it also reminds the student to walk his horse before tightening the girth for mounting.*

Adjusting the Stirrups from the Ground

Stirrups must be adjusted to the proper length in order to be useful. Stirrups that are uneven can be dangerous because they destroy your balance, leg contact, and Basic Seat position.

To make an approximate length adjustment for an English stirrup, face the saddle and put your fingertips on the stirrup buckles. Hold your arm

Making an approximate adjustment for an English stirrup.

straight, and the stirrup iron should reach to your armpit. When you adjust the stirrups from the ground in this manner, a minimum of further adjustment will be needed from the saddle.

Mounting—English

First check the girth, making sure that it is tight but not uncomfortable for the horse. It is almost impossible for a woman to get a saddle pad too tight. However, when using a saddle, you should be able to insert three fingers comfortably between the girth and the horse's barrel. If you cannot, or if the horse's skin is wrinkled anywhere under the girth, the saddle is probably too tight.

Take the reins in the left hand along with a lock of mane. This is important for the beginner. It will keep you from pulling on the horse's mouth in mounting because your hand is fixed in position. A sharp jerk that pulls the horse's head suddenly to the side can unbalance him and cause him to stumble sideways, or it may even completely throw him. (This may sound unlikely, but we've seen it happen.)

Adjust the reins to have an even bearing on the horse's mouth—not too tight, but you want to be in control of your horse while mounting. It is disconcerting—and often disastrous—to get partway up and find that the horse has gone on without you. The bight of the reins (the part of the reins that falls beyond your hand) should fall on the off side.

Stand by the horse's left shoulder and face slightly toward his hindquarters. You should be able to watch the forehand as well as the hindquarters. Horses can bite as well as kick. With your right hand turn the stirrup toward you. Put your left foot in the stirrup, firmly on the ball of your foot. Be careful, as you mount, not to let your left toe dig into the horse's elbow or barrel. You can help avoid this by pressing your left knee against the saddle as you mount.

Fig. 7 Mounting, English: put your left foot in the stirrup.

Spring off your right foot (your right hand should be on the off side of the cantle), and balance on your hands with your legs together. Do not pull yourself up with your right hand on the cantle: This will put too severe a strain on the saddle, pull it off center, and eventually twist the tree. Bend your right knee and pass your leg over the horse's croup without touching him. Sink down easily into the center of the saddle and put your right foot in the stirrup. This should be a single fluid motion.

It may be easier said than done the first time. Unless you are lithe and athletic, it is generally best for a beginner to hop on the right foot and face the horse before springing into the saddle. This will not only give you a little extra bounce, but will put you into a better position to maintain your balance until you get the feeling for it. Try for a continued movement from the

Fig. 8   Balance on your hands with legs together.

original mounting position, through the hop and spring into the saddle, then assume the Basic Seat position.

INSTRUCTOR: *First demonstrate how to mount for your student. Emphasize the importance of swinging your leg well over the horse to avoid touching him. With a nervous, poorly trained, or green horse, touching him behind the saddle or kicking him in the hip is liable to start a rodeo on the spot. A good horseman is never lazy, no matter what kind of mount he is on.*

Emphasize also that the student settle lightly into the saddle. Often a beginner will land with a thump and a sigh of relief at having made it. This is poor horsemanship, hard on the horse, and again, may start more than the rider can finish.

Dismounting—English

Place your left hand in front of the saddle pad as in the initial step in mounting. (This hand will hold the reins and a lock of mane.) Place your right hand on the off side of the pommel. Remove your right foot from the stirrup, shift your weight onto your left foot and right hand, and swing your right foot, with leg bent, over the croup. Your right foot should now be even with your left foot in the stirrup. Your left knee is resting against the saddle, your body is inclined slightly forward, and your weight is on your hands.

Remove your left foot from the stirrup and slide to the ground, landing lightly with knees bent. (AHSA rules, 1991 Hunter Seat Equitation Section, now state that riders may either step down or slide down.) The size of the rider should be taken into consideration in determining the appropriate dismount.

INSTRUCTOR: *First demonstrate dismounting for your student, holding (for emphasis) the position where you are balanced on your hands before dropping to the ground. Make sure he understands that he should remain balanced during dismounting and that the horse is constantly under control. In other words, the dismount is an orderly procedure, not an "abandon ship."*

You should emphasize also that the student bend his knees on landing—if not, he may get an awful jar and lose his balance as well.

Adjusting English Stirrups from the Saddle

As you sit in the saddle, relax and let your legs hang naturally. The stirrups will usually be correctly adjusted on an English saddle if the stirrup iron touches your anklebone. (Be sure you are sitting squarely in the saddle.)

You may adjust the stirrups on a saddle pad or an English saddle as you sit in the saddle. A helper can assist you the first time. If he stands in front of your horse, he can see that your stirrups are even. Many people have one leg slightly longer than the other (this may be the first time you've noticed that yours don't match), so take this into consideration.

To adjust your left stirrup, take the reins in your right hand, keep your foot in the stirrup, and with your left hand unbuckle the stirrup leather just enough to slide up or down a hole. Reverse the process for the right stirrup. With just a little practice you'll be able to do this quickly by feel alone.

There is a right and a wrong way to put your foot into the English stirrup. As you look down on the left stirrup, both leather and iron hang parallel to the side of the horse. Point your toe in toward the girth and pick up the stirrup. You may help by turning the leather with your left hand so that it lies flat against your leg. If you were to pick up the stirrup from the inside (your toe pointing out), the leather would be twisted and would rub badly against your leg.

Adjusting the English stirrup from the saddle.

Review Work

Mentally check over your Basic Seat position, and review the walks, halts, turns, reverses, and voltes. Remember to concentrate on coordinating the aids. Now, of course, you'll be using the stirrups. Push lightly into the stirrup irons, keeping your heels down.

Review the exercises, except for the Up-down exercise. Cross the stirrups in front of you over the top of the saddle pad as you do these. This keeps your stirrup irons from painfully banging on your ankles, and from swinging against the horse.

INSTRUCTOR: *Use your judgment when doing review work and exercises. These are necessary and important, but avoid boring the student with them.*

Sooner or later you will come across the student who has trouble reining and mumbles under his breath, "Turn, you stupid horse!" Finally he will say to you, "This horse won't do anything!" You cannot allow a student to attribute his own difficulties to the horse. An excellent rider will get a good performance out of almost any horse. Make sure that the student understands this explicitly. Tell him that you don't expect him to coordinate his aids perfectly yet—that is why he's taking lessons. But unless he realizes that his own control needs improvement, he will never be able to manage a horse. If necessary you may have to mount his horse and prove the tractability of the mount.

Emphasis of the Lesson—Introducing the Trot

You will be spending considerable time with the trot. This gait is important to the rider for developing control.

The 1–10 Exercise

As an assistant leads your horse in a slow trot around the ring, sit relaxed to the gently bouncing motion. Were the horse to increase his speed, the gait would become rougher and be more difficult to sit. To make the normal trotting gait easier on both rider and horse, the rider will post, or rise in the saddle to the rhythm of the horse's gait. The Up-down exercise has prepared you for the posting trot.

Review the Up-down exercise, at a walk, first without stirrups and then with. We have been doing the exercise to the count of four, rising and sitting on each count. Keep a light rein so as to avoid the temptation to pull yourself up by the reins.

Now stop your horse and repeat the exercise double time, or about the cadence of a normal trot. While your assistant leads you around the ring, repeat the exercise several times, counting to ten instead of to four. Try to rise and sit in a fluid, not jerky, manner.

INSTRUCTOR: *It will take the student awhile to learn to manage the stirrups properly. He will have to put some weight into his stirrups or he will lose them. But, as with no stirrups, the main pushing pressure for the Up-down exercises should come from the knee-thigh area.*

The student should use a very light rein while you lead the horse at a walk. Or you may prefer to have him fold his arms across his chest. To help him catch the increased rhythm of the 1–10 exercise, walk backward and use a lifting motion of your hand on each rising count.

In the next few weeks, start with these exercises before you begin working on the trot—1–4 without stirrups, and 1–10 with.

Posting to the Trot

Now try to post at a normal trot while an assistant leads the horse. The horse will determine the rhythm of your up-down movement. At first you will probably do a bit of double bouncing before the rhythm is established. Remember that you must work *with* the horse. Try to let the horse push you up, then return to the saddle in rhythm.

After doing the exercise, many students are able to post correctly on their first try. Other people require considerable time to coordinate their posting to the rhythm of the horse.

You will notice that it is more difficult to maintain the rhythm through the turns and corners. If you have trouble catching on to posting, listen to the beat of the gait. Say to yourself "One, two, one, two," then, "up, down, up, down." It will come with practice.

As you tire, practice other maneuvers at a walk, then try the trot again. Avoid letting your muscles get overtired, but give yourself a chance.

INSTRUCTOR: *When you begin the fourth lesson phase, give your student a horse that has a cadenced trot. Many horses that have had improper training never learn to stabilize their gaits. Their strides may be uneven and they may speed up and slow down continually. This kind of horse is difficult and undesirable for a beginner.*

Make sure, too, that the horse has a pronounced trot. Some horses have such smooth gaits that anyone can sit their trot with ease. It is difficult to teach a beginner to post on this type of horse, simply because he doesn't have to: He can feel no upward impulsion.

If the student does fairly well as you lead his horse around the ring at a trot, mount your horse and ask the student to follow you. He will still keep his reins long so as not to pull on the horse's mouth if he loses his balance. Many weeks of practice will be necessary before he can approach capability at the trot. Give plenty of practice at both walk and trot, and be lavish with encouragement. If the student appears tired, halt and go over the parts of the horse. Especially with small children, much variety and repetition are needed.

Improving Your Seat

Now that you have some experience with the Basic Seat position, you can work to improve your seat.

1. Sit as far forward as is comfortable for you. This should put your seat bones in the center of a well-balanced saddle. You should always be able to feel a hand's breadth behind you to the edge of the saddle (whether pad, English, or Western).
2. Holding the front of the saddle or a lock of mane in one hand, *pull yourself deep* into the saddle (or the horse's back—this exercise is especially good bareback).
3. To improve the position of your thighs and seat,
   (a) Keeping your legs straight, rotate them from the hip joint (the right leg clockwise, the left leg counterclockwise),
   (b) and then roll them forward against the saddle and into the proper position. Look at your thighs. Now you can actually *see* (and also feel!) what is meant by keeping the "flat of your thigh" against the saddle.
   (c) Do not grip with your legs.
4. Keep your knees supple, the bone of your knee against the saddle (or the horse).
5. Place your feet in the proper position, lower leg back so that your toe and knee are in line (or so that you cannot see your toe over your knee), with your weight on the inside of your heel.
6. Sit tall and straight, yet relaxed, head up and eyes forward.

You will feel the new pull on your muscles. Good! Don't overdo, but do keep practicing. You'll soon feel the improvement in your seat and security.

INSTRUCTOR: *If you don't already have a school horse that will work on a longe line, do train one to do so. This is the only way you can maintain complete control of a horse while training the rider. For the student, it is the best possible method of improving his seat because, since he does not have to control the horse, he can devote all his concentration on his riding. Arrange the reins as shown in Figure 9.*

Exercises to be done on the longe line:

Have your student sit as explained above. Teach the exercises first at the halt, then at a walk.

1. *To strengthen thigh muscles, stretch toes down toward the ground, then up. Repeat on the count of ten or more.*
2. *Supple ankles by turning soles of feet in, then out, keeping heels down.*
3. *With left hand, pull up on a lock of mane or the front of the saddle to deepen seat; rotate right arm slowly in a full circle, palm up when*

ADJUSTING REINS FOR LONGEING:

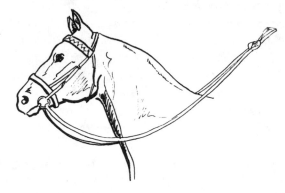

1. knot reins

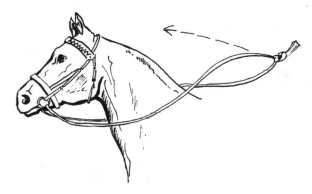

2. figure-8 reins

3. position knot under neck (loop of
rein may also be caught up
in throatlatch of bridle)

Fig. 9

coming forward, palm down when going back and down. Repeat with left arm while pulling into seat with right.

4. *Reach up with both arms as high as you can; then put arms on head, hold them out to the side, put them on hips, then reach forward and down without losing seat. Repeat.*

5. *Hold arms out to the side, keeping them parallel to the ground. Rotate shoulders to the right so that arms are in line with the horse's backbone and you are looking full to the right. Rotate shoulders a full 180 degrees to the left. Hold position for eight strides and rotate.*

Reestablish leg position as often as is necessary while doing the exercises. When the student is ready, do them at the trot. The student will be able to do No. 3 at a trot the first time; however, he may need considerably more practice before he can do No. 4 or No. 5 at a trot. For more exercises, see Chapter V, "Riding Western," and Appendix C, "Exercises for the Rider."

Consistent Practice

You learn to ride only by practice. As you begin something new in each lesson phase, you must add it to your accumulation of knowledge and constantly practice the cumulative review.

Cooling the Hot Horse

INSTRUCTOR: *Now may be a good time to explain how to tell when a horse is "hot" and then show how to care for him.*

Feel the horse between his forelegs—if he is "hot," his skin will feel hot to your hand.

Because a horse should cool slowly, do not remove the saddle and blanket immediately. Loosen the cinch, walk the horse awhile, remove the saddle (not the blanket), walk awhile, then finally remove the blanket and walk the horse until the area between his forelegs is cool. (It can still be damp, but not hot.) Walking your horse at least ten minutes before the end of a ride will ensure coming in cool; it saves hand walking and is the safest procedure for the horse.

Explain to the student that he should not put cold water on the horse's back when he is hot. After the horse has cooled, he should be rinsed with warm water and dried. A soft brushing will feel pleasant to him.

Exercises on the longe line help the rider to improve his seat (Exercise 4).

Students practice Exercise 5.

Part 2 · Fifth Lesson Phase

Emphasis of the Lesson—The Posting Trot

As soon as your posting has progressed beyond the up-and-down-any-old-way stage, you will want to work on posting correctly. You will have to learn when you should be "up" or "down." There is a definite rule for this, called posting on the correct diagonal. Read over again the paragraphs on the trot in Chapter I and in Part 1 of this chapter.

Problems in Posting

Be sure to go through the 1–4 and 1–10 exercises before starting to trot. You have had enough experience now so that you will be able to keep up a trot for longer periods of time. By interspersing slower gaits, exercises, and drill, you will keep your muscles from getting too tired and also keep your horse from becoming bored.

Think about your posting as you trot around the ring and try not to post too high. Doing so is not only unnecessary, but it destroys the purpose of posting—to make the trot comfortable to horse and rider. Extreme motion out of the saddle is exhausting as well as being a forced movement that has lost fluidity. Stay as close to the saddle as you can, and incline your upper body forward. Try to push up with knees and thighs (not feet) and keep lower legs as quiet as possible.

INSTRUCTOR: *Your student is now able to control his horse passably well. Before teaching diagonals, he should be able to post evenly and consistently on turns. If you are mounted for this lesson, you will be able to demonstrate how to post close to the saddle.*

Learning to Post on the Correct Diagonal

You have in mind now the theory of how a horse trots, what the gait looks like and how it sounds, what diagonals are, and the fact that, when working in a ring, you want to post to the outside diagonal—that is, *you rise as the*

Posting on the outside diagonal—the rider rises as the horse's outside shoulder moves forward. Posting is exaggerated, and rider's torso should be inclined more forward.

horse's outside shoulder moves forward, sit as it comes back. If you rise as the right shoulder moves forward, you are on the right diagonal.

An assistant for this lesson is helpful. As he leads your horse in a circle at a trot, stand on the ground outside the circle. When the horse trots to the left, watch his right foreleg. As it goes forward say "Up," and as it hits the ground say "Down." This sounds absurdly simple until you try it. Now reverse. As the horse moves around the circle to the right, watch the left foreleg. Say "Up," as it goes forward, "Down" as it hits the ground.

Now mount up and trot just once around the ring. Watch the outside shoulder. Try to spot which diagonal you are on—whether right or left. Are you posting (rising) as the outside shoulder moves forward? This is correct. But don't worry if you're on the wrong diagonal—the important thing is to recognize which one you are on. Stop and try again.

While you are posting, try also to notice the feel of the gait and any difference in the feel of the left and right diagonals. An advanced rider is able to tell which diagonal he is on by the feel only; he doesn't have to look down. Develop your feel of the gaits as soon as possible—truly harmonious horsemanship can be achieved only when both horse and rider are looking ahead, not down.

INSTRUCTOR: *Generally the clearest way to teach diagonals is to demonstrate. You may have to exaggerate your posting to make it easier for the student to spot the diagonals—explain that you are exaggerating, that he should not really post that high.*

Ask the student to call out which diagonal you are on. Ride in figure-eights and have him call out either "right" or "left" as you change.

Then it is the student's turn to mount, trot, and try to recognize which diagonal he is on.

Changing Diagonals

Although you may be able to see that you are posting on the wrong diagonal, it may be easier said than done at first to change to the correct diagonal. Properly, you change the diagonal by sitting *one* bounce.

To sit just one bounce requires control, and this you will have to develop. Usually a student will sit two bounces, or a whole series of bounces, and still be on the same diagonal he started with. If you have difficulty with this, establish a rhythm as you post, saying "Up, down, up, down." Then as you change say "Up, down, down, up, down, up."

Again, practice is the key to mastering the problem. To practice posting on the correct diagonal and changing diagonals, and to work on control and steadiness at the trot, the figure-eight is an excellent exercise (see Figure 21). Incorporate it into your daily review work.

INSTRUCTOR: *Demonstrate how to change diagonals by sitting one bounce as you ride the figure-eight. Although you can change by rising the extra bounce, it seems that this is hard to teach and more difficult for the student to see and execute.*

When the student is able to tell correctly which diagonal he is on, have him try changing diagonals by sitting a bounce as you have demonstrated. Don't expect him to catch on immediately—he'll probably have to bounce several times at first.

When the student is able to post on either diagonal and change diagonals smoothly, drill him at the trot on circles and figure-eights, but slow to a walk often and review previous work.

Improving Your Hands

So far you have been working to keep your hands steady, to use the rein aids correctly, and to keep from hurting the horse's mouth by any dependence on the reins for balance. When your seat has become fairly secure through the walk and all phases of the trot, you are ready to improve your hands: to use them more sensitively.

Up until now your reins have been fairly long. You have had to pull back a little when stopping. You've turned by moving your hands together across the withers. Now shorten your reins just enough so that you can feel a very light pressure. In this way you have made light contact with the horse's mouth. Release again and this time see if you can, with your knees and calves, push the horse forward to make contact with the bit. When this is correctly done, the horse moves up into the bit and stops, rather than you shortening the reins to make contact. This will be more difficult to achieve with Western horses because they have been trained to a longer rein and lighter control. However, the light contact is still necessary for control.

An assistant should lead your horse around the ring at a walk. Keep your hands still, but maintain light contact with the horse's mouth. This will require you to "follow the horse's head," or to move your arms slightly forward and back in rhythm with his head as he walks. You are using your hands *passively*, or we say you have *passive hands*.

At the halt, close your fingers lightly on the reins and at the same time flex your wrists slightly. Release immediately and repeat. If your horse is well trained, he will "give," or flex, in answer to your rein pressure. Close the fingers and wrist of your left hand, and the horse will turn his nose slightly to the left. Try it to the right. You are now using a *direct rein*, putting pressure directly in line from the bit to your elbow. The direct rein is one type of rein action.

You have also used the *opening rein*: You put pressure on the bit by moving the rein in the direction you wish to go. (To move left, your hand moved the left rein to the left.)

The *indirect rein*, sometimes called the bearing rein, neck rein, or following rein, bears on the side of the neck opposite to the direction in which you wish to turn. To turn left, touch the right rein against the right side of the neck. This is neck reining, and most horses that are ridden Western style are trained to neck rein responsively.

Put your horse into a walk by using the normal aids, but release the reins with your fingers instead of moving your hands forward. Use your hands passively in the walk until it is time to turn in a corner. Close the fingers and wrist of your inside hand *actively*, and let the outside hand follow passively. Practice turns, voltes, and reverses while trying to maintain light contact. To halt, use both hands evenly, and of course release as your horse begins to halt. These are *active hands*.

When you can use your hands sensitively at a walk, try it at a trot.

Be conscious of how you are using your hands. It will require practice to

Improving your hands—demonstrate rein pressure by letting the student feel how your fingers move on the reins.

develop the sensitivity necessary to increase your understanding of your horse and progress toward your goal of harmonious horsemanship.

INSTRUCTOR: *Do not try to develop good hands in your student until he has a more secure seat. The cardinal sin is to hurt a horse's mouth; it is not possible to maintain sensitive hands if the seat is not secure.*

At a dressage clinic we heard one of the world's top dressage instructors say to a rider: "Your horse's mouth is absolutely sacred. If you murder the mouth I will take your bridle and you can manage without." She made her point in a way that one was not likely to forget.

But when the time does come that your student is ready to use his hands more actively, how can you best put across what you mean by "slight pressure," "closing the fingers," and so on? By demonstration. Detach two reins from a bridle and give them to your student to hold, just as he would if he were on a horse. Tell him his hands now represent the horse's mouth. Stand facing him, hold the reins correctly, and give the aids as you explain them. The student can see how your fingers move on the reins as he feels the pressure on his own fingers.

Then ask him to give the aids. You can feel if he is using his hands too strongly, and see if he is moving them incorrectly. This is often very enlightening to a student and worth far more than endless verbal correction.

CHAPTER FIVE

Riding Western

Sixth Lesson Phase

Many Americans throughout the country, especially children, prefer the relaxed informality of Western equitation for casual riding. By learning correct Western horsemanship early, the possible development of poor riding habits can be avoided. It is always easier to learn correctly from the beginning than to correct bad or faulty habits once they have become natural and confirmed.

As soon as the basics of control are understood in English equitation, you may begin work in Western horsemanship. The basic principles are the same, and both seats can be developed simultaneously. The slightly different emphasis of each (discipline in English, suppleness in Western) serves to complement the other. Your mastery of both seats is hastened, and your horse is benefited by increased versatility and usefulness.

Saddling and Unsaddling Western

Proceed as with the English saddle. When using a double-rigged Western saddle, the two cinches should be fastened together by a narrow strap under the belly to prevent the second cinch from slipping back.

Set the saddle on gently. If you place the off stirrup over the horn before saddling, it won't bang down against the horse's ribs. Go to the off side to smooth the blanket and make it even, to be sure the cinches are hanging square, and to take down the off stirrup.

On the near side, push the blanket up into the gullet and make sure the saddle is placed correctly. Secure the front cinch first. Then pull up the rear cinch so that it is snug; if it is too loose, the horse could catch his foot when kicking at a fly. Walk the horse before cinching tightly. When unsaddling, always release the rear cinch first. The right way to carry a Western saddle is shown on page 61.

INSTRUCTOR: *Demonstrate the order, tightness, and safety factors when using two cinches on a double-rigged saddle. Instruct your student to make sure the cinch rings are even with each other on both sides—not higher on one side and lower on the other. Have the student place the left stirrup over the horn to remind him to walk the horse before cinching tightly. Never cinch tightly without walking your horse first! This can lead to being "cinch-bound."*

Adjusting Western Stirrups

You will not be able to adjust the length of stirrup on a Western saddle while you are in the saddle. In fact, adjustment of the Western stirrup can be tedious. If you have your own saddle, you may find the proper length and lace it to stay. If the saddle must be used by several people, buy quick-change buckles to make stirrup adjustment more convenient.

The Western stirrup is usually adjusted an inch or two longer than the English, and should touch an inch or two below the anklebone. You can check the length by standing in the stirrups. If your seat just clears the saddle, the stirrups should be about right.

Mounting Western

Hold the reins evenly (along with a lock of mane) in the left hand. The bight of the reins should fall on the near side. (When using a romal, the bight is on the left when mounting, then falls on the right—or the side opposite the rein hand.) Face the horse and put your left foot in the stirrup. Spring off the right foot and at the same time grasp the saddle horn or off swell of the saddle with the right hand. Bend your knee as in English, swing over lightly keeping your body close to the horse, and put your right foot into the stirrup.

When riding ranch horses for seasonal work with cattle, it is especially important not to hit the horse with your foot when mounting. Range horses are not ridden frequently during the year, and they are more jumpy about being touched than are stabled horses. If they were trained by older methods, they will be more inclined to buck.

INSTRUCTOR: *If you demonstrate mounting and dismounting in slow motion as well as at normal speed (this holds for both English and Western), the student will catch on more quickly. The demonstration helps the student to see just what he should do and helps him become more fluid in his motion.*

Make sure that your student has contact with the horse's mouth while mounting.

Dismounting Western

Place your left hand in the same position as in the initial stage in mounting. Rest your right hand on the horn or the off swell. Remove your right foot from the stirrup and with bended knee swing your foot over the croup and all the way to the ground. Step down looking toward the horse's head. When using split reins, you may take down both reins, or leave the right rein over the horse's neck.

Review

You may begin your first Western lessons by using the saddle pad as in English. Review previous lessons, maintaining a good English Seat. Review your riding at a walk, slow trot, and trot. Work continually on fluidity of your position, smoothness and timing in giving the aids, maintaining rhythm and cadence, anticipating and working *with* your horse—in short, harmonious horsemanship.

Exercises for Western Equitation

Before beginning work on the Western Seat, go through this group of four exercises. They were designed and used for training the United States Cavalry, and their specific purpose is to help relax and supple the muscles, especially through the loins or from the hips up. This suppleness is especially important in Western riding.

The first three exercises may be practiced at the halt, walk, and jog. The fourth should be executed only at the halt.

1. Begin by taking the correct English Basic Seat. Take both reins in your left hand. Swing your right hand around to touch the horse's *near* point of shoulder. Keep your arm straight. You will have to lean

ARMY EXERCISE 1: swinging your arm to touch the horse's opposite point of shoulder.

ARMY EXERCISE 2: swinging your arm in a circle.

considerably to the left to accomplish this properly. Come back to your Basic Seat position. Take the reins in your right hand and repeat the exercise to the right, touching the horse's off point of shoulder with your left hand. While your upper body is very mobile in this exercise (your shoulders will pivot 180 degrees), your legs and feet should maintain the Basic Seat position from the hip joint down. Don't allow your legs and feet to wander.

2. Hold the reins in your left hand. Extend your right hand out in front of you with your palm up. Keeping your arm straight, swing it up and around in a complete wide circle, smoothly, rhythmically, and vertically. Repeat for several circles with each arm. You should feel the muscles in your back and shoulders.

3. Take the reins in your left hand and keep your legs in position. Make a fist with your right hand. Bring your fist back to your right shoulder and then strike out straight ahead. Be careful, of course, that you don't hit your horse if he holds his head high! Repeat this several times with each fist.

4. This exercise is for suppling the hip joints. Maintain the Basic Seat position with your upper body.

ARMY EXERCISE 3: striking ahead with your fist.

Drop your left stirrup and, keeping your leg straight, describe a circle with your whole leg from the hip joint to foot. Repeat a few times, then describe circles with your right leg. Finally, repeat with both legs at once. This exercise can be tiring: Begin slowly with just a few circles and work up gradually to more.

INSTRUCTOR: *You may be interested in the following quotations on the reason for suppling exercises. These are from the United States Cavalry manual* Horsemanship and Horsemastership *(Academic Division, the Cavalry School, Fort Riley, Kansas, 1935, and edited by Gordon Wright, Doubleday, 1962) in a special chapter on suppling exercises:*

"The mounted instruction of the inexperienced rider is hindered at the beginning by an unreasoning and instinctive fear of the horse, over which he feels he has no control, and a resulting revolt of his nervous and muscular systems, which leads to contraction. This fear is overcome by establishing the confidence of the rider in himself and in his horse by means of mounted gymnastics and suppling exercises. . . .

"In attempting to obtain suppleness it should be remembered that good humor is conducive to relaxation, which in turn leads promptly and directly to confidence.

"The suppling exercises, like all physical culture exercises, depend for their good results upon the regularity and thoroughness with which they are practiced daily. . . .

"The suppling exercises engage the rider's attention and lead him to ride without conscious effort, thereby bringing about relaxation of the muscles. . . ."[They] have for their object the assistance of the rider in developing the strength, pliancy, and easy control of the parts of the body most affected in riding. These are the neck, shoulders, loins, hip joints, knees, and ankles."

The Western Basic Seat

Now you are ready to begin work on the Western Basic Seat. If you are using a saddle pad, lengthen your stirrups a notch to allow you to sit the Western Basic Seat properly. Although your stirrups are longer, you are not riding with a straight leg. Your lower leg remains vertical (not pushed forward), and your heels must still be down.

Take the reins in your left hand, but hold your hand an inch or two higher than you do in English. This is to clear your presently hypothetical saddle horn. Your hand should still be low, however. A high-held rein hand often combines with flapping elbows and lack of control—common faults in Western equitation.

The Western Basic Seat.

Achieving Rapport

It is helpful to use the saddle pad—or even ride bareback—during these beginning lessons. One of the most important parts of learning to ride, beyond technical proficiency in the saddle, is the feeling of rapport you achieve with your horse.

In riding, this rapport must be gained by experience in combination with theoretical knowledge. It is an amalgam of understanding and intuition. Some riders, in fact, never achieve it, although they may always do "what is correct" in the saddle.

Harmonious horsemanship is the essence of riding. It is as important in Western equitation as it is in English. Perhaps more so, because nowhere else in the field of riding is so much left to the judgment, decision, and training of the horse himself than under true Western working conditions.

INSTRUCTOR: *Most children are avid to use a Western saddle, but this should not be rushed. Make sure that the student understands why he is using the saddle pad or riding bareback. His understanding will help him to achieve the rapport that is so desirable.*

Incidentally, by using a saddle pad until the fundamentals of the Western Seat are learned, you avoid the beginner's temptation to grab for the saddle horn (called "pulling leather"), which can bring penalties or disqualification in Western equitation classes.

Use of the saddle pad (rather than a Western saddle) holds a special benefit for the instructor: It is much easier for you to see exactly what your student is doing with his legs and feet, whether he is applying the aids correctly and properly maintaining his position. The heavy Western saddle leathers (fenders) are not turned correctly on some saddles, or are so stiff that the rider's legs must conform to them rather than the saddle conforming to the legs. (For more information on tack, and especially on repositioning stiff fenders, see Basic Horse Care, *"Extra Tips on Tack Care #6.")*

The Walk

You are now "sitting tall in the saddle" in the Western Seat position. Move out at a walk around the ring by using the same aids as you did in English equitation. (See photo on page 4.) These should be natural to you by now. (If they aren't, go back to Chapter II, Part 5 and Chapter III, Part I for a quick review!)

Make sure that your reins are of even length. It seems amazingly easy, when first learning Western riding, suddenly to find that one rein is much longer than the other. Western equitation favors an easy rein, but you must maintain enough contact for control. You'll probably have to do a bit of experimenting before you find the length most desirable for you and your horse. (Horses are different and have definite preferences for the degree of contact.)

INSTRUCTOR: *When you are satisfied with the student's position, have him move out at a walk. Watch closely for stiffness of the back, heels high, moving the rein hand, and moving the free hand.*

Length of rein is a problem and should receive special attention. (In Western Pleasure show classes, the degree of "light rein" has always created a problem in definition.) Much depends on the horse himself— his training, his preferences, his bit—but beginners should certainly have enough contact for proper control. Watch also that the student keeps his reins even—the tendency seems to be for one to slip out longer than the other.

Watch that the shoulders are carried straight. The beginner tends to push the rein hand forward, bringing that shoulder forward; and this in turn tends to incline the body forward. As this disrupts both position and balance, it can become a difficult habit to break.

The Reverse (Half-Volte)

A Western horse is trained to respond quickly and expertly to neck reining. If your horse is not used to neck reining, you may have to exaggerate your aids at first. Remember to use the concept of increasing aids and to reward your horse by ceasing the pressure as soon as he begins to respond.

To reverse to the left, move your left hand to the left several inches. The left rein will be somewhat loose or bear very lightly on the bit, and the right rein will be resting or bearing on the horse's neck. Use your weight and leg aids simultaneously as in English equitation.

To reverse to the right, move your rein hand straight across the withers to the right, while giving the appropriate aids.

Always be sure your reins are even in length, or you and your horse may both become hopelessly confused on the turns.

Make sure also that in reining left or right you do not lift your rein hand. This is a common mistake made by beginning Western riders. Your rein hand should move horizontally.

Practice walking around the ring, reversing in both directions (toward the center of the ring). Remember to make proper reverses—following a half-circle of about twenty feet in diameter at a walk, continuing with an even rhythm back to the rail. Your horse should not pivot or otherwise interrupt the rhythm of his walk. Try some voltes and finally practice walking through a figure-eight.

INSTRUCTOR: *Demonstrate reining for your student. Demonstration often shows what a world of explanation will not, especially for young children.*

Problems to watch for in your student:

1. *Holding the rein hand too high when turning.*
2. *Holding the rein hand too far forward, bringing the shoulder forward and throwing the body out of balance.*
3. *Reversing in large, ungainly patterns.*
4. *Failure to keep the horse in a composed, even walk—interruption of rhythm.*
5. *The free hand coming off thigh or moving around.*

Practice with reverses and voltes, then have the student follow you through figure-eights and serpentines (see Figure 21) if you are mounted. He should follow about a horse's length behind you.

The Jog or Jog Trot

Use the same aids to obtain the jog as you did for the slow trot (equal leg pressure, slight forward inclination of the body, slight forward movement of the rein hand). If you have begun work to improve your hands, try to give and take on the reins with wrist and finger movement instead of moving the entire hand. Ask for the jog from a brisk walk, not a standstill. Practice transition in gaits by varying the walk and jog several times around the ring.

Next put your horse in a relaxed "trail" jog and try to obtain completely uninterrupted rhythm for several times around the ring. (Some horses have never learned to stabilize their gaits. If they have trouble keeping to a steady rhythm, see Part 3 of Chapter X, "Uneven Cadence in Gait.")

When you find this to be comfortable and easy, practice jogging through reverses, voltes, and figure-eights. You may have to make your circles larger than at a walk, but most important, keep them even and strive for an uninterrupted rhythm. Eventually you may strive for well-patterned, even voltes of the standard size.

Relaxed "trail" jog.

Your position remains upright as during the walk, or you may incline forward very slightly. On the turns, however, you'll notice that you will be leaning into them more than you did at a walk because of the slightly increased speed.

Problems to watch for at the jog—rein hand coming up, free hand coming off thigh, bouncing, heels coming up, no hat.

INSTRUCTOR: *Demonstrate the jog, calling attention to the speed of the gait and your position in the saddle both at the initiation of the jog and while circling the ring. A relaxed trail jog is best to begin with.*

Call for the walk and jog alternately, and watch the student's position in the saddle carefully. He may have great problems keeping his free hand on his thigh at first. If the hand comes up it tends to bring on flopping elbows, hunched shoulders, and other faults. If you have been using a pad or riding bareback, now is a good time to begin using Western tack.

Trail Riding

Every now and then the formal lessons should give way to a change of pace. What could be better than a trail ride? The student, the instructor, and the horses enjoy this change. A trail ride relaxes the student and gives him a chance to "forget self" temporarily while concentrating on a different aspect of riding. At the same time he is unconsciously practicing what he has learned in the ring lessons.

Trail rides fall into a number of different categories, depending upon length. For our lesson, the ride will probably last short of an hour. Longer rides—anything over half a day—should not be attempted until you have worked up to them. Both you and your horse must get into condition for a long ride—or what was supposed to be an enjoyable change could become miserable and even injurious both to you and to your mount.

We'll assume, for the sake of this lesson, that your horse is experienced on the trail. But if he has never been ridden beyond a ring or a civilized bridle path before, even if he's as steady as a rock wall, you may want to check the references on training your horse for the trail. You may be riding your horse for a longer period of time than usual and away from familiar surroundings. You can't afford to let him get by with unmannerly behavior. (See Chapter VIII, especially "Manners and Safety.")

INSTRUCTOR: *As soon as your student feels comfortable and confident using the Western Seat at the walk and jog, begin using Western tack instead of the saddle pad. Review the lesson in the corral or ring until he is familiar with the new tack before going out on the trail.*

The first few rides are better taken at the walk. During the ride, you'll want to emphasize important points as they come along. Most of these will treat directly with manners and safety. The horses you are using as mounts for your beginning trail riders should be good steady horses that follow each other nicely.

When ready to begin, make sure it is understood that you will lead and the others will follow behind in a line, in a preestablished order. As you start out, you will of course walk. Emphasize now that it is important to walk for at least ten minutes before moving into a faster gait. This will give the horses time to settle down and warm up to the ride.

Emphasize the importance of keeping proper distance between the horses: a horse's length is best, and generally safest, at a walk. Increase the distance by one or two lengths for the faster gaits. By traveling too close, one horse could get nipped or kicked by another; or if a horse shied, he could start a chain reaction; and if a horse stumbled and threw his rider, the following horse could run over the grounded horseman.

On the other hand, if the distance between horses is too great, a horse may suddenly hurry to catch up with the gang. The rush of hoofbeats may frighten or excite the other horses, thereby creating trouble for the inexperienced rider. If the last horse in line were to get far behind and have some difficulty, the other riders would be long gone before anyone noticed he was missing. On a trail ride with more than a few riders, it is important for each horse to keep the proper distance and maintain a steady pace. It is wise for more than one experienced horseman to ride with a group—one to lead, one behind to ensure the safety of the group.

Create an opportunity to go through gates. Dismount, open the gate, and have your students go through far enough to be out of the way. Then have them halt and wait while you close the gate and mount up. (Or you may choose this time to demonstrate how the well-trained trail horse will help you to open the gate while you remain in the saddle.) Again, this is good manners and proper safety.

While out on the ride, you might pick a haystack or clump of trees to ride around while you go through the beginning exercises—a bit of unemphasized ring work.

On the way back, stress the importance of walking home, especially during the last ten minutes. This should not be difficult to get across to the students because they will notice their horses' increased alertness and speed as they turn toward home. The horses would like to get home in a hurry, and if they take off, now is the time. Emphasize this to your students. Another reason for walking home is that it enables your horse to cool off gradually. If you come into the yard at a gallop, presumably still in one piece, you'll have to walk him anyway until he's cooled out.

CHAPTER SIX

The Canter and Lope

Seventh Lesson Phase

Part 1 · The English Canter

Review

You are now able to sit the Basic Seat properly—both English and Western—and to manage your horse fairly precisely at the walk, jog, or trot. Before beginning the canter, review what you have learned in English equitation. Give attention to your position at all gaits, especially when stopping, moving out, and turning. Strive continually to improve your application of the aids, and work to obtain precise responses from your horse.

Recognizing the Leads

Read again carefully the section on the canter, lope, and gallop in Chapter I. Unless you know how the horse should look—how his legs work—it is difficult to give the correct signals at the right time. And timing now becomes of the utmost importance. If your timing is off, your horse will not respond correctly to your aids.

Study photographs of cantering and loping horses and try to tell which horses are on the left lead, which on the right. Go to horse shows, rodeos, and

The right lead.

The left lead (showing different phase of canter). In both of these photos, note bend of horse around inside leg.

gymkhanas to watch—really *observe*—how horses and riders move in the different gaits.

INSTRUCTOR: *Demonstrate a medium-slow, well-controlled canter. Call attention to the way you are sitting the horse: Your buttocks remain in contact with the saddle and your back is supple. Demonstrate that some of your weight is resting in the stirrups; perhaps you could also show that too much weight in the stirrups destroys seat contact and that with too little weight in the stirrups you are liable to lose them.*

Starting into a Canter (The Canter Depart)

There are several methods of initiating the canter. The two most common in the United States today both require the horse to begin the canter on a specific lead, not one of his own choice.

One system of aids for obtaining the desired lead advocates turning the horse's head away slightly from the direction in which he is going. If you are in a ring, taking a circle to the left, you would turn the horse's nose out, or to the right, slightly, as you give the other aids for the canter. This is said to free the horse's left shoulder and therefore "throw" him into the left lead. This method is popular in some areas of the country and is sometimes a bit easier for the beginner to master.

We will learn to use the other method, however, because it is more consistent with the basic theory of equitation. It is the method most often used by dressage riders and Western horsemen. It differs from the other method chiefly in turning the horse's head slightly into the turn instead of away from it, thus keeping the horse laterally and evenly flexed into the turn.

The canter *can* be achieved by continuing to urge the horse forward, faster and faster, until he finally is trotting his fastest and so necessarily must break into a canter or gallop. Also, he is liable at this point to break away from you completely. In the canter we are not asking for speed, but for a specific pattern of hoofbeats. The canter can be obtained from the halt or the trot, but it is usually most desirable, at least in the beginning stages, to obtain it from a walk. Your horse should, however, be capable of taking a well-controlled canter from a trot.

How Your Aids Initiate the Canter

Walk your horse briskly and prepare him to take the canter by collecting him, or "putting him on the bit." That is, give equal leg pressure to increase his forward impulsion but restrain him with the reins to keep him from breaking into a trot. (See Part 2 of Chapter XI for explanation of collection.)

- Displace your weight to the inside. Earlier you were leaning to the left or right as a weight aid. But now you should begin using your weight more subtly. Displace your weight to the inside by sitting deeper in the saddle on that side—in other words, by putting more weight on the inside seat bone. This does not mean to shift your body position. However, your inside knee bones will drop slightly due to your deeper push on this side. Avoid the tendency to lean forward when sitting deeper on the inside. Also, avoid collapsing your inside hip (bowing your body to the inside without the correct seat-bone pressure).
- Put pressure on the inside rein, turning the horse's nose just slightly to the inside. In combination with the other aids, you are telling your horse to flex, not to turn inward. The horse's forelegs and hind legs should follow on the track, not deviate to inside or outside.
- Give pressure with the outside leg about a hand's width behind the girth. (Some horses will require more pressure, some even a kick.) This leg flexes the horse slightly, putting him in the proper position for the canter, and therefore signals the canter.
- Give steady pressure with the inside leg on the girth. This leg supplies the impulsion and keeps the horse's hindquarters from shifting inside the track.
- Simultaneously with the above four aids, release the rein pressure— that is, give with your fingers (though of course keeping contact). You are allowing the horse to go forward as directed, translating the impulsion into a canter.

Coordination of the aids requires considerable practice, and it may be some time before your timing is good enough so that the horse knows what you want. If your horse breaks into a trot, slow him and try again.

INSTRUCTOR: *Demonstrate the leads, and explain how to recognize which lead your mount has taken by glancing down at his shoulders. Demonstrate the aids, especially your position in the saddle as you take the canter, and have the student tell you exactly what he would do to obtain the left lead.*

It may be exhilarating—perhaps even frightening—when the student tries his first canter. The new feel of the gait and the surge of motion combine to give him enough to think about. Let him get the feel of the canter before worrying about correct leads. Avoid overdoing—a few short canters will be enough to start with.

Longeing your student at the canter is an excellent introduction to the feel of the gait. Because you control the horse, the rider can concentrate on the motion, thereby building both confidence and skill.

Begin by riding ahead of the student and lead him into the canter. Or better yet, have a good rider lead him, leaving you free to instruct from the center of the ring. Your school horses should follow well and thereby eliminate the need for precise control at this early stage. You may have to use voice aid to help the student's horse into the canter until the student has coordinated the aids well enough to tell the horse what to do. Do not canter for too long at a time; be ready to stop if the student should look the least unbalanced. You should also set the speed of the canter and keep it from becoming too fast.

Problems at the Canter

When you watch a good horseman circle the ring in a controlled, collected canter, it looks like the most comfortable gait in the world. He is sitting absolutely still on his horse (or so it seems!). His legs are quiet, his seat remains snug against the saddle, his shoulders are still. Look more closely. You may notice a suppleness in the small of his back and a give-take motion in his hands and arms, both of which harmonize with the rhythm of the horse.

You've just had your first canter and you bounced all over the saddle. Your feet went back; your heels came up; you felt jarred in the back of your neck; your horse surged ahead too fast, and you grabbed the mane with your hands.

What happened?

These are typical problems for beginners at the canter. The key to the solution of this situation is in your back. As you sit and relax in the saddle at the walk, you can feel motion through your pelvis. This same motion is stronger at the canter. Exaggerate the motion as you ride at the walk and then try a canter again. As you go into the canter, try to relax and let the horse's movement establish your own. Only then will you be able to sit the gait without losing contact with the saddle. This of course requires practice.

Watch for the following problems or tendencies as you learn to canter, and work to correct them:

1. Leaning too far forward—you should be vertical in the saddle during a collected canter or leaning slightly forward if the canter is more extended.
2. Leaning too far back.

Problems to watch for at the canter or lope—leaning too far forward, seat coming out of saddle, pulling and lifting the reins, toes pointing toward ground. Also, rider has no hat or safety helmet.

3. Pulling ("holding on") and lifting the reins.
4. Not enough contact with the legs and seat—this is usually connected with putting too much weight in the stirrups or poor leg position. Gripping too much with your legs will force you out of the saddle— much like gripping a wet bar of soap forces it out of your hand.
5. Losing stirrups—one or both.
6. Pointing your toes toward the ground in order to hold your legs to the saddle—this generally combines with the first fault. You don't realize it, but in your efforts to stay on, you are squeezing your horse into added speed.

The canter is very tiring when you are first learning it. It will be tiring to your horse also until you learn to harmonize with his movements and cease to be an ungainly weight. Be sure to alternate walks, trots, and exercises between canters. You will find that exercises which ease the tension in your legs, such as the Forward-back, Flexibility, and One-two are especially helpful.

INSTRUCTOR: *When the student has acquired a feel of the canter and has improved his balance so that this is no longer a prime consideration, he will no longer need to be cued by the horse ahead. Instruct from the center of the ring and watch his position carefully for the faults mentioned above.*

If Your Horse Does Not Respond to the Aids

Beginners usually have difficulty in coordinating their aids. With some students, this is more mental than physical. There is a certain "fear of the unknown" involved, and they communicate this fear to the horse. The horse becomes hesitant and will not perform. This fear is usually dissolved when the student tries a few canters and has the feel of the gait. Sometimes a short canter uphill on a trail ride is most effective in overcoming the beginner's first fear and hesitation.

It is usually easiest to obtain a canter if you give the aids as you are entering a corner. The horse will prepare himself to take the correct lead.

If your horse has been trained by a different method of aids from those we are using, he may not take the canter readily unless the other aids are given. Try using the method whereby you put enough pressure on the outside rein to turn the horse's nose a bit toward the rail. Also, lift the inside rein an inch or two, and apply the inside leg on the girth, the outside leg behind the girth. When the horse begins to canter, turn his nose to the inside position, flexing him properly, and keeping him on the track. He will soon respond to the regular aids.

Coordination of the aids themselves is important, but they are even more effective when used in conjunction with proper timing. By this we mean, *when* is exactly the right time to give the aids?

Here a knowledge of the horse's gaits is especially valuable. You remember that the pattern of the canter is initiated by the opposite, or outside, hind leg (on a left lead, then, the right hind leg). If you apply the aids for a left lead at the instant your mount's right hind leg makes impact with the ground, he is immediately able to thrust forward into the canter. To accomplish this, of course, you must *think* about your riding, *work* at getting the feel of the horse's gaits. Close your eyes and say "Left, right, left, right" as your horse's *hind* feet make impact with the ground. Look down and check yourself—it's not easy! Learn to know by the feel where each of your horse's feet is placed. This may be a tall order, but it will refine your riding immeasurably.

INSTRUCTOR: *Mount your beginning student on a responsive horse so that when he does coordinate the aids, the horse will respond by willingly taking the canter. An unresponsive horse will soon discourage the student.*

As an instructor, you should be thoroughly familiar with your horses and try to ride each of them on a regular schedule. If you notice several students having trouble initiating the canter on any particular horse, it would be well worth your time to give him extra attention and some intensive review training.

Part 2 · The Western Lope

When you are familiar with the feel of the canter, are able to remain well balanced, and have learned to coordinate the aids so as to obtain an immediate response from your horse, you may begin riding the Western Seat. The canter and lope are the same gait, though some horsemen insist on the distinction that the canter is collected, the lope more extended. In the show ring, the canter and lope are both shown collected.

The Aids

You have learned to coordinate the aids in English equitation. The same aids are used in Western riding except for the difference in handling the reins. To put your horse into a lope on the left lead.

- Push your horse into a brisk walk, keeping him alert and on the bit.
- Displace your weight to the left by pushing more heavily on your left seat bone.
- Turn your horse's head slightly to the left.
- Give pressure with your right calf or heel about a hand's width behind the cinch to signal the movement, and give pressure with your left leg on the cinch to provide impulsion.
- Simultaneously release with the left hand.

If your horse is not responsive to calf pressure, and if you cannot use your heel because of stiff fenders on the Western saddle, you may have to use a crop. If this is the case, remember the principle of the increasing aids. Give the aids as above and follow immediately with a smart snap with a crop. You will be training the horse and eventually he will respond to the aids before the snap. Be sure to reward him by release of pressure (and of course no crop).

Many horses are trained to respond to spurs, and this is often the solution for difficulties due to stiff Western saddles. Remember that spurs are not intended for punishment, but as a signaling aid. They demand good control in the rider and, as a general rule of thumb, should not be used until the rider is capable of training his horse to their use.

Problems in Riding the Lope

Watch for the following faults in your Western position:

1. Flapping elbows—this is a common fault when you are "ahead" of your horse; that is, you are urging him on with the upper part of your body instead of your legs and seat. You have shifted your weight too far forward, and if the horse stops suddenly, you'll probably keep on going.
2. Leaning into the rein hand—as mentioned in Chapter V, "Riding Western," this is a serious problem because it twists the body, disrupting balance and proper use of the aids. Because once established it is difficult to correct, make sure that you keep your shoulders square.
3. Tendency to hold the horn.
4. Tendency to push toes out and feet forward (generally because of pushing buttocks back onto the cantle).
5. Too loose or uneven reins—a fault associated with being "behind" the horse—that is, your weight is behind the horse's center of gravity. You are out of balance, and if the horse moves forward suddenly you are thrown back. To stop the horse, you may find your rein hand hitting your chest or coming back over your shoulder. If the horse should shy sideways, you undoubtedly will be grounded. Be sure also that your reins are not twisted—they should lie flat along the horse's neck from bit to hand.

INSTRUCTOR: *Do not let the above errors pass when you are teaching the lope. If ignored, they too easily become nearly unbreakable habits.*

Refer again to Improving Your Seat in Chapter IV, Part 1. Repeat the longe line exercises using the canter as well as the walk and trot.

CHAPTER SEVEN

The Horse Show

Beyond the need for transportation, each era through the centuries has developed its own use of the horse as a partner in glory. Horses have long been a means of expression, satisfying man's need for challenge and stimulation. From earliest times, riding races, chariot races, various polo-type games, hunting, jousting, and similar sports have been dependent on the horse for their very creation and existence. These sports in turn stimulated owners and breeders to keep and reproduce the best horses for their particular purpose.

The horse show is one of today's answers to man's need for challenge and his demonstration of accomplishment. In today's primarily recreational use of the horse, the horse show takes many different forms; but its overall effect is to stimulate the owner, breeder, exhibitor, show committee member, and spectator toward better breeding, better care, and better horsemanship.

Horse Show Associations

The American Horse Shows Association was formed to unify the diverse interests in the horse world; it is recognized as an accepted authority on horse shows in the United States.

The *Rule Book* and news sheet "Horse Show" keep AHSA members informed of the amending of rules and the adoption of new ones. A section in the *Rule Book* is devoted to each of the popular breeds (for example, the

Arabian Division, Saddle Horse Division, Shetland Pony Division) and to types of performance (Cutting Horse Division, Dressage Division, Equitation Division, and so on). The *AHSA Rule Book* lists, among other things, duties of show officials and employees, conduct of recognized shows, recognized judges, stewards, amateur and professional status, class definitions and general procedures, show classifications and requirements.

Membership fees may be found in the current *Rule Book*; membership blanks may be obtained through the AHSA secretary or in the catalogues of recognized shows.

The American Quarter Horse Association does not show under AHSA rules. It publishes its own handbook, although many of its rules and contest patterns are similar to AHSA's. The handbook includes recommendations concerning youth activities, corporation bylaws, and registration regulations for American Quarter Horses.

The rules and regulations printed in the official handbook must be used at all approved AQHA shows and contests unless otherwise approved by the Executive Secretary of the AQHA. Only horses registered with the AQHA are eligible to compete in these approved shows and contests. The AQHA handbook lists duties of show officials, class definitions, general procedures, and show classifications and requirements (tack, reining patterns, contest measurements, etc.).

To keep members and the public informed, the AQHA publishes an illustrated monthly magazine, *Quarter Horse Journal*, and other publications.

The numerous breed and national riding magazines also promote interest in showing, and they list ribbon winners around the country. Breed magazines contain information concerning current breed specifications, uses, schooling, facilities for horse and rider, stud service, sale horses, trainers, and horsey people in the news. Any show is more interesting and informative when you know something about the owners and riders, as well as about the horses.

Why Show?

Why do you want to show? If you have worked hard to improve your riding, or if you feel your training methods have produced especially good results, you may want to measure your progress against other competitors with an impartial, knowledgeable person as judge. Perhaps you would like to meet others with the same interests. Or perhaps, with the horse show as a definite goal, you find you work more consistently and enthusiastically with your horse.

The prospect of showing your horse, especially in performance, should in itself encourage hard work and better riding. It can be harmful, however, if preparation is left until too late and then shortcut methods and overwork are employed to try to shape up your horse in time.

A ribbon or trophy should not be the goal for showing your horse; these should be happy incidentals acknowledging a job well done. Have some constructive goals in mind and your enjoyment of the horse show—as both exhibitor and spectator—will be a reward in itself.

A halter class at Estes Park, Colorado.

Competing in halter showmanship.

Familiarize Yourself with Horse Show Procedure

Let's assume you have never shown a horse either at halter or in performance. How do you enter, prepare for, and conduct yourself at a show?

If you have never attended a horse show as a spectator, now is the time! If you have friends involved in showing, all the better. Accompany them to a few shows, observe the various classes, help with your friends' horses, and talk with some of the contestants.

In short, learn all you can about the overall operation of showing a horse. The ideal type of show to attend is sponsored by a 4-H club, riding school, or riding club; many times there will be critiques for the exhibitors after each class or at the end. While observing the various classes, either halter or performance, compare the performance and condition of the horses shown to the experience, condition, and performance of your own horse. Is your horse ready to compete in that particular class? If not, make notes on what you and your horse should practice. Has your horse the quality, presence, type, conformation, and condition to compete successfully in halter classes? If not, and if you are under eighteen years of age, you can still compete in Junior or Senior Showmanship where *your* performance as a showman is judged. Naturally, your horse must be trained for this event even though his conformation is not judged. If your horse has been on pasture and is not in "show" condition, it will take many weeks of good nutrition, daily grooming, loving care, and practice work at halter to accomplish this goal.

Thinking Ahead

First learn what shows will occur in your area—through horsey friends, riding schools and clubs, breed magazines, 4-H club meetings, and tack shops. If you belong to a breed association, you undoubtedly will receive notice of the shows involving your breed. When you gather this information, plan a simple show circuit (a schedule of the shows you plan to attend). Some of these shows may be local day shows, where you can ride your horse to the show grounds; others may be two-day shows or large three-day or four-day events where you must trailer your mount and arrange for overnight accommodations. It is, of course, wise to attend some small day shows before entering "the big time." Types of contests include open shows (all breeds can participate), breed shows, fairs, playdays, clinics, gymkhanas, and riding club shows.

Riding in a parade.

Exhibitions and Parades

For those folks who like to show their horses but do not have the time to train and practice for ring competition, parades and exhibitions may fill the bill. For this type of showing, your horse must be used to all manner of strange sights and sounds. If you are ever chosen to carry a flag, your horse should be accustomed to the sight and noise of the flapping cloth.

Many of the larger fairs, rodeos, and horse shows provide a parade to generate spectator interest. Here is the chance for the parade horse to show his fine parade gait, his costume or silver tack. Usually the divisions in a parade will be by breed. Arabians are usually shown in native Bedouin costume, Morgans in Western tack, Appaloosas in Indian costume, and Palominos with extravagant silver parade tack.

The Prize List and Entry Blank

The next step is to obtain prize lists (sometimes called premium lists) for the shows you wish to enter. These are usually available at least one or two months in advance. Prize lists include the all-important entry blank, AHSA or AQHA membership blank, information on show officials, list of breeding and performance classes, the information on prize money, general information on such things as rules, registration, stall, tack room, fees, admission passes, date entries close (some of the small local shows accept entries the day of the show), exhibitors' dinner, veterinary inspection, hay and grain availability, farrier, and so on. If there will be a jumping class, reining class, or other such specialized event, the prospective courses and patterns may be diagramed in the back of the prize list. Courses and patterns may also be posted at least an hour before the scheduled class.

When filling out the entry blank, first make sure that you are eligible and that your horse is suited to the classes you wish to enter. Fill out all blanks, and be sure to sign the form.

If you are a minor, a parent or guardian must also sign to give consent to your entry. Because at most shows stalls are assigned in the order the entries are received, send in your entry as soon as possible.

Most large shows bring out-of-state exhibitors; therefore they usually send a map of the city, giving the location of the show and a list of motel and hotel accommodations available for exhibitors and spectators. The prize list also gives the necessary information for those who wish to advertise in the show program. Breeding farms, tack shops, and training facilities usually take advantage of this means of advertising.

Make yourself familiar with the rules for each specific show. Are post entries accepted? What tack do I need? What do I wear? On what are my classes judged? The questions should be answered well in advance of the show so that you have time to train your horse, and so that you have time to break in any new tack or attire that may be necessary.

Preparing Your Horse

If you plan to show, begin preparing your horse three or four months ahead of the show season, even if you have no idea which shows you will enter.

He will need an ample, nutritious grain ration with vitamin and mineral supplement, and good-quality hay or alfalfa. Salt and water should be readily available. Parasite control is very important: All the good food in the world won't help your horse's physical appearance or mental outlook if parasites are infesting him. Take a sample of feces to your veterinarian for a report on the parasites that are present. The vet may suggest worming with a stomach tube, followed up later by diet worming.

Several weeks before the show try out the fly repellent you expect to use at the show. Some repellents may irritate your horse's skin. We know of one case where the horse was so affected by the repellent that he had to be scratched from the entire show.

Your horse will need thorough daily grooming. Call the farrier and have your horse shod about ten days to two weeks before the show so that he will have time to adjust to his shoes. If his feet are dry, apply a hoof dressing to help condition them. Clip the hair from the coronary band to above his fetlocks; trim about his throatlatch; trim off his face whiskers; clip the bridle path if the breed calls for it, and trim around his ears. It is up to the owner whether or not he clips the inside of his horse's ears. If your horse will not be subject to insect-nuisance, clipping the inside of the ear will not bother him; but it is thoughtless to clip inside the ears and leave him to the mercy of mosquitoes, flies, or gnats. It is true that most professionals thoroughly clip their horse's ears. If you feel it is necessary, you can buy a scrim ear net at most tack shops to protect him.

If your horse has never been away from home before, you have no idea how he will react to different water. Get him used to drinking from a pail at home, add a few drops of molasses or mint extract, and be sure to take the same pail (and molasses or mint) with you. See Chapter VIII for more about your horse away from home.

Preparation of Equipment, Attire, and Tack

A trunk or tack box that you can transport to the show is necessary and convenient for most exhibitors. In this you will collect such things as your show grooming tools, clippers, nails, screws, snaps, hammer, cloths, extra halters, ropes, saddle soap, leather conditioners, animal shampoo and coat dressing, scissors, saddle blankets, sheets, chaps, spurs, Vaseline or other medical supplies, extra pieces of leather for repairs, some twine, wire cutters, leg and tail wraps, rope for saddle, longe line, slicker, second cinches, extra show brow bands, bridles, show halters, and whips (if tack box is large enough), as well as extra parts for saddle and bridle.

After collecting everything, print a list of the items and attach it to the lid of the tack box; this will help you avoid forgetting things either before or after the show and will serve as a check list for forthcoming shows. Undoubtedly you will change the list from time to time. It is wise to print your name on most items with indelible ink. You may purchase and use a leather-burning outfit to mark your tack. For maximum protection, register branded tack and other valuables with your local sheriff's department.

Of course, your tack box will contain only the smaller items. Let's now think of the larger miscellaneous equipment you'll need: pitchfork, rake, shovel, buckets, grain pans, stall sign, and folding chairs. At most shows there will be a bale of straw in each stall and you can purchase hay and grain. However, if you wish to take your own, be sure to add it to your list. Don't forget your saddles and bridles! Most of the above items will be packed the day before you leave for the show; but as the last day is hectic, to say the least, make your list early and check off items as you pack them in.

Preparing Yourself and Your Horse for Specific Classes

Now that you know the classes in which you will compete, you can start working your horse in his show ring routine. Proper procedures may be found in current magazines, 4-H horse project books, or AHSA and AQHA rule books.

When working young horses in patterns and routines, practice the elements of each, but rarely run the whole pattern in sequence. If you do, your horse will learn the routine and anticipate your aids, thus spoiling your test pattern.

Showing Your Horse at Halter

Because more fine horses are produced each year, halter horse competition becomes stiffer at every show. To compete successfully, we must not only produce a superior individual, but we must also show him to his best advantage. To the inexperienced eye, this may look easy, but halter show-manship is an art. A lot of training and practice are necessary before the halter horse and showman can win.

Let's look at some of the general rules for showing at halter. First, consider the general appearance of the horse: his condition (nutrition, parasite control, proper exercise), his grooming (clean, well brushed, trimmed according to breed standard, hoofs clean and trimmed or shod correctly), and the condition and adjustment of his tack. The showman should dress to complement his horse—wear neat, clean, appropriate apparel for the class.

There are several differences between 4-H halter showmanship and professional showmanship. Among other things, 4-H'ers usually do not use a whip or touch their horse while on the line, and they do not show stallions.

Ring procedures vary with each judge, but most agree that the horse be shown in hand at a walk and trot and that he stand squarely (or stretched, depending on the breed). Lead the horse with your right shoulder at his left shoulder. Carry the lead, neatly coiled in a figure-8, in your left hand (along with the whip, if you use one). Usually, the judge wishes to see the class move around him counterclockwise after entering the ring. Lead your horse briskly and in an animated fashion.

Next, you will be asked to line up your horse facing the judge. You will be told how and where to stand your horse by the steward. Usually horses are lined up side by side, eight to ten feet apart. The judge should have room to walk safely between horses and to stand back far enough to obtain a clear profile of each animal. Set your horse up (put him in show stance), and keep an eye on the judge. The alert showman watches the judge unobtrusively but continually during the class. He makes sure that the judge receives an unobstructed view of his horse at all times, whether or not he appears to be looking.

Show management should designate the pattern to be used, considering the size of the class, space available, and judge's preference. When working your horse (leading him at a walk or trot) for the judge, follow directions and move directly and squarely. Do not pull your horse's head around or otherwise disturb his natural gait. You should have trained your horse before the show to perform on a loose lead and to move at the same speed that you move in an obedient and brisk manner.

Usually, you first will walk away from the judge, then reverse, and trot to him or past him. When moving away, keep your horse going in a straight line. This can be done by using the steward or some vertical object as your reference point. When reversing to return to the judge, turn to the right, thus giving the judge an unobstructed view of your horse. Remember that you are trying to show your horse to his greatest possible advantage. You should look proud of the animal you are showing and adopt a posture that is as alert and worthy as his.

In the final or second lineup (after all horses have been worked individu-

Showing at halter.

ally), the judge sometimes selects several horses and places them head to tail in a line. Listen to your ringmaster's directions and, if selected, keep adequate space between horses and be sure your number is readily visible. The judge will be comparing horses and giving his final decision. When he has handed in his card, keep alert and wait until your number is called before moving out to receive your ribbon. Thank the ribbon girl and move briskly out of the ring. If there are photographs to be taken, take every care that you and your horse are positioned correctly.

If you were not among the winning horses, accept the fact gracefully. Now would be the time to objectively compare your horse with others in the ring. In what area—training, conditioning, or grooming—can you improve?

Western Classes

While training for your Western classes, wear your Western attire. Your horse should be familiar with such things as flapping batwing chaps, and especially with spurs (use of which is optional). If you expect to wear gloves, use them when practicing, and by all means wear your hat. You'll find out whether it has a tendency to fly off (if so, how to keep it on)—as well as to

Proper Western attire and good working tack. Angel of Paris, owned and ridden by Jan Kirkpatrick of Boulder, Colorado. Reins are held in California method.

WESTERN WEAR

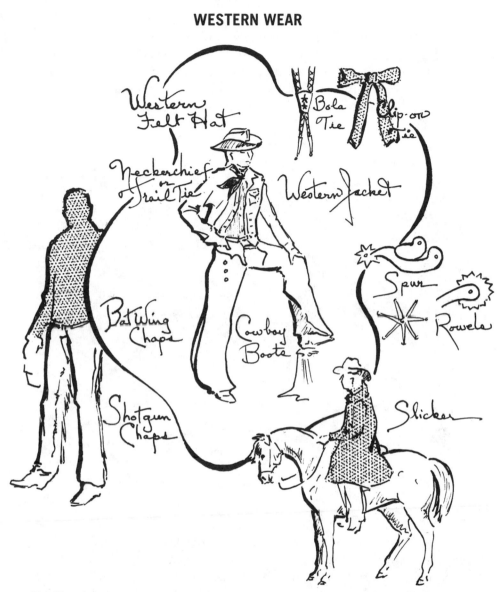

Fig. 10

accustom your horse to the sight of flying hats, which he's almost certain to encounter at the show. If you haven't looked at any of your show attire since last season, it's possible it may need mending, altering, or cleaning. Also, if your saddle is double-rigged and you don't usually use the second cinch, now is the time to start using it. Hang your lariat correctly, tie a slicker, hobbles (when using closed reins, hobbles are required), or any other required appointments on your saddle, and generally accustom your horse to everything possible at this stage. He'll have enough new to contend with at the show.

For Western classes, decorated silver equipment and other geegaws should not count over a good working outfit, but remember that your blankets, cinches, and leather should be clean.

Standard method of holding the reins.

A horse must be steady, well trained, and obedient to win in a trail class. Practice riding over obstacles, opening and closing gates, loading your horse in a trailer (several strange trailers, if possible), jumping over hay bales, backing through barrels or poles laid parallel on the ground, and any other obstacles you can devise. Your horse should also be used to fording streams, letting you put on a slicker while mounted, being mounted from the off side, dragging wood on the end of a rope, allowing you to lift a sack of cans, passing an animal hide or skin, and ground tying. (You should be able to drop your divided reins and leave your horse twenty feet or more while he stands motionless.)

When training to drag wood or a sack of cans, don't dally the rope around the horn until you are sure your horse is steady—just hold it in your hand. You may hobble your horse if using the single rein with romal. However, since hobbling is time-consuming, it is seldom used in the show ring.

In trail classes it is mandatory to open, pass through, and close a gate correctly. This shows your horse's maneuverability and demonstrates his willingness to perform this useful task.

Since trail classes usually have a time limit set on each obstacle, you should study the gate and ask yourself such questions as: Where will I position myself (is the gate hung on the left or right; does it open toward or away from me)? How will I unlatch the gate (does it have a sliding bar latch, hook and eye, or some other type latch)? How will I maneuver so as to take the fewest steps possible (thus using as little time as possible)?

You must at all times retain control of your mount and the gate. In other words, your reins are in one hand, and the other hand must remain on the gate throughout the entire maneuver.

You should be able to open a gate from either the right or left side, either toward you or away from you. Also, you should be able to open the gate only far enough for horse and rider to pass through. The horse's body should block the opening at all times so that, if you were actually moving cattle or other stock, the horse would prevent another animal from slipping through.

One way of opening a gate is as follows:

The gate is hung on the left and opens toward you on the right. In this case, as in most cases, it will be easiest and quickest to back through the gate. Position your horse parallel to the gate, facing the hinge, so that you can reach the latch with your right hand. (In shows, latches are usually at least forty-eight inches from the ground.) Undo the latch and move your hand to the top of the gate. Direct your horse to sidestep to the left: Your right hand will pull open the gate. Now direct his haunches to the right and back around the end of the gate. Your horse now faces the latch. Then sidestep again to close the gate. Your hand will still be on top of the gate. You may have to back or go forward a step or two in order to reach the latch.

Most obstacles in a show trail class are set up to judge a horse's willingness and training. See Chapter VIII for more about preparing your horse for the trail.

Be prepared to follow instructions, since even in trail classes most judges ask that the horse be worked at the walk, jog, and lope both ways of the ring as in a Western Pleasure class. If possible, trailer your horse to a strange ring and practice your ring routine. Although he may give an excellent performance at home, in strange surroundings he may fall apart (especially if young and inexperienced).

It is not usual to post in a Western saddle in the show ring. However, on long trail rides, cattle drives, and other informal Western rides, you will often see riders posting or standing in a Western saddle.

When you enter equitation classes (only for contestants under eighteen), you are judged not only on your ability to perform the usual ring procedures for a given class but also on your ability to describe any additional maneuvers the judge may ask. You will also be judged on the way you use your aids, your seat, the performance of your horse, your appointments, and the suitability of your mount. (This refers primarily to size—a small person on a large horse, for example, might indicate unsuitability.) Also, the temperament of horse and rider should complement each other. In equitation classes the individual is the competitor and wins the award, whereas in other classes the horse is the competitor and wins the award.

English Classes

In English Pleasure classes your mount must be smooth, relaxed, and willing. Manners are very important here: A horse that wrings his tail, lays back his ears when other horses pass, fidgets in the lineup, shies at unaccustomed sounds and objects, plays with his bit, or otherwise acts nervous or unwilling usually does poorly in an English Pleasure class. Study the *AHSA Rule Book* to answer such questions as: At what gait do I enter the ring? In what order are the gaits usually called? Is breaking gait considered a major or minor disobedience? What type of bridle should I use? What type of girths are acceptable with an English saddle? Are spurs, whips, crops, and martingales optional?

In English classes the judge should distinguish the quality of the different trots—for instance, the brisk, smart, cadenced, and balanced cross-country type of trot and the smooth, well-balanced fast trot. Don't confuse your slow trot with a jog. You post to both English trots at the present time. (Rules change—always check your rule book.) Take care in your transition from one gait to another, accomplishing the gait changes smoothly and quickly. Always give the judge the impression that you have complete, gentle control of your mount. This takes practice at home!

If you do not normally wear spurs, do not use them in the show ring. Use the saddle girth that you expect to use at the show. Girths stretch (especially if dampened by sweat), and you should learn just how tight it must be to keep your saddle in place. Make sure your riding habit is roomy enough in the knees to permit you to mount and dismount gracefully. Also, wear your suit a time or two after it is returned from the cleaner—it could shrink a bit

ENGLISH WEAR

Fig. 11

during cleaning. Clean and condition tack thoroughly, as mentioned under Western classes.

Trailering your horse is discussed in Chapter VIII, but there's one facet of trailering a horse that's especially important to think about when going to a show. Clean the tail chain rubbers (sometimes called butt chains) of your trailer. Some horses "sit" on their tail chains especially when traveling in hilly country, and if manure dries on the rubbers, your horse will arrive at the show with sore and unsightly hindquarters.

Washing Your Horse

Many show folk wash their horses at the show; however, amid all the confusion and waiting in line at the wash rack, we think it saves time and tempers to accomplish the wash job before you leave home. Your show blanket and sheet should be clean and dry so that they can be put on your horse immediately after he is bathed and dried. We use a clean white bed-sheet to make a cover to use under the show blanket. This keeps the dirt and dust from coming through the larger weave of the blanket. Clean a set of brushes and curries to use after the washing, and make sure the stall is clean and amply bedded—it's worth every precaution to be assured you'll have a show-ready horse the following morning.

There are many horse shampoos, coat conditioners, and dressings on the market. It is wise to use livestock shampoo rather than household soap or detergent. Any residue from the latter can make your horse itch and rub. You'll need several buckets of warm water, a big sponge, shampoo, a hose with adjustable nozzle or a washer-groomer comb (made especially for washing horses and available at tack shops), a sweat scraper, Turkish toweling, at least one helper, and a warm day in a place out of the wind. It's especially convenient, though of course not necessary, to crosstie the horse between two helpers.

Sponge him all over with warm water and, when thoroughly soaked, generously lather him up (except for his head) and scrub. His head should be gently washed with the sponge, keeping soap away from his eyes. Several warm-water rinses without any soap at all may be adequate. His mane and tail should be given special attention with lots of scrubbing down to the roots. Be sure to wash the hocks, the top of the rump, under the tail, and between the hind legs and forelegs.

When you think he's been scrubbed adequately, start rinsing with the hose, using only a gentle stream of water at first. After each part of his anatomy has been rinsed, use the sweat scraper (or as a substitute, a coat hanger with hook removed, or the smooth side of a hacksaw blade) to squeegee the water, soap, and dirt from his coat. The color and soapiness of the water will tell you whether he is really clean and thoroughly rinsed. Check his feet (especially white feet) as there may be some ground-in mud or dirt that needs to be scraped off; it is easier to remove while the hoof is wet.

Gray horses can be rinsed with bluing, after the wash job, to "get the yellow out."

When you are convinced he is thoroughly bathed and rinsed, towel him off and walk him in the grass until he is absolutely dry. Then his coat, mane, and tail can be brushed and brushed. Check your trimming job, put on his clean white sheet and return him to his clean, well-strawed stall with a prayer that he'll look that way the next morning.

Besides washing your horse, there are many other chores to perform the day before you leave. Does your car or truck need gas, oil, or a tire check? Are all your equipment, attire, and overnight personal effects ready to be packed? Pack whatever you can and cross each item off your check list. Load up the tack box, clean saddles and other tack, and stable-cleaning tools into the car or truck.

Leaving for the Show

Undoubtedly the day of the show will find you up and around early. Give your horse plenty of time to eat and drink and try to stay calm so that he will be calm also. Hitch the trailer to your vehicle and recheck all mechanical equipment. Groom your horse lightly and resheet him. If it is cool, you can

Ready to leave for the show.

put his show blanket on over the white sheet. Then wrap his tail and legs. Stick-together leg wraps called "Velcro closing" do not require the time and labor of the conventional wrap and they give excellent protection. Most tack shops carry both kinds. Take care in wrapping the conventional type sometimes called "track bandages": Leg wraps that are too tight will cut off circulation. Tail wraps can be bought or made. Your valuable animal deserves this care while traveling.

When you are completely ready to leave, quietly load him into the trailer. It is not a good idea to load up and make him stand where other horses may nip him or confusion may upset him. Now you're on your way— well organized and filled with enthusiasm.

At the Show Grounds

When almost to the show grounds, look for the "exhibitors' entrance." (You'll find one at most shows.) As you enter, note the parking area for horse trailers and vehicles—after unloading you will want to park in that area. Fire laws usually forbid vehicles to remain closer than twenty feet from a public stabling building. First make a visit to the Barn Manager's office, where a stall assignment plan is posted. Before unloading your horse at his stall (which usually is marked with your name), take your pitchfork and spread the bale of straw that was left for you in the stall. If there is no bedding, you will have to contract for some on the show grounds. Check the stall for any protruding nails, sharp splinters, wire, or other problem spots. Also check the gate latches for strength.

After leading your horse into his stall, take off his tail and leg bandages and blanket if it is warm. Provide him with some hay and water and let him rest. If your trip was a particularly long one, you may wish to walk or longe him before stalling him. It is better not to grain your horse until he has settled down to his new surroundings, and then grain him only lightly. (Nervousness may lead to bolting grain; this in turn causes colic.)

If the show secretary's office is open, you can procure your envelope, which encloses your numbers, program, passes (allowing each exhibitor to enter the grandstand during performance classes), and necessary announcements. Some show managements provide a cardboard list of classes to tack on your stall door. You can then highlight your own classes to save time and let interested spectators know when you will perform. Prepare a personal check list for each class: Do you have your number, hat, rope, and spurs for Western classes, etc.?

You will now want to unload some of your hay and grain, your tack box and stable implements, after which you can park your vehicle and trailer.

Horse show mother. Painting by Rich Rudish; courtesy of the artist and *Arabian Horse News*.

Many exhibitors affix a crosstie in the stall for convenience in grooming and saddling. You will also want to tie a water bucket in place and install a grain tub and hay net. The latter is very practical, if not tied too high. (Hay chaff falls down into a horse's eyes when tied above his eye level.) On the other hand, if tied too low, your horse could catch his foot in it, especially when it is empty. Stable signs can be put up and some comfortable folding chairs set out in front of your stall.

If the show will last for a weekend or longer, now would be a good time to check on your own accommodations.

When you return to the show grounds, you may wish to lead your horse around the grounds to familiarize him with the strange sights and sounds. If you have plenty of time, it would be wise to practice a short time in the show ring, especially under the lights if your horse is not used to working at night.

At large shows the exhibitors' dinner is usually held the night before the show commences. During the dinner you meet other exhibitors and show officials. While it is not mandatory to attend the dinner, it can be enjoyable and informative.

Before leaving the show grounds for your accommodations in the evening, check your horse's water and hay and notice whether he seems contented in his new surroundings. And make sure the stall latches are secure.

Show Grooming

Show grooming includes a few points that you do not ordinarily bother with for daily rides. If your horse has white socks or stockings, dampen the white and pat on some cornstarch. When the hair and cornstarch are dried, brush it out and you'll be amazed at the brightness of the white. If he has orange or yellow stains on his body white (from the latigo of your Western saddle or some other dye mark), sponge the spot with lemon juice (or other citrus fruit), soap well, and follow with the cornstarch treatment.

Check over your clipping job (muzzle, hairs at the base of the tail, fetlocks, coronary band, inside of the knees and under the jaw). How about hoofs? You may need to wash them again and perhaps scrape or sand off the dirt marks. Then take a neutral shoe polish and rub it in well. Don't use anything on the hoof that will catch dust or dirt. Also, extremely black dye on dark hoofs will give them an artificial look.

The next step is to brush and wipe your horse (with toweling) to make him shine. Oil your hands lightly with coat dressing, and run your fingers through his mane and tail to separate all the hairs; follow by brushing. Oil your hands again and rub over his coat; avoid putting an excess of oil on any one spot or he will look greasy. Oil applied around the muzzle and eyes (to look larger) helps him look well groomed and typey. Some coat dressings have fly repellents added; this can be very valuable if you are in fly country and must show at halter. A horse switching his tail, stamping his hoofs, and throwing his head does not make a good impression on the judge.

Entering the Show Ring

When your horse is ready, it is wise to ask a helper to watch him (or leave him cross-tied) while you change from stable clothes to show attire. Don't forget to attach your horse's number to your back (or wherever the management suggests). Go through your class check list before entering the paddock.

It is customary for the paddock manager to announce the class over the loudspeaker (which is heard by the exhibitors in the barn area) thirty minutes before the performance begins. A second call will come fifteen minutes prior to the time the class will enter the ring, and the third and final call is made five to seven minutes before, when the specific missing numbers are paged. The paddock manager checks the horses into the paddock against the correct check list and must verify that each contestant carries the proper number. If you have a helper at the paddock, you can give your horse a last-minute brush, wipe off your boots, or make an adjustment in your girth or other tack.

Good sportsmanship requires manners and courtesy at all times. Be on time for your class, don't crowd at the gate, be willing to help others, be friendly, and follow instructions.

Enter the ring as instructed by the steward; in case you are first and can't follow the leader, you should know ahead of time whether to enter at a walk or other gait and whether to circle clockwise or counterclockwise. In the ring, try to place yourself advantageously (called "ring generalship") so that the judge can see you. It takes practice and good sense to avoid being hidden by a pileup of riders. Anticipate and prevent shying or cutting a corner. Do your best, and be a good sport. If you don't place, remember that not all judges see the class the same way; you've learned a lot, and there will be other shows. If you do win, enjoy yourself, but don't get overinflated.

Cool out your horse after each class before putting him in his stall.

At the end of the show, return your number(s) and attend to any unfinished business matters. Return any borrowed items, pay your grain, hay, or straw bills, check with the photographer if you ordered pictures or wish to choose one taken during the show. Take the same care of your equipment while packing and the same good care of your horse (preparing to load and loading) that you did before leaving for the show. Take time to cool your mount before loading into a trailer for the homeward trek.

Several of the most important questions to ask yourself now are: What were my strong points while showing? My weak points? Now I must start to work on these points—how will I go about it? Have I the correct tack and attire and how can I improve my appearance? Did I enter the correct classes or is my horse better suited to others? If you were showing with friends, a critique-sort of round-table discussion is very valuable. Perhaps your friends (participants and spectators) noticed something that could help you. Use your horse show experience as a stepping-stone to further perfect your riding form, the training of your horse, and enjoyment of the sport.

Trail Riding

Trail riding may be considered the most natural and basic reason for horseback riding. In this country, trails were ridden long before the construction of roads made transportation by carriage and wagon possible. Trail riding reached its most colorful and romanticized phase in the famous Western cattle drives along such routes as the Chisholm Trail, in the westward migration routes such as the Oregon and Overland trails, and in the Pony Express.

Trail riding today is a popular, healthful recreation. In fact, vacationers who otherwise never come near a horse take trail rides to combine pleasant outdoor activity with enjoyment of clear air and off-the-beaten-track scenery. Trail rides and pack trips are often the featured attractions of national and state parks, dude ranches, and summer camps.

Trail rides today may be divided into several different categories. Noncompetitive trail riding includes organized or informal pleasure and social rides, cattle drives, and pack trips. Competition trail riding includes two distinct categories: endurance riding and competitive trail riding.

Noncompetitive Trail Riding

Noncompetitive trail riding includes everything from informal Sunday-afternoon get-togethers to highly organized rides involving hundreds of horses and riders. Whether large or small, these rides are generally social

Trail riding in the pines.

events, planned by horsemen who enjoy riding in each other's company. Planning and organization are necessary even in informal outings, but for the big rides, careful and complete organization is of paramount importance to the well-being of participants and horses and to the overall success of the ride.

Local riding clubs may sponsor trail rides for members and friends, or sometimes breed associations may promote a trail ride as the special event of the year. A route must be decided before the ride is begun, and, to avoid confusion, at least one person should be familiar with the route and the time factor involved in distances. Committees can handle such problems as food for a noon meal and decide ahead of time whether to carry the food along or be met by a car at a designated point. Trail manners and safety should be carefully observed at all times by any group; clubs often adopt a list of safety rules suited to their particular needs.

Some of the larger social trail rides, such as the Old Spanish Trail Riders (sponsored by the Shelby County Sheriff's Posse of Center, Texas) and the Desert Caballeros, Wickenburg, Arizona, take several days and cover 150 to 200 miles or more. These are highly organized with special rules and regulations of their own.

The American Forestry Association promotes trail riding through its division called Trail Riders of the Wilderness. Annual pack trips for ten days to two weeks are organized through wilderness areas of the United States such as the Sawtooth Wilderness in Idaho, the Wind River Mountains of Wyoming, the Pecos Wilderness of New Mexico, and the Great Smoky Mountains of North Carolina. Trips are limited to thirty riders and fifty to seventy horses, as a rule; the AFA provides horses, equipment, guides, and cooks, thus making the trips available to nonhorse owners. Of course riders should have sufficient riding experience to be comfortable on the trips and not present a hazard or detriment to other riders.

Certain conditions apply to trail riding in general; and knowledge of trail manners and safety, as well as what to wear and how to ride on the trail, is important to your own and your companions' enjoyment and safety and to your horse's well-being.

Basic Trail Information

Proper Attire for the Trail

Your attire should be workmanlike and well suited to riding a trail, whether on a short ride or an overnight trek. Avoid loose, flapping clothes that may catch on brush or a low limb. If you ride on a trail during hunting season (in some areas this can be dangerous or even deadly), be sure that you and your horse are sufficiently covered with bright red or orange. The weather, season, type of trail (through woods, prairie, rivers, buckbrush, rocky mountain slopes, and so on) will have a bearing on the clothes you wear.

In today's West the cowboy hat is worn not only to ward off the sun, but also to keep rain from dripping down one's face and neck. Because of its practicality and style, the Western hat is now frequently seen in the East, also. In the old days the "ten-gallon" hat was used to drink from, to fan a bronc or campfire, to protect from the sun, and for an umbrella in the rain. During snowstorms the old cowhand tied the brim of his hat down over his ears for warmth. Today any hat that is protective and fits well is acceptable. Your hat must not be too tight for comfort, but it must fit firmly enough to stay on in the wind; if it flies off in a gale, it could frighten your horse or someone else's. Some riders like to have their hats fitted with a tie-string that goes under the chin. This helps keep the hat on in a wind, or allows it to rest out of the way on your back if you tire of it.

From time to time it is considered stylish for both men and women to wear kerchiefs around the neck. This style grew out of practical use. In the old West, the bandanna was tied around the neck as a bit of handy, all-purpose equipment: to protect from the sun, as a sweatband, to cover the nose and mouth in dust or extreme cold, as an emergency bandage, blindfold, hobble, towel, sling, signal flag, or emergency anything.

When going on a short ride in hot weather, short-sleeved shirts are fine. But for a long ride, you should have some protective clothing, such as a sweater, vest, or jacket, tied to your saddle or around your waist. (The old cowboy wore a vest because his pants pockets were useless when riding, and he carried matches and the makin's in his vest pockets.) When tying a jacket or sweater to carry on the saddle, roll it up so that there are no loose ends to flap. Taking a jacket on and off while mounted can be unsafe. If your horse is not proven in this situation, dismount. Freak storms do come up and extra clothing can make the difference between an enjoyable ride and a wretched one. You should carry a slicker (or some type of rain wear) with you; but be sure your horse is used to a slicker: Half in and half out of one on a spooky horse can spark a wild ride. Short slickers that just cover you to the knees and spread over the cantle of the saddle are comfortable and easy to carry.

Take a pair of gloves with you, even if you don't like to wear them all the time. Gloves give you a better grip on the reins, especially in damp weather when leather is slick. They are handy to wear when opening wooden gates, or when dragging brush to the campfire. Leather gloves can be used to relieve a

Trail riding in the rain—your horse should be used to a slicker. (Photo courtesy the Colorado Game, Fish and Parks Division and Freda Lavigne)

saddle sore, or you can sit on them to protect yourself from damp ground. In winter, lined mittens are more comfortable than gloves.

In the West, Levi's or jeans (sometimes the stretch variety) are most popular among men, women, and children. The material for these pants is comfortable, tough, wind-resistant, and easily laundered, and Levi's are considered stylish as well. Make sure they fit correctly (big enough and long enough). Most Westerners wear their pants outside their boots to keep water, snow, and other foreign material from going down inside.

When riding in buckbrush, on cold days, or just because you like to wear them, chaps are useful, warm, and protective. Chaps keep you clean and dry, and can save your legs from friction burns.

When riding with English tack, English jodhpurs with jodhpur boots (or breeches with high boots) are good trail clothes. Stretch jodhpurs are very comfortable and allow you to mount easily. Most pants are worn with a belt, and often your belt can double for a broken strap, halter (you can lead your horse with a belt looped around his neck), or emergency knee strap. Hang your jackknife, compass, watch, or other gear on your belt for a good way to keep them handy.

Proper footwear is important. On a trail ride it is always best to wear boots of some kind, rather than moccasins or tennis shoes. Your boots should fit well and be high enough to protect your feet from water, rocks, mud, and coarse brush. They should have pronounced heels to keep your feet from slipping through the stirrups—an important safety measure. Where rattlesnakes are a problem, high boots are a must. If you wear your pants outside your boots, it is nearly impossible for a snake to get through to your skin.

Spurs are optional. But if you wear them, you should know how to use them and your horse should be used to them.

Packing Extra Gear

Wilderness rides and pack trips require pack horses and mules to tote the tents, food, bedding, and other extras. Packing an animal for these rides involves a detailed knowledge that is beyond our scope here.

Suggested items to take along on an overnight (or several days') trip:

For You	*For Your Horse and Gear*
Jackknife with hole punch	Tack (saddle, bridle, pad, halter)
Pliers	Hobbles, nosebag, leadropes
Compass	Saddle soap and oil
Flashlight	Extra leather thongs for gear repair

For You

Piece of plastic to cover your head and gear

Chocolate bars, raisins, oranges

Water-purifying tablets

Filled canteen, collapsible cup, trail silverware

Can opener

Insect repellent

Salve for sunburn or chapped lips

Matches in waterproof container

Small first-aid kit with Band-Aids

Whistle

Toilet/personal kit (pills, money, washcloth, towel, soap, toothbrush, toothpaste, etc.)

Sunglasses

Camera, small notebook, pen/pencil, other personal items

Extra socks, underwear

Extra clothing for warmth

Poncho/slicker for rain

Snakebite kit

Sleeping bag

Campsite equipment (including tarps, food, ax, tent, toilet paper, trash bags, grille, extra rope)

For Your Horse and Gear

Spare cinch and curb straps

Hoof pick and grooming tools

Antiseptic powder/salve, first aid supplies including sterile gauze pads, soft cloths, rolled gauze, Ace bandages or other wrap, scissors

Fly spray or wipe

Wire cutters/pliers

Blanket

Feed

Tools for picketline area (including shovel, rake, rope, V-supports and/or flat-headed anchors)

Of course, you have more opportunity to pack extras on a Western saddle than on most English saddles; however, you can pack many small items in your coat or sweater when it is tied to your saddle. Saddlebags can be an asset on any trail ride for toting the extras. We like the inexpensive canvas saddlebags that stretch and do not harden with age.

Water for drinking purposes can be a problem. Even the clearest mountain streams may carry sheep fluke, giardia, or other impurities that can either spoil your ride now with an upset stomach or lead to more serious physical problems later. If you don't know the water, carry a canteen or a purifying agent (available at most drugstores). You can always boil water at an overnight stop.

On a long ride in unfamiliar country, especially in the West, it may be wise to carry wire cutters and a few feet of extra wire. You'll be glad to have the wire cutters if your horse should become entangled in a coil of abandoned

Pack trip into the wilderness. (Photo courtesy the Colorado Game, Fish and Parks Division and Freda Lavigne)

and partially buried barbed wire. It is conceivable that you may find it *necessary* (not simply convenient) to get through a fence and not be able to find a gate. If you should have to cut a wire—this, of course, is an emergency operation and should not be done unless absolutely necessary—always repair the fence tightly and well.

Carrying extra gear on the saddles for an overnight camping trip.

Tack

Now for your horse and for the start of your trail ride. While grooming him, check him over for saddle sores, scratches, sore mouth, or other problems. Give special attention to the condition of his feet.

Now tack up; but again, take special care. Because the trail is usually uneven and there will be hills, sharp or sudden inclines, and obstacles of various kinds, it presents an entirely different type of riding problem than you encounter in the ring. The long-range comfort of the horse is paramount. A slight crease in the saddle blanket may not mean much on an hour's ride in the ring; but on a trail ride this same slight crease could produce a serious saddle sore that would mean discomfort for your horse, no more riding for you, and perhaps a long walk home. This is true not only because of the rider's longer time in the saddle, but also because, due to the uneven riding terrain, the saddle will be constantly shifting or tending to shift. A tighter girth will be needed. This is one reason why the Western saddle is practical for the trail; the heavier weight of the saddle is more evenly distributed over a larger area of the horse's back than with the English saddle, and therefore it is easier for the horse to carry. The saddle must fit the rider, of course, and be comfortable for him. But to be suitable for a trail ride, it must also fit the horse well, without any points of stress. Be sure that the gullet width of your saddle is in relation to the set of your horse's withers. A narrow gullet on a heavy-withered horse, for instance, will fit poorly and cause sores, and vice versa.

Your saddle blanket should be heavy, absolutely clean, and folded smoothly. We like a horsehair or thick felt saddle pad next to the horse's back, covered with a Navajo blanket for maximum comfort for the horse. Set your saddle on properly with about three to four inches of the saddle blanket showing in front of the front edge of the saddle because blankets tend to slide back. It may be necessary to use a breast collar to keep the saddle in place, depending on the horse or on the nature of the terrain planned for the trail ride. Be sure that the breast collar fits well and is well padded. Be sure also that your girth is strong, clean, and not twisted. Always check the off side of your horse's tack when saddling.

The bridle must fit well and therefore be comfortable at all points on the headstall. A well-fitting halter (preferably flat web or leather) should be worn under the bridle. The leadrope can be coiled and tied to the saddle, or it can be worn around the horse's neck with an acceptable knot. Don't try out new equipment on long rides; it could be agonizing for your horse and yourself.

Insect Pests

Mosquitoes, flies, ticks, and other pests can make rides or overnight camps completely miserable for both man and beast. Find out ahead of time if you are likely to encounter insect pests in quantity. You may have to carry insect repellent for yourself and your horse, or in some cases mechanical devices, such as flaps of burlap or leather strips hanging from the bridle to protect your horse from botflies. Find out from your state university or county extension office the best control methods for insect pests in your area.

Where to Ride

One of the most important considerations on an informal trail ride is, of course, where to go. Often this will not be up to you. Through wilderness areas and on many planned rides throughout the country, you will simply follow your guide. However, you should have some idea of where you are and where you are going at all times. Discuss this with the guide before leaving, or study the mapped route, if available. If something unforeseen should happen to him—unlikely, but a dead tree limb *could* fall on his head—you might be left with the responsibility of finding your way back to civilization and getting help for him quickly. Leave your itinerary with a Forest Ranger so that your group can be located if necessary.

Learn to read and use maps; you might sometime have to read and follow one to find the correct route. Be observant on the trail. Record landmarks and trail signs on your memory so that you can retrace your steps even if you can't "track" or "follow a trail." This means looking *all* around you often, and especially behind you.

Most riding establishments have their own trails mapped out, or they have gained permanent permission to use trails that go through private property. Permission must be gained from the landowner *before you begin* any ride that goes through his land. This is absolutely essential, not only from the standpoint of courtesy, but also because he may have special plans himself for that day. If he is driving a herd of spooky heifers from their summer pasture and you suddenly appear in the way, scattering the herd, not only might you have to spend the rest of the day rounding up cattle, but you would probably be denied permission ever to set foot or hoof on his land again. In most Western states, the landowner's fence means "private property—no trespassing" unless by owner's permission. Common courtesy requires that trail riders respect private, local, state, and federal laws.

When a landowner gives you permission to ride on his property, he expects that you will understand and respect his land, stock, and crops. *Always leave gates as you find them*—if you open a gate to go through, you must close it behind you. Ask if you may build campfires and use that area designated by the landowner. Do not smoke where there is danger of fire, and make sure fire is *dead* before you leave. Stay off cultivated fields and soft irrigated meadows, and do not interfere with livestock. Ask the landowner where he prefers that you water your horse. If you obtain permission to go through his cultivated land or soft meadow, ride single file at the edge of the field. Above all, don't be a litterbug! A responsible, experienced trail rider can be assigned to check gates, litter, and other problems on large trail rides.

Manners and Safety

Trail manners are very important: Manners and safety go together. Keep the following points in mind:

1. A careful safety check of each horse and rider is a must before proceeding. Include: girth check for tightness, bit adjustment, length of stirrups, equipment check for security (sleeping bag tied on properly, etc.). Saddle strings may loosen during a ride and should be checked often. If inexperienced riders are included in the ride, show them the proper length of rein for their individual horse, and how to turn and stop their horses.

   Be sure your horse is "slicker trained" and is used to carrying a canteen on the saddle. (The noise of sloshing water can spook some horses.) Longeing with canteen and slicker secured to the saddle will help train a horse to these necessities of the trail.

2. Warn other riders behind you of danger on the trail such as rockslides, wire, holes, rattlesnakes, depth of muddy streams, or boggy areas. Whoever is riding at the head of the group should keep an eye on the end of the line and stop if there are problems or when necessary for slow horses to catch up. A "drag" rider makes sure no riders are left behind.

3. Don't ride too close to the horse in front of you or lag too far behind. Crowding, as we mentioned before, is dangerous. Lagging behind is just as bad, especially in a long line of riders: Those at the end of the line won't be able to keep a steady pace. If your horse has a tendency to kick other horses, tie a red ribbon in his tail to warn other riders to stay clear.

4. Avoid letting branches snap in the face of the rider following you. This is another reason for keeping at least a horse's length between you and the horse ahead.

5. If you must adjust equipment, or take a picture of the gorgeous view, ride out of line so that you don't hold up the group. This goes, too, for checking or caring for your horse's feet. Check them often if riding in rocky areas.

6. If it is necessary to pass a line of horses, first give warning and call out your intentions. Don't gallop past, but trot or walk by quietly and courteously.

7. On steep or treacherous footing it may be wise to get off and lead your horse. If your horse should fall or stumble while carrying you in a dangerous place, it could cause havoc or injury to a line of horses and riders.

   Mounting and dismounting on steep slopes can be a problem. Always mount or dismount uphill from your horse, since this is more easily accomplished and less likely to throw him off balance. Obviously, you have a great advantage if your horse has been trained to stand for mounting from the off side. If he does not, you may be able to turn your horse around to mount him from the uphill side. If this is not possible, travel on farther until you come to a wider place. Look ahead and keep alert to avoid getting into situations that you may have trouble getting out of.

8. When you ride on steep trails, what is your best position in the saddle? You may have to lean forward or back in relation to the topline of the horse to actually maintain a vertical position.

   It is easier for your horse to travel uphill if you stand in your

On steep or dangerous footing, stand well to the side of your horse and keep your arm fairly straight as you lead him. If he should stumble or fall toward you, you will be pushed out of his way.

Mounting from the uphill side on a steep slope.

stirrups and balance forward. Do not let your horse rush uphill (as inexperienced horses have a tendency to do).

On a steep downhill slope, sit straight and guide your horse in a straight line—not sideways. Let him have his head enough so that he can see to balance himself—slow and sure is best on downhill riding.

When you tire, be careful to maintain a good, balanced position. By slouching and unevenly distributing your weight on the horse's back, you will not only tire him unnecessarily but will also produce saddle sores. This is one reason why you must condition yourself, as well as your horse, for a long ride. Rest your legs by taking your feet out of the stirrups, but don't displace your weight. On long rides, it rests your horse to dismount and lead him for a few minutes every hour or so.

9. When facing road-crossing hazards, such as bridges or right-of-way crossings—especially if you are unfamiliar with the area—it may be wise to tie your horse and check your route on foot. Look for hazardous trash, old post holes, coiled wire, soft shoulders beside the pavement, and blind approaches to the highway, and scout out a safe route. Control your horse firmly.

In potentially treacherous areas such as a very narrow bridge, it may be best to lead your horse. If you do ride in such areas or on short, steep stretches, let one rider get all the way across before following. The riders should wait on the other side until all are safely across. Danger areas should never be attempted unless all horses and riders are capable of negotiating the spot safely. Other considerations are slick pavement and poor visibility—stay alert and cautious. Avoid riding along highways whenever possible; however, if this is necessary, see number 15 on page 146.

10. Some horses may balk at water crossings, especially when swift and noisy. An experienced horse ahead of your balky one will usually give your horse the confidence he needs. If you still have trouble, another rider can lead your horse across. But *don't* get off and lead him across, or let another person on foot lead your horse. The horse may panic in the water, lunge, and jump on you or your helper. Again, keep enough space between horses.

In high water you can raise your feet up to keep them dry. In swift, high water, face your horse slightly upstream. A horse must stretch out his neck to swim; make sure his head is not restricted by tight reins (if his nose is pulled under, he could drown) or by tied reins (they could hobble him or catch on a snag). If you swim across with your horse, hold on to the horn or other part of the saddle, or hold on to the horse's tail. Swim on the upstream side and don't get in front of him.

Some horses like to roll in the water. A horse with this intention will give you advance warning by lowering his head and hindquarters, and pawing the water. Use your legs actively; command with a sharp, stern voice, and slap with the reins if necessary to keep him moving forward.

Wet or drying cinches will probably stretch and shrink—be aware of this, and loosen or tighten the cinch accordingly.

11. When leaving your horse during a rest stop or for overnight, do not tie him too close to another horse. Tie him securely and safely near a horse he knows and will get along with, or tie him entirely alone, but within your sight and hearing. Never tie on concrete or slippery footing, as his feet can go out from under him if he should pull back. Tie to a rugged post or upright (never horizontal poles or rotten branches) at a level with his eye. If the leadrope is tied too low, a horse can be permanently injured if he pulls back—he can also put a foot over the rope. Never tie a horse with the bridle reins. See also "Overnight Care of Your Horse on the Trail."

12. Avoid horseplay around horses. Don't ride double, run under your horse, throw objects near a tied horse, or in general make any horse uncomfortable.

13. One of the pleasures of trail or cross-country riding in English tack is that usually many opportunities are offered for jumping. The leader should know the jumps ahead of time, or check them before actually jumping. (There might be a whopping badger hole just beyond that log.) Jumping blindly is foolhardy unless all horses and riders are expert. Keep enough space between horses, but do not let them get too strung out. It may be best to wait and jump one at a time until all are safely over, then continue the ride. The leader should never attempt a jump beyond the capabilities of the most inexperienced horse and rider in his group.

14. Storms can be a safety hazard, and you (or your guide) should check weather reports before the ride. Light rain and mist may be enjoyable, but heavy rain, sleet, or hail can be uncomfortable and dangerous, especially in the West where storms can be sudden and violent, and can erupt without warning.

In the event you are caught in a thunderstorm, avoid ridges, rocky slopes, or exposed areas if possible. If lightning is close, dismount and lead your horse—or release him, get as far from him as possible (he's a prime target for lightning, especially if shod with metal shoes), and assume a tight, kneeling position to make yourself as small a target as possible. See also page 220.

15. Riding along roads or highways involves special considerations (and should be avoided if possible):

    (a) If pavement is wet, shod horses will tend to slip. Always be alert, and walk cautiously. You may decide to dismount and lead your horse.

    (b) When riding along the shoulder or borrow pit, watch for holes, glass, wire, and other hazardous trash. When horses are in a line, the first rider should call back over his shoulder, " 'Ware glass!" or whatever. (" 'Ware" is short for "beware.") Each rider should pass the warning on back.

    (c) Face oncoming traffic with all riders on the same side of the road. Pass back the warning of oncoming traffic.

    (d) When crossing a highway with a group, use the "flank turn" (which should be practiced ahead of time at home). See Figure 12. If the crossing is exceptionally hazardous, dismount and lead horses.

16. Last but certainly not least of practices is to help those who need assistance. Perhaps a rider on a young, skittish horse will need help at a stream or gate. Be alert and generous. Inexperienced riders and young children might welcome good, tactfully given advice on surmounting some obstacle along the trail, or on what sort of gear to take, or on how to arrange and pack gear on the saddle.

Opening and Closing Gates

As mentioned before, it is good manners (and very necessary) to reclose gates after going through them. Gatework requires control and training. Your horse will have to pivot, two-track, and back with ease. Practice often at home, and go through as many different kinds of gates as you have (or can construct). This does not include wire gates, however, which are not safe to handle from the saddle. See "Western classes" in Chapter VII for more on going through gates.

Care of Equipment on the Trail

Sturdy, good-quality horse equipment is expensive. It pays in many ways to take good care of it. Equipment that is well cared for reflects on you as a

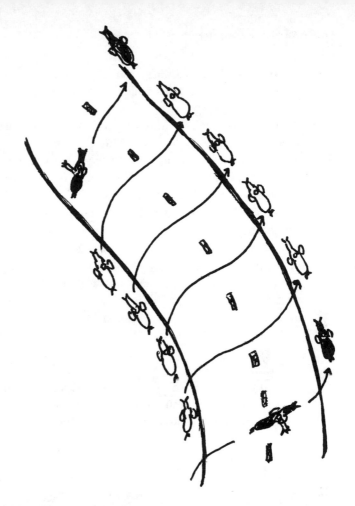

Fig. 12   A group of riders using the flank turn to cross a road safely.

horseman. More important, your safety depends on the good condition of your equipment as well as on the comfort of your horse.

Here are a few items to check before you begin your ride and at stopping points throughout the trip:

1. Your saddle blanket or pad should be clean and heavy enough to do its job properly—provide for the comfort and protection of your horse's back. Check occasionally to be sure no wrinkles develop. Your cinches or girth should be strong and clean.
2. Find the points of wear on your saddle (around stirrups and stirrup leathers, fenders, latigos, and so on), and make sure that they are saddle-soaped and oiled. You may need new lining on your saddle.

The points of the saddle's contact with your horse are especially important. Watch for worn hair around cinches, latigos, pads, blankets, and breast collar.

3. As with the saddle, the headstall and all other leather tack should be saddle-soaped and oiled often. After each use the bit should be wiped dry; any accumulated dried saliva or grass should be scraped off and the bit scrubbed and dried. The points of wear to watch for on a bridle occur wherever the leather is joined: connecting places for reins, noseband, browband, leather curb strap, cheekpieces, and throatlatch.

4. You should know how to carry your saddle and bridle, how to store your equipment, and how to set your saddle on the ground. (It should rest on the gullet with saddle leathers or fenders close to the saddle, so that your tied horse will not catch a foot.) After your saddle has been on the ground, be sure to check the cinch, saddle lining, and gullet for burs, twigs, or sticks before saddling up. When storing your saddle overnight or for longer periods, hang it from a rope or set it on a saddle rack of some kind. Make sure all leather pieces are lying flat. Allowing stirrup leathers to remain twisted, stacking saddles one upon the other, or dumping them helter-skelter into a truck are abuses which will quickly add to the general wear and tear. Cover

The correct way to set your saddle on the ground.

your tack and equipment with a tarp or poncho for heavy morning dews and for rain or snow.

Overnight Care of Your Horse on the Trail

When stopping for the night remember that your horse's comfort comes before your own. First find a good place to keep him for the night. On organized trail rides, a picket line is usually provided. This consists of a well-stretched rope on which individual lead ropes are attached. The picket line may be anchored with V supports and flat-headed anchors that are driven in flush with the ground. Be sure that any picket line you make or buy is *very* strong. Your picket line area should be some distance from the water source and from cooking and sleeping areas, though well within your sight and hearing.

On some trail rides, a rope can be stretched between trees, or horses can be tied to individual trees. When tying to a tree, make sure to remove any dead limbs to protect his eyes and face from injury. It is usually better to tie to an overhead "green" limb than to the trunk of a tree. Any troublemakers should be tied securely and alone to a good stout tree.

If your horse has been trained to hobbles and does not wander exces-

A well-managed picket line on a large ride. (Photo courtesy of *The Western Horseman*)

sively (some horses really learn to travel with them), he can move about in the area and find his own feed and water. However, if there are other horses on a picket line, be sure that your horse will stay away from them to avoid any horsing around and possible kicking or biting. If you hobble him where there is good grass, he will seldom wander.

After finding suitable quarters for your companion, you should look to his physical comfort. Remove the bridle and put on halter and lead rope.

If your horse is very hot, he should be cooled out before watering or tying him. An inexperienced rider may wonder what "hot" means. A horse can be hot on a cold day after a hard ride, but he might not be hot even on a very hot day after a leisurely ride. Feel the horse between his front legs. If he feels hot to your touch, or if you have any doubts, loosen the cinch but leave the saddle and blanket on his back. This will relieve the stress areas of his back and allow circulation to return gradually. If you were to take the saddle off immediately, the blood would rush into the stressed areas, causing swellings or "hot spots." Walk him awhile, lift saddle and blanket to allow air to circulate under them, then continue walking him until he feels cool and acts relaxed. Then you may water him.

Many times horses will not drink strange-tasting water. Several days before the trip, put a tablespoon of molasses or a few drops of oil of wintergreen into their drinking water. If you then add it to the strange water, they'll never know the difference and will drink readily. Don't use strange buckets or communal water tanks unless there is running water; they may be germ carriers.

Now tie your horse and remove the saddle and blanket. Tie him short enough so that he cannot get a leg over the rope but long enough so that his nose can reach the ground. Use a quick-release slipknot (see Figure 29) so that in an emergency he can be freed immediately, yet you are sure of this knot holding him securely when you are not in attendance.

Give him some hay or cut grass. (A jackknife can be handy for cutting the deep, rather tough mountain-valley grass.) While he is munching away peacefully, groom him completely and sponge him lightly where the saddle and girth were in contact with his body. Check his feet thoroughly and remove any foreign material. Any little cuts can be treated with antiseptic powder or salve.

Then you can grain him. When using a picket line, it is wise to grain all the horses at once to avoid jealousy. A nose bag is excellent for graining on the trail because the possibility of jealousy is minimized and because the grain won't be wasted. Be sure to be around when he is finished to remove the bag. He also can be grained on the saddle blanket. It is best not to put the grain on top of hay because horses tend to paw their hay under them in an effort to find more grain.

If your horse is used to pelleted or cubed grain, you'll find the use of this feed to be handy, and little is wasted on the ground. "Cake" is a Western term for the cubed feed that is usually prepared as a protein supplement for cattle and sheep. If you are unable to get pelleted or cubed feed, good-quality whole or rolled oats or a commercial horse feed are excellent. On very hot days, heavy feeds (containing corn, molasses, and other heatening foods) can cause colic. Don't change your horse's diet drastically. Fatigue and a different diet can also cause colic. For more on feeding, see page 163.

After cooling, grooming, watering, and feeding your horse, leave him to relax. If this is the first trail ride for either you or your horse, it won't do any harm to check him often. Your slipknot may have loosened, his hay may be all gone, he may have wound himself up in something, or a hobbled horse may have wandered.

Breaking camp is as important as arriving at the campsite: Cover the latrine, douse fires completely, pack and carry out your trash, rake and scatter manure. Groom and check your horse, especially his feet. Pack your gear, check and balance your tack as you saddle up, and prepare for an enjoyable trip home.

Trailering Your Horse

Often a trail ride will start out at such a distance from your stable that you will want to transport your horse to the starting point. While a truck may be used, a part of the education of most well-trained horses includes loading into a trailer. A horse that loads well into a truck or pickup won't necessarily load well into a horse trailer. Be sure that your horse will load easily and ride quietly before you hitch a ride for him in someone else's rig; there are also insurance considerations when trailering with others. (See *Basic Horse Care*, Chapter 9, "Transportation and Insurance.")

There are two types of trailers: the ramp type and the step-up type. A horse should be familiar with both types; if he is trained only for one, he will not necessarily load easily in the other. If your horse is not trained to load into a trailer, or if he gives you trouble, see Chapter X, Part 3, "Hard to Load into a Trailer."

When transporting a horse into a different county or state, it is usually necessary in Western states to obtain a brand inspection. This is very inexpensive and is required in some states regardless of whether or not your horse wears a brand. Brand inspections are for your own protection. Some states also require a health certificate and a negative Coggins test (for equine infectious anemia, or EIA), also for your protection. The health certificate is usually good for ten days and therefore can be obtained several days before you leave. The Coggins test (which requires the veterinarian to draw a blood sample) takes *at least* ten to fourteen days to obtain. This test is required in most states and is good for six months or a year, depending on the state. Your veterinarian can advise you.

Be careful when trailering your horse! Don't take curves too fast, or stop or start too quickly. Take into consideration state laws, signs, traffic, and weather conditions.

Beyond the many things to consider when going on a trail ride, such as appropriate dress and tack, good manners and safety habits, some just plain horse sense will help make for an enjoyable experience.

Cattle Drives

Contrary to some Easterners' impressions, cattle drives are not a thing of the past. Although the days of the long, long drives to market are over, many ranchers now drive their cattle to and from summer ranges in the national forests and elsewhere. Often part of the distance must be traveled along public highways. Motorists often are taken aback at the sight of several hundred cattle solidly blocking the road, and their reactions vary from stopping altogether to panicking and scattering cows, calves, and cowboys alike. It is not always necessary for the tourist to stop completely. He should slow down and drive into the herd, waiting for cows and calves to move aside for the car. If a particularly cussed old cow stops in front of the car, the driver should keep inching forward and perhaps bang the side of the car with his hand. A light tap of the horn is permissible if the cattle still won't move, but ranchers will not appreciate long bellowing blasts. Bulls may look fierce with their heavy necks, big horns, and tiny eyes, but they react the same as the cows in this situation and will move aside for a car.

Occasionally greenhorns have the opportunity to help out on cattle drives. There is a knowledgeable way to drive cattle and, if the newcomer is familiar with the ways and means, he will be able to help instead of hinder.

When driving cattle either on the highway or across the range, it is usually best to move the animals along in a compact line. They are easier to handle when strung out in the direction of movement than when bunched or strung out perpendicular to the direction of movement. It is easier to drive cattle up a fence line when moving cross country, and the same is true along a highway. Occasionally there will be great difficulty in getting cattle to cross a yellow or white line on a highway.

Yells, yippees, whistles, and swishes of a whip or branch keep the cattle moving at a steady slow walk. Avoid rushing them or setting too fast a pace, especially if there are calves. Part of the object in moving cattle is to have

Driving cattle along a fence line.

them arrive in good condition with little or no weight loss, so it is best if they remain calm and untroubled. Don't crowd the animals at gates, bridges, or other narrow areas that they must file through. Only so many can go at a time, and to crowd them causes injury and unnecessary riding after animals that break away.

Animals as well as people seem to have "tolerance range" that, when broken, causes anxiety. You know how distressing it is to talk with someone who comes very close to you. Feeling uncomfortable, you back up until the distance suits your tolerance range, but invariably your companion moves in closer again. Apparently his tolerance range is shorter. With cattle, if you remain a certain distance from them, they seem to be undisturbed and will travel calmly. If you break the tolerance range by crowding, they become excited and try to break away in any direction.

The "drag" men keep the cattle moving from the rear. To keep animals from leaving the trail or straying off to the side, "swing" and "flank" riders ride alongside the herd turning back any animals that tend to become separated. Again, this is generally a calm process though it may require spurts of fast riding to put your horse in the correct position to turn back a cow. Usually an old and wise cow will lead the herd if the trail is familiar. "Point" men may ride at the head of the herd to guide the cows, but they stay out to the side; if they were to get in front, the cows would probably stop. Each rider should keep his eye on the whole herd so that he can best judge his own work, anticipate where he will be needed, and ride to aid another rider if necessary.

Cattle are subject to moods and conditions, sometimes moving along easily and cooperatively, sometimes seeming to go in every direction but the right one. By giving them enough room and avoiding crowding, you are in a better position to work animals that separate from the herd, and the cattle themselves are more likely to be calm and move as they should. If an animal breaks from the herd, you will have little success in running it down to turn it back; it is better to circle and come at the animal more from an angle in order to turn it. Never allow yourself to drift in front of the cattle as they will not usually follow a rider but will turn or stop.

Hunting from Horseback

Pack trips are often organized for hunting parties. These are usually in the care of a guide who leads the party into the proper game districts and shows the group the most likely areas in which to find big game. The guide provides the horses that are used to gunshots and are not afraid of packing game. Generally horses must be trained to pack game and many remain wary of it, especially of the big cats and bear. Because it is so easy to become lost or confused in the vast wilderness of the Western states, out-of-state hunters usually hire (or may be required to have) a licensed hunting guide who knows the current regulations and knows the trails and landmarks of his hunting area.

Competition Trail Riding

Competition riding consists of two basically different types of rides: competitive trail rides and endurance rides. The competitive trail ride does not push the horse and rider to his limits of stress, while the endurance ride approaches the limits of stress for both horse and rider.

The endurance winner would be an exceptional animal, whereas any healthy, well-conditioned horse could compete and win in a competitive trail ride. The same holds true for the rider: Anyone successfully competing in an endurance contest would be a very capable and knowledgeable horseman. The endurance rider may do almost anything he wants with his horse; the competitive trail rider is restricted during the ride as well as afterward. On both distance rides, however, there are veterinary checks so that ignorance or cruelty will not ruin a horse.

In most competitive trail rides, warming up your horse is not allowed prior to the ride; an endurance horse may be warmed up in advance. The endurance rider may walk on foot occasionally to save his horse, but in most competitive trail rides, the rider must be in the saddle every forward step of the way.

In the 1920s the United States Army conducted a series of three-hundred-mile endurance tests for the purpose of finding the best type of horse for cavalry use and the best methods of conditioning horses for long and strenuous rides. The rides were grueling affairs, covering sixty miles a day for five days straight. Horses carried minimum weights of two hundred pounds (240 pounds on two rides), and were required to finish each day in not more than ten hours, not less than eight. Because a total of only 148 contestants rode in the eight rides, averaging eighteen horses in each ride, results were not considered conclusive as far as the preferred breeds and types were concerned. However, the fact that fewer than half of the starters finished the tests indicated the importance of conditioning and training.

Perhaps the most valuable contribution of the old army endurance tests was to serve as a model for later endurance and competitive rides, both in purpose and physical organization. One of the early competitive rides took place in Vermont, and with this as a precedent, the Green Mountain Horse Association organized its first endurance ride in 1936. Organizers didn't want to promote an extremely severe ride that would allow only a few professionals to qualify, but rather a more popular ride that would nevertheless require thoughtful training and good horsemanship.

Since 1936, the GMHA has conducted distance rides every year. Many other contests have been organized throughout the country, especially in recent years, and in all of these, the general purpose of improving care and horsemanship is paramount. Most rides are strictly and competently judged and controlled to prevent or punish abuses. The contestant must be thoroughly familiar with the rules of the particular contest he enters.

The Trail Horse

If you are interested in competitive trail riding and endurance riding, you have two primary considerations: first, your own purposes and goals for entering the contest; and second, your horse: Is he capable of carrying you on either an endurance ride or a competitive trail ride, and if not, can you find a horse that is?

Your own goals should closely approximate the goals of the ride itself: to improve your horsemanship, to condition and care for your horse in the best way possible, to enjoy a beautiful outing that is a pleasure for both you and your horse. Unfortunately, there are always riders whose main interests seem to center on winning a prize—often to the point of abusing their horses. Keep your goals clear. When you first enter an endurance or competitive trail ride, remember that this contest should act as a trial run to show you what it is like. Don't expect to be a winner the first time out. As in any other contest, coming up through the ranks is the usual procedure for most contest winners.

When it comes to your horse, you will have to judge whether or not he is capable of the rigorous training necessary to compete in an endurance ride. If done properly, the conditioning should improve the health and fitness of any horse, up to the limit of his individual capabilities. You should know when this limit is reached. Many horses may make perfectly satisfactory family mounts, capable of any ordinary demands, but not capable—either physically or temperamentally—of sustained hard riding. This does not make the horse any less valuable for his main purpose; it does mean that you had best find another horse if you are interested in competing in endurance rides.

Age, size, conformation, temperament, training, soundness, gaits, breeding, and intelligence all have a bearing on the potential capability of a horse for both endurance and competitive trail riding contests. Even so, the final measure of endurance can be determined only by actual test. Also, remember that you and your horse must like each other and enjoy working together. All the physical attributes in the world won't help unless you "live together" well.

In sizing up your own horse or in selecting a mount for distance riding, keep in mind the following points as *most likely* to be found in a good distance horse. The points will at least serve as standards against which you can measure your own horse's possibilities and limitations.

Age. It is best to have a mature, fully developed horse. Young horses (under five years of age) may not be fully developed in bone or muscle, and although they may be able to take the conditioning and hard riding, they are more likely to succumb to injury or unsoundness because of it. Ideal ages are from six to twelve, and if the horse is an exceptionally sound and well-conditioned animal, he could be used in competitive trail rides when older than twelve.

Size. Generally it seems that a medium-size horse (under 15.2 hands and under 1,200 pounds) is more successful in distance riding. Too small an animal (under 14 hands or 750 pounds) would have to move his legs faster to accomplish the distance and, therefore, could not maintain a rhythmic speed easily. Too large or heavy an animal uses too much energy moving his bulk around and is more inclined to have hoof and leg problems.

Conformation. Details of good conformation are generally listed with each breed ideal and in every treatise on selecting or judging horses. In general, these conformation characteristics may serve as an ideal for a trail horse. Specific physical qualities especially desirable in the distance horse are:

1. Good legs and feet: strong-boned, straight and clean, short cannons, long but not extremely long sloping pasterns, good quality hoofs; generally long muscled and well muscled; a horse is only as good as his legs.
2. Deep, sloping, well-muscled shoulders.
3. Short back, close-coupled, well ribbed out to the hips, with long muscles covering the kidneys.
4. Broad powerful chest with large, solid, strong muscles; well-sprung ribs (indicating good heart and lung capacity).

Soundness. If you have doubts about the soundness of your horse, have him checked by a veterinarian. If you are selecting a horse for distance riding purposes, give careful consideration to a vet's examination. It would be a heartbreaking waste of time to go through weeks of conditioning and training (supposing the horse could take it) only to have the vet disqualify him before the ride begins because of irregular pulse rate or some other problem of which you may be unaware.

Gaits and action. How a horse moves determines the amount of wear and tear he can take. If his action is free and smooth he will expend less energy in moving, and therefore will be less liable to fatigue. Naturally, the animal should not interfere or stumble, and he should be balanced and flexible, with little noticeable concussion.

The walk should be flat, elastic, and fast, with a straight, reasonably long stride. As high action means unnecessary expense of energy and quicker fatigue for a trail horse, it is not desirable.

The trot should also be square and true, fast and lasting, with the diagonal feet striking the ground at the same time. The gaits must be comfortable for the rider, and the horse should have the ability to keep his gaits stable; lack of these qualities would mean that you could become very tired just in the process of riding him, which in turn would affect his performance.

Breeding. Although almost any breed may produce a good trail horse, many people feel that a horse of good breeding will have more intelligence and physical capabilities than one whose breeding is questionable. Actually, many half-bred and crossbred horses are of excellent type for trail use. Ponies and some horses with pony breeding also seem to do exceptionally well. Breeds that have proved especially popular for endurance riding include Arabians, Morgans, Thoroughbreds, and Appaloosas.

Intelligence. Intelligence is an important characteristic in a trail horse because he must be able to look out for himself, work alertly and calmly, accept conditions without fuss (eat and drink what you give him and when, rest when he can on the trail or in the stable, and so forth), and occasionally keep his rider out of trouble by avoiding dangerous footing in boggy areas or elsewhere. Many riders have been glad they trusted their mount's judgment in dangerous or uncertain situations. Generally a good head—wide at the top, with broad, flat forehead and large, low-set, and expressive eyes—is indicative of intelligence.

Temperament. Some horses are temperamentally suited to distance riding and some are not. A good competitive trail horse should be calm, easygoing, alert, curious, and move freely either alone or in a group of horses. He should be able to lead out willingly or follow other horses without concern. Animals that are either nervous and excitable or constantly in need of spurring to move at all will tire both themselves and their riders. Horses with more serious vices such as kicking, biting, boring, or bolting should not be allowed on this type of ride; and if the horse has bad habits such as weaving, cribbing, or wind sucking, his good points must be strong to warrant his use.

The endurance horse is allowed more latitude in temperament because he is judged on the time and condition factor almost exclusively; he should, however, be bold and sensible.

Training. The trail horse should have a good background of basic training which leaves him mannerly, responsive to the aids, able to rein and back easily, and stand quietly for mounting and dismounting as well as when mounted. Special trail training—encountering obstacles, opening and closing gates, low jumping, and so on—would certainly be helpful. If the horse is basically well trained, he should automatically receive as much extra work as he needs during the conditioning period. The conditioning process itself is the training for these contests.

Conditioning Horse and Rider

Conditioning is the process of strengthening a horse to his peak of physical and mental fitness. It is similar to the conditioning of any athlete—and vital to an acceptable final performance. It requires regimen and includes scheduled exercise, diet, and management. During conditioning, a horse's muscles improve in strength and tone, his body loses excess fat and becomes firm and hard, his lung capacity is improved, and he develops to a peak of vigor. As a result of conditioning, he performs at his best with the least amount of fatigue. To attempt a distance or endurance ride without proper conditioning would be akin to leaving the office chair to shovel three feet of snow off all the driveways on the block before noon—it could be fatal.

Conditioning of the rider is as important as that of the horse. If the rider is not in proper condition and allows himself to become tired, ride sloppily, or become stiff, he will handicap his horse seriously, perhaps even to the point of injuring him, especially in the endurance contest. Happily, the conditioning of horse and rider is easiest and best done together, and the process of working together regularly and with a purpose can bring unexpected joys in understanding and companionship.

How long does it take to condition a horse? Depending on age, previous condition, and general temperament and training, three to four months could be considered a bare-bones minimum for a competitive trail rider. Six to eight weeks should probably be planned on to allow time to suit the final conditioning program to the individual horse. The endurance horse may need over a year of planning, training, and conditioning.

First Steps to Take

First of all, you will want to decide what ride or rides you wish to participate in. Send for a program. When will the ride be held? If this fits in with your vacation or time-off schedule, the next thing to consider is its location. Can you ride your horse to the starting point? If your horse must be trailered to the starting site, is he prepared for this, or will trailer training have to be part of his conditioning schedule? If it will take several days of trailering, this too should be prepared for ahead of time. Financial considerations should not be overlooked, especially if there is a possibility they might be limiting; a realistic advance estimate of costs could save embarrassment or actual discomfort for you or your horse later.

If all bodes well for the intended ride, it's time to evaluate your present situation. This begins with yourself even before your horse. Are you willing and are you able to take the time necessary to condition yourself and your horse properly? Conditioning is hard work and a schedule must be adhered to on a daily basis—weekend workouts will not suffice. To cut corners on the conditioning program is to take chances with your horse's health, and the cards are stacked against you.

If all signals are still go, evaluate your horse. We'll assume that his age, gaits, temperament, conformation, and so on are such that he has the potential of making a good endurance or competitive trail horse. What is his present condition? Has he been out on the range all winter, perhaps a bit run down and in need of some flesh and energy? Or has he been stuffing himself in stall and paddock with only an occasional short ride so that he tends to be fat and is overall soft? Has he been worked regularly so that he already carries some degree of condition? What shape are his feet in? It's a good idea to call a reliable farrier before beginning conditioning; explain to him what you are planning so that he can trim and shoe your horse's hoofs properly and regularly. Check the trail ride program with him to see if there are any qualifications or restrictions on shoeing. Make a date with him to return several days before the ride: If new shoes are necessary the horse will be able to get used to them before the big event.

Check the program again for tack. Are there any special tack requirements or limitations? Are there minimum weight requirements? (Will you have to pack extra weight to meet the minimum, and if so, what's the best way?) You should train in the tack you will use on the ride. If you need a new bridle or want to try a new bit, start out with it when you begin training.

General Considerations in Training And Conditioning

Training and conditioning consist of regular exercise that gradually increases in severity and duration—in other words, lots of work over a long period. Proper evaluation of your horse's condition and capabilities and an understanding of the conditioning effects of the terrain over which you are to travel are important in setting up your training schedule. Too light a schedule will not work the horse out sufficiently to develop his muscles and wind. Too heavy a schedule is a worse offense, for it will exhaust or injure the horse rather than improve him. Keep the work within the limits of the horse's strength, and encourage his confidence in himself and in you.

If possible, train in an area similar to that which you will encounter on the ride. If you live on a featureless plain and the contest is all up and down hills (or vice versa), your horse will be at a severe disadvantage since he must use different muscles and a different type of action. Take advantage of any physical land features in your area that approximate conditions of the ride and do extra work in these areas. Assuming the ride will include both hills and flats, training in both areas will develop the muscles properly.

If a severe altitude change is necessary, you may have to arrive at the site of the contest several weeks ahead of time, and work your horse lightly at first to give him the opportunity to adjust.

Your horse should be used to working in all kinds of weather. Let him stay out in rain or shine to become hardened to weather changes. However, use common sense and don't chill your horse in a cold wind or rain after a hard workout.

Good muscle development is attained by day-by-day hard training at a fast walk and a steady, fast trot, and wind is improved by occasional brisk gallops. Training in deep sand, plowed ground, and over steep hills develops both wind and muscle.

As to speed, in competitive trail rides this is usually worked out for you with minimum and maximum times allowed. In endurance contests, since eight miles per hour is an average speed, you will probably have to ride ten miles per hour to maintain this. In other words, you will have to maintain a trot over most of the course.

Variety in the training pattern is vital to maintain your horse's interest. The same repetition of scene day in, day out can sour a trail horse quickly— in fact, you're likely to become pretty bored, too, and your feelings will be communicated to the horse. Vary the routes you take as much as possible. Try to ride near traffic one day, and well off in the wilder areas another day, if you can. Change your gaits often enough to keep him alert, and ride at night occasionally as well as during the day. Endurance horses often have to move at night, so they should be used to traveling sure-footedly over obstacles and strange trails in the dark or in and out of moon shadows, and they should not be upset by night noises, headlights, flashlights, and other night phenomena.

Arrange to ride with other horses part of the time; occasionally you may keep your horse back while others go ahead, or pass the group and push your own horse ahead. At any rate, he should behave calmly with other horses; any chance he has of becoming used to them before the ride can be beneficial. It may be possible to stay overnight in other stables—perhaps you and a friend could work out alternate arrangements to give your horses experience in unfamiliar surroundings. If both horses will be entered in the contest, work them together occasionally and then stable them near each other at the ride; this will help keep them contented.

Some horses may find work itself monotonous and will benefit greatly by a day off once a week. Other horses might lose ground if given a complete day of rest. If your training schedule involves months, as is necessary in endurance contests, perhaps a week of rest in a pasture would be beneficial after about three months. You'll have to determine what's best for your horse and try to keep his welfare in mind rather than a restful day for yourself at the beach or for catching up on the yardwork.

The Rider

You will have to become so familiar with your horse's way of working that you can judge the most efficient way to put him over any stretch of ground. This means staying alert, keeping your horse alert, and constantly anticipating the course to determine how best to ride it. Discipline yourself to stick to a schedule. Thus you will be conditioning and training yourself as well as your horse in the months before the contest.

The Basic Seat, in which you sit erect but relaxed, deep in the lowest part of the saddle, is easiest on your horse. In distance riding it is imperative to sit square and in good balance, especially toward the end of the day or contest. Slouching, shifting weight, swinging legs, and any other acrobatics attributed to poor horsemanship will destroy the rhythm of your horse's gaits and breathing, thus tiring him rapidly. "Look ahead of your horse" and "tall in the saddle" are phrases that help approach the spirit of successfully riding the trail contest. Standing in balance in your stirrups relieves stress on your horse's back and is acceptable in distance riding.

You should not need to carry a whip or crop or wear spurs on an animal that is eager to go. Know how to use your legs to push your horse forward with his legs well under him, and learn to keep your horse's gaits even and smooth.

The way you select and care for your tack tells whether you are a knowledgeable horseman. Any selection of and experimentation with tack should be completed months before the ride. At this early date find out whether your horse works best in a hackamore, snaffle, Pelham, or other bit. Which fits your horse better—Western, English, or McClellan saddle? (See "Tack" in Chapter 4 of *Basic Horse Care* for more on proper fit of saddles.) Many riders groan at the mention of the McClellan as it has been said that it is easy on the horse and hard on the rider. But if ridden correctly and in balance, we have found it comfortable; certainly it allows air to circulate across the horse's back. This saddle is worth trying out for distance riding. There are many worthy distance saddles on the market.

Your girth or cinch, whether leather, web, or horsehair, should be viewed with the contest in mind; so should the type of blanket, pad, or combination of both. All your equipment should fit extremely well—take the time to know exactly how it should be adjusted, not only for your horse's best performance but for your own as well. Adjustment slightly on the tight side is better than loose and rubbing. Any accessory equipment (saddlebags, canteen, slicker, and the like) should be tied securely; in fact, you should carry the accessories when you train as well as on the contest ride.

The main objective in the care of your equipment is to keep it spotless, supple, and strong. This is especially true of any part of your equipment that touches the horse: The blanket should be free of even a piece of straw, the bit should be clean without any dried saliva or hardened-on oats, the girth should be strong and flexible, free of twigs or hay. Always check your equipment before you tack up. Attention to detail in every aspect of the contest is the difference between the winner and the also-rans.

Furthermore, you should also be willing to study and read. Study the results of endurance rides: Learn how to take pulse, respiration, and temperature, and check your horse often enough to know his normal readings under certain types of stress, weather conditions, and altitudes. Learn how to rate your horse. Study the different kinds of tack and the methods of caring for it, and be willing to experiment and learn.

Rating Your Horse

"Rating" is the practice of riding measured distances within a certain time span. For instance, pick a measured distance of five miles and try to cover it in one hour—as close to sixty minutes as you can. Make yourself conscious of time by doing this over a variety of distances and in different terrains. You will get used to estimating time and mileage at various speeds for your individual horse. In competition trail riding, you are penalized for coming in too early or too late—learning to rate your horse is essential to success.

Feeding for Conditioning

Adequate, beneficial, and well-scheduled feeding combines with proper training and care to condition a horse successfully. Your goal is to develop a horse that won't shrink unduly under the abnormal stress of competitive trail or endurance riding; he should stay about the same weight with the hardness and fitness of a true athlete.

Hard hay (well-cured mixed meadow grasses) seems best for producing a watery sweat under stress, which is desirable. Alfalfa or other legume hays tend to keep a horse soft and produce a lathery sweat. (Legume hays also tend to be laxative.) Alfalfa (or other legume) is very palatable, however, and is acceptable as a small percentage of his ration, say 5 or 10 percent. Roughage should be available whenever your horse is at rest.

As to grains, we prefer oats to bring a horse to fine fettle and hard condition. For us the ideal combination seems to be a ration of one-third rolled plain oats, one-third whole oats, and one-third rolled mix (variety of grains with molasses). Check with your vet to establish an economical grain ration of similar value for your area. Graining your horse three times a day is more beneficial than once or twice. A horse has a relatively small stomach for his size and will digest his ration more completely in smaller amounts given more often. The total grain ration should be increased gradually (to not more than one pound per hundred pounds of body weight) as the exercise is increased. If your horse is rested one day a week, his grain should be reduced on that day. A bran mash before his day of rest is very beneficial. Costly supplements, quick cures, tranquilizers, and vitamin shots are usually not necessary and may be detrimental if not administered under a vet's care. Keep your grain ration simple and reasonable.

Water and loose-form minerals and salt should be readily available. Be sure to check the mineral deficiencies of your area with your vet before buying your minerals. Salt may be obtained plain or iodized. (Again, which you buy will depend on your area.) As noted before, some horses have a problem with the palatability of water at strange locations. Several weeks before any move, put some molasses or oil of wintergreen into the water and let him drink from a pail. When at the new location his strange water, with additive, will taste the same as at home, and the pail will be familiar.

Of course, your feeding schedule (or plan) is worthless if your horse is infested with worms. Take a sample of feces to your vet to determine whether your horse needs a vermifuge and, if so, what kind for what parasite. The severity of worming medicines necessitates this check; don't worm just for the sake of worming. Maybe it isn't necessary.

Observation and good judgment are the keys to proper feeding.

Daily Schedule

With all these considerations in mind, set up a tentative training schedule. Use a calendar to determine each day's goal and write it down. This needn't be inflexible, but a written schedule does wonders for one's own self-discipline and keeps upsets to a minimum. Revise the schedule if need be as you go along, but a well-thought-out plan that includes routes, time, and type of work each day should stand as a basic framework for your conditioning program.

As you follow the schedule, keep a diary for each day, recording feed, mileage, how certain terrain affected your horse, and so on. This information will help you later in rating your horse for the contest.

Begin each day with a thorough grooming. Besides promoting good condition in itself, grooming gives you the chance to check your horse thoroughly for any signs of soreness, lameness, or blemishes. Pay special attention to his feet and legs, both before riding and when you come in. If you ride twice a day, groom lightly the second time, but don't shirk on checking his feet. A good grooming stimulates, massages, and toughens the skin, encourages proper circulation, prepares the horse for work, and promotes a feeling of comradeship.

There are so many different factors to consider when setting up your training schedule that it would be almost impossible to fit your own conditions into a formula schedule. The following seven-week schedule is intended to be a sample only, to show you *one* way in which a schedule could be planned. It is set up for a normally exercised horse and is planned for a competitive trail ride; an endurance horse would require many more months—even a year or more—of intensive scheduling. A soft horse that has been used little during the winter and spring would need from three to four months of training. If your horse is active and is kept in a large, hilly pasture, he would need less preparation time. Or, if your horse is already in good condition and used to regular riding, a three-day-a-week schedule (instead of six days with one rest day) could prove effective, at least for several weeks. Please remember, this schedule is planned for a competitive trail ride and is intended to be used only as a guide in setting up your own plan.

FIRST WEEK   vary routes, include gentle slopes

1st–3rd days	½ hour twice a day; walk, a little jog or trot to relieve monotony
4th–5th days	40 minutes twice a day, mainly walk, a little more trotting
6th day	45 minutes twice a day, more jog and trot, occasional mild canter—cover 3 to 5 miles
7th day	rest

SECOND WEEK

1st–2nd days	45 minutes twice a day, more jog and trot, occasional canter
3rd–4th days	60 minutes twice a day, try hillier ground, work up and down medium slopes at walk (stop and rest when horse gets winded—take time)
5th–6th days	1 hour twice a day, increase pace on slopes if horse is ready
7th day	rest

THIRD WEEK

1st–2nd days	1 hour twice a day, more trotting, try steep slope, take time
3rd–4th days	1½ hours morning, 1 hour afternoon; more jog and trot, some canter
5th–6th days	1½ hours morning, 1 hour afternoon; as much jog and trot as possible; medium and some steep slopes; some long, easy canters; cover approximately 10–12 miles morning, 8–10 miles afternoon.
7th day	rest

FOURTH WEEK

1st–2nd days	1½ hours twice a day; same as above, some sharp, fast canters
3rd day	20–25-mile ride
4th–5th days	1½ hours twice a day
6th day	20-mile ride
7th day	1 hour twice a day

Keep track of your mileage and the time necessary to cover ground at different gaits and through different terrain—this will give you a working guide for rating.

FIFTH WEEK

Try to approximate contest conditions: If it will be in hilly country, increase up-and-down work; if in sandy country, walk, trot, and canter in sand.

1st–2nd days	1½ hours twice a day
3rd day	20-mile ride, more steep slopes
4th–5th days	2 hours morning, 1 hour afternoon
6th day	30-mile ride
7th day	2 hours morning, 1 hour afternoon

Rating on long rides: If you have twenty miles to ride in four hours, try to ride according to terrain to come out within the allotted time.

SIXTH WEEK

More practice rating, much trotting, steep slopes

1st day	20-mile ride
2nd–3rd days	2 hours twice a day
4th day	20-mile ride
5th day	2 hours twice
6th day	30-mile ride
7th day	2 hours twice

SEVENTH WEEK

Let up and rest before the big ride so that your horse will be fresh and ready. Ride an hour twice a day.

Is Your Horse in Condition?

When a horse is in condition, he has:
- alert eyes and ears
- a fine, glossy, silky coat

- good muscular development
- a good covering of flesh
- a smooth, free, springy, vigorous stride
- a watery sweat
- a quick return to normal breathing after hard work
- a good appetite
- willingness and eagerness to start the day

Before the Ride

You've completed your conditioning program and the Big Contest is coming up. Plan to arrive two days (more, of course, if there is a considerable change in altitude) before the contest, allowing your horse the opportunity to rest up. If he doesn't sleep well the first night from nervousness in the unfamiliar surroundings, by the second night he will be more at home.

Before leaving home, give your horse a thorough last-minute health check; it will probably be necessary to obtain both brand and health inspection certificates. (Check on county and state laws.) Be sure that your negative Coggins test is current.

Preparation for the trip and what to do when you arrive at the site of the contest have already been discussed in Chapter VII.

Some rides provide stabling only during the ride and for one day preceding and one day after the ride. If you arrive earlier, make sure you arrange ahead of time for stabling for your mount. You should know also whether to bring your own feed or if feed will be provided—some competitive trail rides provide all feed so that conditions will be the same for all the horses.

If you arrive several days ahead of time, don't let up on your exercising routine. (This *is* exercising now, not training—it's too late for training!) Let your horse become acquainted with the country by riding him at least an hour to an hour and a half each day. Or if this is not possible, ride him in a corral, riding ring, or similar small area; if this is not possible, longe him in the stable yard. You may have to cut back on his grain ration if exercise is curtailed.

These days may be pleasant and relaxing for both you and your horse if you keep your schedule as well as his. Don't be tempted by the stimulation and excitement of a gathering of horsey people to overdo, change your personal eating-sleeping schedule radically, or otherwise jeopardize your ride. Here is opportunity to spend even more time with your horse while keeping tack spotless and oiled or just enjoying the companionship.

During the Ride

Give your horse at least an hour to digest his food after he has finished eating. This may mean an early feeding—perhaps 5:00 A.M. Give him his fill of water first, a little hay to calm him, and finally his grain—approximately the same amount he has been getting unless you've had to cut down the last week because of lack of exercise. Avoid any radical change. The largest grain serving should come in the evening when he has plenty of time to digest it thoroughly. However, he'll need enough now to see him through the day.

Groom him as usual, taking particular care with every spot that will be in contact with saddle or bridle, and with his feet. Check tack carefully also, shaking out and brushing saddle pads or blankets to be sure that there is not the tiniest hayseed that will eventually develop into trouble on the long ride. Place blankets or pad on his back so that they are absolutely smooth and without wrinkles. Check girths carefully before tightening—and avoid over-tightening in the excitement. Western cinches especially are easy to over-tighten: It should be tight enough to mount without turning but loose enough so that you can easily place three fingers between it and the horse. You should know your horse well enough to know just how much (if any) he swells.

Bridle your horse a few minutes before starting time. You will probably have to line up with the other contestants. When your turn comes you will probably have to trot out past the timekeeper, giving the judges a better opportunity to check your horse for lameness or signs of fatigue. Then walk for fifteen minutes or so to warm him up gradually.

By now you have made your plans and have a good idea of how you will cover the course. Each horse-rider team is competing as an individual, so don't be influenced by other riders as to gaits or rate of going. Your main interests now are to keep your horse fresh as long as possible while covering the course in the properly allotted time. The horse should come in on time and in the best possible condition.

Some hints that may help you:

Take advantage of level stretches to trot or lope since you must push along if you are to come in within the time limit.

Trotting downhill may be hard on a horse's legs, but if he's in good condition, his wind will probably last longer trotting and cantering downhill than uphill.

Walk when footing is especially rough.

Change gaits fairly often—this is where knowing your horse is important. He may be able to jog, trot, or lope easily and comfortably for five miles at a stretch—if so, you can take advantage of his preferred gait.

When trotting, change diagonals often, or stand balanced in your stirrups.

Occasional rest periods (at the top of a long, steep hill, perhaps, or if the weather is very hot) will allow the horse to regain his wind and you to stretch your legs while you loosen the girth for a few minutes and check him over. Don't stop so often, however, that you spoil your rhythm.

Water your horse lightly but not too often; certainly don't let him overdrink. Drinking when hot won't hurt him if the amount is little and if you continue working; sometimes just sucking a sponge is beneficial.

Ride your horse in a relaxed way that leaves him free to conserve his energy for the trail rather than use it up worrying about what you want him to do. Remain balanced and alert.

At the lunch stop, water your horse and loosen the cinch, but leave the saddle in place—though you may lift it several times to let air circulate. Be sure not to disturb or wrinkle the blankets. Have a sandwich and drink but don't stand around too long—when warmed up, it's best to keep going.

Try to rate the ride so that you can walk in the last mile or two, arriving with your horse already partly cooled out. Why add an hour of walking at the stables to the miles already traveled?

If your horse becomes lame on the trail or stumbles badly, check to see if a stone has become embedded in his hoof, or if there are any bad scratches, scrapes, or cuts. Report these to the judges when you see them. If he is seriously lamed or otherwise injured, ask a passing rider to notify the judges. A veterinarian will check your horse to see what should be done next.

After the Day's Ride

When you take your horse into his stall, you have arrived at one of the most important times of the day. Good care at this stage is vital to the continued well-being of your horse. Being able to take TPRs (temperature, pulse, and respiration) will help a horseman to evaluate when his horse has cooled off sufficiently to be watered. (For more on TPRs, see *Basic Training for Horses*, Part 4, Chapter 2, "Training for Competitive and Endurance Riding.")

Remove his bridle, loosen the cinch or girth, and massage his legs. Give him just a little water and some hay, or you may merely wet the hay if he is still hot. Your horse doesn't have to feel hot to be hot. On a cold, windy day he could come in dry and then sweat up later. Leave him alone to rest for a bit or chew hay if he so wishes. After half an hour, loosen the cinch again, lift the saddle to allow gradual return of circulation, and replace it. Check his feet and shoes thoroughly and again leave him for half an hour. When you return this time, remove the saddle. Leave the blankets on while you get him a small amount of water and massage his legs again. Then remove the blankets and set them to dry. In another fifteen or twenty minutes give the horse another half pail of water and, if his back is dry, groom him thoroughly, especially massaging his back. The care you give your horse will depend upon the weather conditions, his TPR, his degree of fatigue, and so on; adapt your own procedure from this general guideline.

Continue giving water in fifteen-minute, half-pail portions or less until he is completely dry and well rested, at which time he can drink his fill. Give him his grain and make sure the stall is well bedded down, his water bucket full, and he has hay and salt. See that he is undisturbed during the night—if the stables are closed and no one is allowed to enter, there will be no problems of this kind.

What Are Judges Looking For?

Horses are judged before the ride, during the ride, and at the stables after the ride each day. If the ride is for more than one day, the judges will usually inspect the horses in the stable after everyone has left each night; on the last day of the ride the horses are inspected about an hour after the finish.

Horses are judged on their condition: Their fitness is based on the amount of time it takes them to recover from stress. The value of TPRs has been proved in helping to judge condition. Keeping a record that reveals the rate of your horse's recovery serves as a basis for future conditioning and training. The Tevis Cup Ride (endurance) publishes this information to its contestants.

During the preliminary checkup by a veterinarian, all blemishes and unsoundnesses are noted. It is wise to point out all blemishes, although they are rarely missed, so that the horse will not be penalized for them at the end of the ride. If serious lameness, wind, or heart conditions are apparent from the TPRs, the judges will bar the horse from continuing. If the problem is not severe, the judges may inform the contestant and leave the decision as to what to do to him. The rider should keep the welfare of his horse in mind, and this will probably mean retiring from the contest. After the first day of the ride, judges will also be watching for signs of fatigue, such as dragging feet or drooping heads.

At established checkpoints along the road the horses are judged on gaits, freedom of movement, and evidence of continued vigor or lameness, especially after hard climbs. The experienced judge will check TPRs at these points, and keep a record of them. Judges may withdraw horses at any time, or warn riders of conditions the rider may be unaware of, leaving the decision of withdrawal to the rider's discretion.

In competitive trail rides, the judges will also have an eye on the riders, noting good sportsmanship, consideration of horse and other riders, horsemanship, stable management, and other qualities for the awarding of individual prizes. Some rides also give "best all-around trail horse" awards that are often difficult decisions for the judges. Proper concern for safety and good manners is always important.

At the end of the ride, the horse is judged on degree of fatigue, the way he eats, the condition of his back, feet, and legs, general physical condition, and of course TPRs. Any soreness, unsoundnesses, or blemishes that have developed since the start of the ride will be noted and penalized. The severity of each weakness or blemish will determine the amount of penalty in relation to the rules of the contest.

Back Home Again

Simply to turn a horse out to pasture when you return home from the contest would be tantamount to riding him over a cliff. He will have to be eased off gradually from the high level of exercise and feed—sort of a debriefing period.

One problem that will likely develop if a horse's regimen is suddenly and completely curtailed is stocking up, a swelling of the legs caused by congestion of blood, especially below the knees. Feed must be cut down gradually, rather than all at once. A sudden shift from hay to pasture may cause colic— he will have to become used to green grass gradually.

It is also wise to watch your horse fairly closely for a week or more after the ride to see if any late-appearing lameness or unsoundness should develop, or if the horse has contracted a contagious disease.

Ease off exercise gradually, riding him an hour or so twice a day for several days, then an hour once a day for a few days, and finally an hour every other day, unless you plan to continue using him fairly hard. Even so, avoid giving him several days of complete idleness followed by a big day of activity. Grain may be cut back to normal rations by a quart or so a day. Work up to pasture by allowing an hour of grazing the first day, followed by several hours for a few days, then half a day of grazing for several days before turning the horse out around the clock.

Naturally, if you are planning to compete in more than the one contest,

NATRC: SCORE CARD

RIDER'S NAME:

Horse's Name

Preliminary

Horse's No.

Heart Rate

Respiratory Rate

IN OUT IN OUT IN OUT IN OUT IN OUT IN OUT IN OUT IN OUT

Score

Soundness (40%)

LAMENESS, RING BONE, SPAVIN, NAVICULAR, HEAT, FILLED TENDONS, CINCH SORES, BACK TENDERNESS, BONE CHANGES, SIDEBONE

Condition (40%)

FATIGUE, CHARACTER OF BREATHING, DESIRE TO EAT AND DRINK, MUSCLE SORENESS, THUMPS, COLIC, TYING UP, AZOTURIA, LOSS OF COLLECTION, PäR RECOVERY

Way of Going (5%)

FORGING, CROSS FIRING, INTERFERING, STUMBLING CONTINUOUSLY, SCALPING, OVER REACHING

Manners (15%)

TRAIL OBSTACLES, RESPONSE TO RIDER, DISPOSITION, KICKING, HEAD TOSSING, PRANCING, STAND FOR EXAMINATION & MOUNTING, BUDDING UP

Horsemanship (100%)

CLEANLINESS, PRESENTATION, PROPER FITTING EQUIPMENT, CARE ON TRAIL, CARE AT STOPS (FEET, SADDLE, CINCH WATER), SPORTSMANSHIP, CONSIDERATION, HANDS, SEAT

Horse's Name -- Reg. No.	Age	Weight	Breed
	Sex	Height	Color

	Horsemanship Penalty Points
	Horsemanship Score
	Horsemanship Place
	Total Score
	Ride Place

RIDE SECRETARY AND/OR JUDGE ... PLEASE FILL IN ALL CATEGORIES

RIDE SECRETARY, PLEASE DETACH AND MAIL TO NATRC ... BALANCE OF CARD TO RIDER

For NATRC Use Only

NATRC Pts.:

Horsemanship Pts.:

Name of Ride:

Rider's Name and Address:

Horse's No.

Name

Age

Breed

Sex

Color

DIVISION: (Check)

☐ HWT   ☐ JR

☐ LWT   ☐ NOV

Judges' Signatures:

Total Score:

Ride Place

Horsemanship Place

Figs. 13 and 13a   Sample score card for a trail ride.

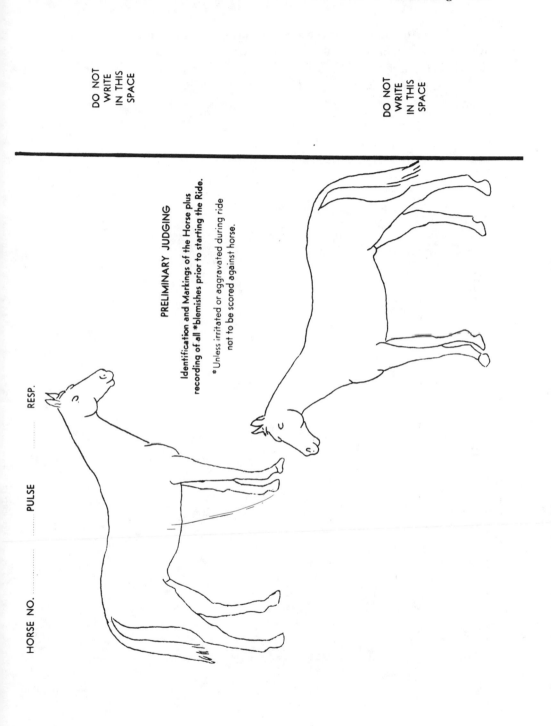

DO NOT
WRITE
IN THIS
SPACE

DO NOT
WRITE
IN THIS
SPACE

PRELIMINARY JUDGING

Identification and Markings of the Horse plus
recording of all *blemishes prior to starting the Ride.

* Unless irritated or aggravated during ride
not to be scored against horse.

HORSE NO. ....   PULSE ....   RESP.

you will have to adjust your schedule accordingly. However, don't overdo your training regimen. Probably as many contests have been lost through overwork and fatigue as through inadequate preparation. (For more information, see *Basic Training for Horses*, Part 2, Chapter 7, "Basic Trail Training.")

CHAPTER NINE

Jumping

There is something about jumping in harmony with your horse that is unique and wonderful. Jumping can be a highly technical and specialized sport. For those serious riders who wish to improve their jumping beyond a basic stage, there is a list of recommended books and videos in Appendix D. The purpose of this chapter is to serve as an introduction to jumping by presenting a basic understanding that may help English and Western enthusiasts to start correctly and safely.

A good rider should have some understanding of how to put his horse into a jump, how to ride the jump, and how to carry through after the jump. Any rider may someday find that a jump is unavoidable; therefore it is wise to learn the rudiments before that time arrives.

As in any other high-flying sport, on-the-ground training, consideration of safety factors, and conditioning are necessary before the flight. What can we do to prepare ourselves and our horses both mentally and physically for jumping?

Evaluating Your Horse

First, let's briefly evaluate your horse in the new light of jumping. Your horse has been doing fine in his regular work of teaching you to ride in the ring and on the trail. Will he do for a jumping horse also? Generally speaking, any horse capable of taking you for a long ride on the trail should be able to take you over natural low obstacles and perhaps do some concentrated work on those interesting low jumps you have out in the back pasture. The major factor is to make sure your horse is sound enough, with suitable conformation and an agreeable temperament, to do some concentrated jumping.

If your "learning horse" is quite elderly and you've been thinking about moving on to a horse with more challenge, perhaps now is a good time to consider one that would be as suitable for jumping as for your other interests. Let's take a moment to stare down the old-fashioned idea that jumping is for "English" horsemen only. Any Western horse should be able and willing to jump several feet, and many Western riders are finding a wonderful new sport in training for and entering their Quarter Horses in AQHA jumper and hunter classes.

What should your versatile jumper look like? First, he should be sound. (A veterinarian can pass him on this, though you would know in the normal course of riding whether your own horse has leg or back problems.) He should be a strong horse, at least five years old, with well-developed quarters, good sloping shoulders, substance, a well-put-together body, freedom in his gaits, and some natural knee action. Let's also hope he has a steady disposition, good manners, confidence, and a certain boldness necessary for a horse to jump well.

To boil it down to simple terms, your horse should be able to take the strain of jumping and to do it willingly. Some preliminary longeing over low obstacles can tell you a great deal about his feeling for jumping.

Rider Goals

Are *you* ready to jump? You should have a secure seat, hands that are able to maintain contact without pulling, good judgment, ability to control your horse in every situation, and the same kind of courage your horse possesses. If you are afraid you don't measure up, don't drop the idea of jumping. Spend enough time on the preliminary exercises to build up your judgment, courage, and control, and you will find that you are progressing smoothly and enthusiastically. Take your time and don't measure your own progress by someone else's yardstick.

More often the problem is just the opposite: Young enthusiasts tend to be so thrilled with jumping that it is all they want to do—more and more, higher and higher. Don't overdo your horse on jumping, especially if you and your horse are learning together. Resist the temptation to take your fences too high too soon, or to make your jumping sessions too long and concentrated. Not only may you strain your horse's legs, but you may also sour him. His attitude toward jumping, as well as yours, is very important. Remember, it is better to clear a low jump well than a high jump badly. The mistakes you make in early training may take months to cure, and may even be irreparable.

It is especially important always to wear your helmet, boots, and safe, sensible clothing when jumping.

Preparing to Jump

Before studying the motion of the horse in the jump, what can the rider do to prepare himself for the new sensation of jumping? At this stage let's consider the adaptation of the English Basic Seat to jumping.

To prepare for jumping, shorten your stirrup leathers by two or three holes—your lower leg should be back far enough so that the stirrup leathers hang straight down. Your heels will take up much of your weight shift when the horse jumps. Your feet lie on the inside of the stirrup iron, and your calves, knees, and thighs keep in close contact with the saddle. Your head should be up and your eyes forward; this cannot be repeated too often as you start jumping, since there is the greatest temptation to look down and this can bring on any number of faults. Your arms, as before, should hang naturally with an imaginary straight line running from the bit, through rein and hand, to the elbow. Your body will incline more forward from the hips than at the Basic halt position—considerably more forward as the jumps increase in height and speed of approach—and you should be out of the saddle as in the posting trot (called two-point contact).

When learning to jump it is important to hold your reins in a special way. This method is to be used strictly for learning, of course, but we find it valuable because: (a) it is effective in preventing injury to the horse's mouth, and (b) it allows your hands to remain more nearly in the correct jumping position than is generally possible for beginners to achieve, enabling you to keep the direct line from bit to elbow.

Take up the reins in the normal manner, and then take the bight of each rein in the opposite hand as shown in the illustration on page 178. In this way the reins make a twelve-inch bridge across the top of the horse's neck. To assume the jumping position, push your arms forward and rest your hands down against the reins, which are crossed over the horse's neck. By moving your hands forward, you give the horse enough rein to free his head for the jump (learning to maintain contact will come later), and your hands are firmly braced to keep you from losing your balance and tearing at his mouth.

Lay several poles on the ground (or between jump standards) a good distance apart so that you need concentrate on only one at a time. Place one safety cone about four feet in front of the pole and another four feet beyond it to use as signals. When you are at the first cone, assume the jumping position

Crossing the reins over the horse's neck and assuming the jumping position. (Ordinarily you would use a snaffle bit—this horse goes well in a Pelham for his experienced rider.)

(rise into two-point contact) and push your hands forward, trying to make a straight line from your elbow to your horse's bit. Hold this position until you arrive at the second marker. Think about each pole as a jump: Keep your eyes up and practice changing from two-point to normal position over the poles (with the cones as markers) both at the walk and later at the slow trot. When you feel confident, dispense with the cones and judge the distance for yourself. Also practice at the trot, posting, and sitting. You want to feel comfortable, light, and well balanced in the jumping position. It cannot be held by muscular strength as this creates the stiffness you are trying to avoid.

The next step is to assume the jumping position over cavalletti or very low cross rails, still at a trot. Rather than stepping over the rails as the horse has been doing, he will probably give a little hop. This will give you your first feel of a jump. Again, your only problem will be to keep your eyes up and looking forward and to hold your position, shifting your weight forward to keep in balance with your horse.

If you are still a bit lacking in balance or in confidence, ask a helper to longe your horse over a series of poles and very low jumps while you ride with your hands on the mane or holding a neck strap. This will greatly improve your balance and feel of jumping.

Continue practicing over cavalletti and low jumps at a trot—several in

Trotting over poles.

succession will give you the timing and feel of the horse's body as he raises his forehand, clears the jump, lands, and regains his normal stride. Take the jumps straight toward the center at an even, moderate pace.

There is no need to rush this stage of your learning. You are trying to become so secure and easy in your position that you will automatically move your hands forward, shift your weight forward, keep your eyes up, and balance yourself in the jumping position. Your mastery of this preliminary stage will prepare you for safe jumping over much higher fences.

INSTRUCTOR: *Cavalletti spacing is important and in general should be as follows:*

> *Walk: 2 feet 8 inches–3 feet 6 inches*
> *Ordinary trot: 4 feet 3 inches–4 feet 10 inches*
> *Ordinary canter: 9–12 feet*

For extended gaits, increase the spacing a few inches; for collected gaits, decrease the spacing. The horse's conformation and length of stride, as well as the experience of the rider, will be considerations in spacing the cavalletti.

Holding the mane to prevent pulling on the horse's mouth.

Holding a neck strap to prevent pulling on the horse's mouth.

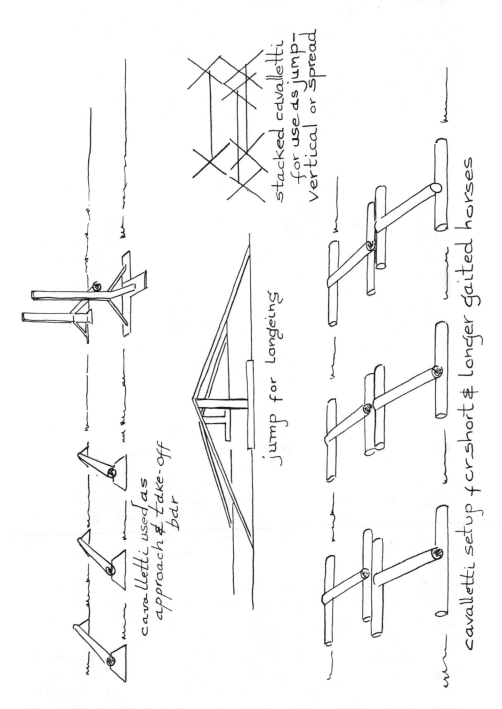

Fig. 14 Ways of using cavalletti to prepare for jumping.

Time Out to Understand Jumping

Let's take time out from actually beginning to jump in order to analyze the motion of the horse over an obstacle. This analysis, together with a discussion of how the rider's form helps or hinders the horse in his jump, should give you an idea of what actually happens when an expert rider and an experienced horse take a good-sized jump.

The movements a horse makes in jumping may be divided into the approach, the takeoff, the flight, the landing, and the departure.

The most important phase is the approach as this is the basis for a successful jump. As the horse comes in during the approach, he extends his head and neck downward and forward, preparing to engage his hindquarters as he judges the point of takeoff.

In the takeoff, the horse lifts his head and forehand, his hindquarters come forward—usually ahead of the point where his leading forefoot last touched the ground, rather like a spring—and then propel him into the air. He again stretches his head and neck forward. In the takeoff, the horse will have his own peculiarities—he may be the desirable type that springs off his haunches, or perhaps the kind of horse that needs speed in order to clear his jump, or he may take his jumps too close. By observing your horse jump on the longe line or in a jumping lane, you can plan and train accordingly.

The flight—or period of suspension—is the time when the horse is in the air. In this phase the horse keeps his neck extended, his legs folded, and his back relaxed and slightly rounded so that his body forms an arc over the jump. The act of rounding his back (the degree of doing so) is termed the "bascule." He may extend his neck forward and downward even more after it passes the jump. While the horse is in flight there is nothing the rider can do to help him except maintain contact with his mouth and not interfere with his action. The flight will be successful if the approach and takeoff have been made correctly.

When landing, the horse touches down (only one forefoot hits the ground first) and his head and neck come up a little. One forefoot often takes off again before the hind feet touch the ground, and the head and neck stretch forward.

This is a difficult period for both horse and rider. There is quite a strain on the horse's forelegs. If the rider interferes by throwing his weight to the rear too soon, or by pulling on his horse's mouth to secure his seat, his mount may fail to takeoff properly with his front feet. This may result in his heels or tendons being badly cut, as well as his mouth and back being hurt. Certainly

approach   take-off   flight   landing   departure

Fig. 15   Phases of the jump.

his attitude toward jumping will not be improved. He may begin to "pop" his jumps and to lose any bascule he may have developed.

During the departure the horse should be in line with his approach and will take his first strides in resuming his gait. The canter should be resumed on the same (inside) lead if the course continues in the same direction. This is the moment the rider resumes normal position and looks toward the direction he wishes to take.

Mechanics of the Jump and the Rider's Form

How does the rider's form help or hinder the actual movements of the horse's jump?

Many theories of jumping exist, but today it is generally agreed that a balanced seat over the jump, in which the rider's weight is well forward over the withers or neck of the horse, interferes the least with his jumping movements. This means that the horse is free to jump without the rider disturbing his balance and equilibrium by sitting on his loins, pulling up his head, or jabbing his mouth. He is free to jump, without punishment, in the easiest and most natural way possible for him.

This does not mean that control is abandoned. Control is very important for speed and direction. In fact, most horses like the security of contact with the rider's hand.

From studying the mechanics of the horse's jump, you can see that the horse modified his position several times, especially as to position of head and neck and to the point of his center of gravity. Understanding these changes is important to the rider if he wishes to help (that is, not hinder) his horse over the jump.

Now let's follow the horse over the jump when mounted. During the approach the rider adjusts his horse's speed, length of stride, and direction to the size and situation of the jump. Depending on the jumping habits and conformation of the horse, more speed may be necessary to provide the thrust and momentum over larger jumps. Direction is maintained to keep the horse coming into the jump in a straight line aimed at the middle of the fence. (On jump courses where many jumps are set up to be followed in succession, or in hunts, steeplechases, or three-day events, it is sometimes necessary to approach a fence from the side and to jump it at an angle. This requires more judgment on the part of the rider and more experience, skill, and courage on the part of the horse.) The rider keeps his thighs flat and close, his knees and heels down; his legs should remain steady against the girth throughout the jump. While maintaining control and direction, his hands allow extension of the horse's neck.

During the stride or two before takeoff, the rider does not interfere with the horse's mouth (the die has already been cast): However, he should maintain contact and follow the movement of the horse's head. As the horse takes off, the movement thrusts the *prepared* rider forward into his jumping position: Ideally his seat comes out of the saddle, his weight goes into his knees and heels, his upper body is inclined forward, and his arms reach forward on either side of the horse's neck to follow the mouth, keeping contact and maintaining a straight line from bit to elbow without pulling or interfering.

This is the most difficult part of the jump for the rider—until he has had considerable experience jumping and is himself athletically prepared to take the jump, he is not ready to accept the horse's thrust into the jumping position. He therefore enters the jump behind his horse, pulling on and hurting his mouth and back, possibly interfering so much that the horse cannot clear the jump properly. For this reason, in the early stages of jumping the rider should assume the jumping position during the approach and hold it for several strides after the landing.

During the flight, the rider maintains his jumping position—seat out of the saddle, legs in position, with body balanced over the stirrups. His hands follow the horse's head and are completely independent of his seat as he maintains constant communication with his horse. The steadying effect of his hands gives a sense of security to the horse. As the horse's head and neck stretch out and downward, the rider's hands follow and his knees and body go forward slightly to keep his balance over the horse's center of gravity. The rider should, of course, take care that he is balanced equally from side to side.

For the landing, the rider should be relaxed, his knees and ankles ready to absorb the reaction of the landing. He should maintain his forward position until the horse has completed his landing and is two or three strides beyond.

During the entire jump the rider has his head up and eyes looking

Rider's form on the takeoff. (William Steinkraus on Bold Minstrel, Cologne. Photo by Karl Schönerstedt)

Rider's form during the flight. (Mrs. Frank Chapot on White Lightning, Hickstead. Photo by Jean Bridel of *L'Année Hippique*)

ahead—to look down or to the side destroys his balance and ability to judge and prepare for the next obstacle. Horses take their jumps differently, and the rider must learn how best to rate each horse for any given jump.

Beginning Jumping—Elementary Phase

At this stage, after getting the feel of jumping through your preliminary exercises, and with the understanding of what happens to horse and rider over a jump, you are probably ready and eager to go ahead and try some real jumping. It is important at this stage for you to have a safe, steady horse—preferably a quiet mount that needs some urging rather than one that you must constantly hold back or fight for control.

Use a low cross-rail jump—one end of each pole about two feet high, the other end on the ground. The jump will be low in the center, encouraging your horse to take the jump straight and in the middle. Now you can begin cantering toward the jump, keeping the gait slow and controlled. Do not allow your horse to rush toward his jumps (see the section "Correcting Vices" later in this chapter).

A low cross-rail jump is good for beginners, guiding the horse to the center of the jump.

About twenty yards before the jump, assume the jumping position. Remember, you must not punish your horse's mouth. Using the bridge-reins method and learning to *push* your hands into a jump, rather than pull, will give you the basic understanding and training you'll need later to follow the horse's head properly into higher jumps. If there is some difficulty in grasping the "push" concept, be sure to use a further aid to keep from punishing your horse's mouth: Use a neck strap (such as a stirrup leather) placed halfway between poll and withers, and hold onto this along with the reins. (See illustration on page 180.) Make sure your reins are even, if you are holding the neck strap.

Maintain the jumping position over the jump and for several strides after the landing—to come out of position too soon, before the landing has been completed, again risks punishing your horse's mouth. Then gently sink back into the saddle.

Important points on which to concentrate in this stage of jumping are:

1. Assume the jumping position during the approach.
2. Keep your head up and your eyes forward during approach, takeoff, flight, and landing, with your shoulders open, not hunched.
3. *Push* your hands into the jump.
4. Keep your weight evenly distributed and your torso inclined forward to keep you balanced over your feet, adjusting to the speed of your horse.
5. Keep your heels down with your feet on the inside of your stirrups. The inner surfaces of thigh, knee, and upper calf should be in light functional contact with the saddle, becoming more muscular in the last few strides before and during the jump.

    The stirrup leather should hang straight if your leg is positioned correctly. Envision good position and try to emulate your mental picture.

    Looking in books and magazines at pictures of good jumping position will help you to sharpen your ideal mental picture.

INSTRUCTOR: *When teaching the beginner, take great care in selecting his mount. In the early stages, any unpleasant experiences will reflect on the student's later interest and courage in jumping.*

Take your time and don't try to rush your students into accomplishing too much too soon. Be generous with encouragement and praise. You will undoubtedly have some timid students and others too bold—the former to be encouraged and the latter to be restrained. It is wise to progress with a timetable geared to the ability of each student.

Teach your students to keep their heads up, to look ahead at their jumps and come into them straight and centered in order to prepare for what's ahead.

Teach them, also, that the moment of the jump while in the air is very fleeting, and all they can do is go with their horse; between jumps they must work to gain impulsion by using their aids and improving the security of their seat.

Problems to watch for:

FAULTS OF THE HEAD: *popping back head on the flight and landing, ducking to side, looking down.*

FAULTS OF THE TORSO: *rounded, arched, or hunched back, shoulders closed or rounded, seat too far out of the saddle, seat that does not clear the saddle when supposed to; rider tipped too far forward, too erect, or lopsided; rider stiff; rider left behind (worst of all!).*

FAULTS OF ARMS AND HANDS: *elbows flipping out (usually happens when wrists break); hands and arms not giving enough over the fence, that is, not pushing into the jump; hands balling up into tight fists (hard hands); curb rein too tight; hands too high or too low; hands breaking either forward or backward at the wrist; fingers spreading out during jump; rider lying down on hands.*

FAULTS OF LEGS: *swinging forward or back; floating lower leg; knees out or pivoting; bracing in the stirrups.*

Common faults in jumping: looking down, elbows out, rider lying on hands, leaning too far forward, toes turned out, bracing in the stirrups, no contact with calf of leg, and horse not jumping the center line of the pole.

FAULTS OF FEET: *heels up; feet on outside of stirrup or "shot home,"* *which is sometimes done by experienced riders but is usually not desirable; broken ankles; only toes on tread of stirrup; toes sticking out east and west.*

You will usually see several of these faults in combination. For example, elbows that flip out and bent wrists are found in riders who hunch their shoulders. A floating lower leg usually combines with unevenly distributed weight and insecure seat.

To correct these faults, take your students back to the preliminary exercises. In some cases, you may want a student to concentrate primarily on assuming the jumping position ahead of time and pushing into the jump. Other areas of practice on which to concentrate, depending on the fault, are balance, flexibility of hip, knee, and ankle, following through in the jump with eyes up and forward, developing suppleness in back and loin, sitting straight with equal weight on each thigh and knee, and maintaining proper position of the legs. Longeing your student over cavalletti and later over low jumps will help position and confidence.

Intermediate and Advanced Jumping

After the beginning stage of jumping has been thoroughly learned—that is, when holding the jumping position and pushing the hands forward have become automatic so that there is no danger of hurting the horse's mouth—the rider can go on to the next phase of jumping. His main concern here is independent action of seat and hands.

Now instead of assuming the jumping position early, he waits until the horse takes off into the jump; the action of the horse's hindquarters as he begins to jump thrusts the rider forward into the jumping position. His hands, working independently, go forward to keep gentle or firm contact with the horse's mouth.

To improve coordination and "feel for jumping" in both horse and rider, set up a series of low (about two feet) jumps eight or ten feet apart. Vary the distance after you can manage a set of two such jumps without difficulty.

The advanced stage of jumping is reached not according to height of jump, but when the rider's hands follow the horse's head with the reins and forearm on each side of the neck, forming a straight line from bit to elbow. There is much more danger of the rider being left behind this way, but even if he is—that is, even if his body is not prepared to assume the jumping position—he should thrust his hands forward automatically, or let the reins

Progressing in jumping: The rider assumes the jumping position as the horse begins to jump. Although still pushing forward against the neck, the rider is not interfering with her horse's mouth. She should be looking up.

slip through his hands, to avoid hurting the horse. This is called jumping "out of hand."

Form, of course, acts as a basis for learning to ride properly and usually provides the framework in which the best can be done most easily. In jumping, as in other forms of riding, and especially over higher jumps, the most important thing is to clear the jump without interfering with the horse. Experience, balance, and knowledge of his horse give the experienced horseman the license to dispense with some formality. However, you will never see the experienced horseman punishing his horse's mouth due to bad form.

Tack

The modern jumping saddle is ideal for its purpose: First, it gives support through knee rolls and with both cantle and pommel higher than those of the old-fashioned flat saddle; and second, it places the rider at the center point of the saddle, thus helping him to keep forward over the center of gravity of the horse, and to rise out of the saddle during the jump.

The bridle should be a simple heavy snaffle even though the student may be capable of using a double bridle. The feel of the horse while jumping is a new experience. It will take time and practice to jump "on contact" or "out of hand."

Other helpful tack for the beginner is the neck strap. It may also be necessary to use a running martingale or dropped noseband to keep your mount from evading the bit. If you are a beginner, have an experienced horseman help you decide what tack to use and adjust it properly for you.

Many Western trail classes in horse shows now call for low jumps over hay bales, low poles, logs, or water. The Western rider should acquaint himself and his horse with correct jumping techniques to be prepared for these classes or for actual obstacles on the trail. Besides, it's fun and adds spice to a training or riding period. The Western rider should also use a simple snaffle bit in practice sessions—certainly not a long-shanked Western curb. When using a Western saddle, shorten the stirrups one or two notches while training, and jump only very low or narrow-spread jumps such as logs or irrigation ditches. If you jump in a Western saddle, be sure the horn is the wide flat type typical of the roping saddle rather than the high old-fashioned type.

Correcting Vices

Jumping vices may be due to the inexperience of horse and rider, being asked to jump fences too big or difficult, loss of nerve due to a previous fall or lack of condition, experiencing pain from saddle or bridle, or remembering pain due to rider error (such as punishing the horse's mouth). The most serious and most common jumping vices are refusing, popping, rushing, and shying out.

Refusing to jump is often caused by raising the jumps too rapidly. Similar lower jumps should be attempted to restore self-confidence, or re-place the jump with poles on the ground. Apply even support with forward-driving legs and maintain contact with the horse's mouth. If he ducks to either right or left (which is usual with this vice), give more tension to the opposite rein on the last few strides; however, use the following hand during the takeoff.

Rushing, or going too fast into the jump, is commonly caused by fear. Many times a fearful, high-strung horse has been ridden by heavy-handed, clumsy riders and he anticipates pain from jerked reins and use of the whip. This horse has learned that it does no good to refuse, so he tries to get over his obstacles as soon as possible to finish the disagreeable task. This can be a dangerous vice because the horse cannot judge the height or the takeoff point with his head in the air.

A sensitive rider will take the horse back to the fundamentals in training:

working at the trot over low obstacles, longeing, cavalletti work, and design-ing a low jump course with turns so that the horse can't get up steam to race around the ring and over the jumps. A hackamore can be used to retrain horses very fearful of pain from the bit. The rider should strive to calm the excitable horse without losing his impulsion.

It can also be effective to begin the approach, but then circle the horse in a large volte before reaching the jump. Sometimes a horse must be circled several times in either direction before taking his approach calmly. You can also try a small figure-eight in front of a low jump. As he ceases to anticipate the jump, his tendency to rush will diminish.

Shying out, or runout, occurs when your mount suddenly shies to left or right (and usually he will take the same direction) within a few strides of the takeoff to evade the obstacle.

The most commonly used method to prevent this is to come into the jump at an angle on the same side your horse shies into. For example, if he shies to the left, come into the jump from the left and straighten him out a couple of strides before the takeoff; vice versa if he shies to the right. You can also design a jump course whereby your horse never knows which jump you intend to take and so cannot anticipate and set his pattern for a runout. Do not have long straight approaches to any jump. Circling to the opposite side before the jump will break the horse's train of thought. Of course, going back to the fundamentals such as were noted above is valuable for retraining in this instance also.

There are some less serious faults due to incomplete schooling or, again, taking jumps too rapidly, too high, too soon.

These are buck-jumping or popping, continually rapping, and exces-sively overjumping. When your horse buck-jumps or pops his jumps, he misjudges and takes off too close to the jump; he almost stops, then bunches up and pops over the jump. This is extremely uncomfortable for the rider, and makes maintaining contact and anticipating the horse's movement very difficult. Use poles or cavalletti on the ground in front of the jump to force him to take off farther back.

There is also the horse that continually raps (or underjumps) his obsta-cles. He should be jumped at liberty in the Hitchcock Pen with some low, solid jumps in order to teach him respect for them.

The horse that overjumps just hasn't learned to judge the height of the jumps. He also may have a fear of hitting the obstacle due to an earlier unfortunate experience. He should be allowed the opportunity to learn and should not be hurried in his training.

Setting Up a Jump Course

Jumps may be divided into two categories—the vertical or straight fences (to encourage high jumping) and the spread fences (to encourage wide jumping). Some vertical, single jumps are the single bar, sloping panel, post and rail, picket fence, gate, cross poles, narrow brush jumps, and the Continental gate. Spread jumps include the hogsback, brick wall (square or round), triple bar, parallel bars, and double oxer. The chicken coop may be either spread or vertical, depending on the width of the top. The spread fences encourage the horse in basculing. This should occur when going over any difficult jump.

Natural obstacles would include hedges, open ditches, stone walls, logs, and the Irish bank. You can make many interesting combinations to give variety to your jump course, using piled wood, bales of hay, a combination of piled wood or barrels and a standard pole jump, slanting panels such as a door set at an angle, stacked logs, and so on. Avoid piles of tires or similar obstacles where a horse could get his foot caught if he misjudges and fails to clear the jump, especially if he falls short at the far side.

A combination of single jumps set eight to ten feet apart constitutes one type of in-and-out. Another type of in-and-out jump is a fenced, boxed area, commonly called a pigpen.

Use your imagination in type of jump and vary the height, direction, and distance between jumps. (See Figure 17.) It's a good idea to design your course on paper first. Then you can measure your distances by walking the course yourself, counting strides, or, of course, by trotting and cantering your horse around it. Be sure to leave enough room between obstacles, especially if your horse is not a seasoned jumper. Again, not enough can be said about jumps being too high or too wide in the early stages of training. If you have open country with opportunity to jump, take advantage of this change from the daily ring work—your horse will enjoy it too.

Walking the Course

When a top show rider walks his course, he paces out the distances between obstacles, mentally noting the best track to take, the degree of difficulty in the turns, and the number of horse's strides necessary to clear the jumps. He studies the detail of the obstacles and the approach to and landing from each one, always taking into consideration the capability and individuality of his own mount.

VERTICAL—SINGLE   **SPREAD JUMPS**

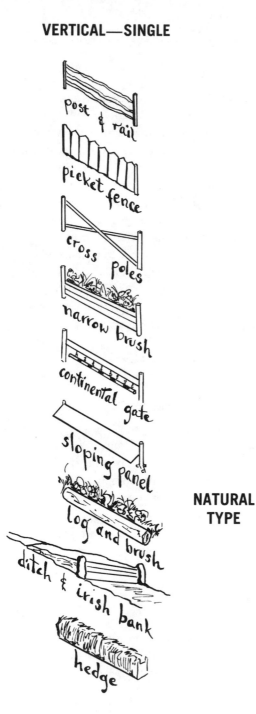

post & rail

picket fence

cross poles

narrow brush

continental gate

sloping panel

log and brush

ditch & irish bank

hedge

**NATURAL
TYPE**

double oxer

triple bar

rounded wall

brick wall

chicken coop

hogsback

stone wall

bales of straw

stacked logs

Fig. 16   Types of jumps.

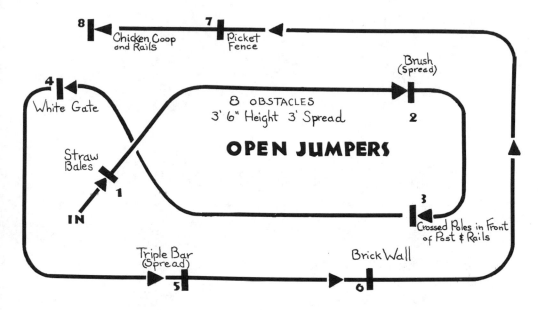

Fig. 17 A sample jump course for the more experienced horse and rider.

What may seem to the untrained eye to be needless detail, such as the slope of the ground or the lighting (shade may obscure the detail of an obstacle), will mean a yard or two loss or gain, and this is what wins or loses in serious competition.

Obviously, you will not be as detailed as competition jumpers; however, you should learn how to translate your paces into the number of strides (remember speed) taken by your horse, so that you can design an interesting and safe course as well as ride a strange one knowledgeably.

The normal length of stride at a slow canter is at least eight feet; at a full canter, the stride may be fourteen feet or more. It should be noted also that the normal horse jumps in a perfect arc; thus if his takeoff is four feet from the jump, his landing will also be four feet from the jump. Even in the best of plans it is sometimes necessary to improvise, but with good judgment, planning, and practice, improvisation will be kept to a minimum.

CHAPTER TEN

Special Problems and Situations

Part 1 · Teaching Your Child to Ride

Attitudes and Goals

A parent who wishes to teach his child to ride should have, or try to develop, the attitudes of the instructor mentioned in the introduction. It will require more patience to teach your own children than to teach those of others.

Parents should have a clear, flexible plan of instruction. You must move slowly and be careful neither to expect nor to demand too much of your child. One of the most important goals is to help the child to love horses and riding. Therefore the lessons should be happily anticipated by both child and parent. Each lesson should contain fun as well as work.

If your teaching becomes forced, or if it is no longer enjoyable to both, turn the instruction over to a professional teacher. When parent-child instruction succeeds, however, the rewards are great, developing mutual understanding, appreciation, and enjoyment.

Parents are sometimes anxious for their children to begin riding at an early age. This is not always wise, as the very young child sometimes loses interest as he grows older. Riding should be a privilege for your child, not a duty. As a rule of thumb, ten years of age is a good time to begin short formal lessons.

Developing Companionship Between Your Child and His Horse

Let your child have some degree of freedom with the horse; and, depending on the child's age, there should be a sense of responsibility and just plain horse sense. We know of a dedicated horseman who never let his daughter near her horse or his horses alone; she was always under supervision. Maybe she would have liked to talk with her horse, listen to him eat, or just observe him.

Naturally, children need supervision, but keep it inconspicuous rather than suffocating.

Use of the Longe Line to Develop the Rider's Seat

If you understand the concepts of longeing and have a well-trained horse, much can be learned by your child while both horse and child are under your direct control. One of the greatest advantages of longeing is that the child may learn to develop his seat before there is any need to direct his horse. When the child begins using his hands, he can do so without hurting the horse's mouth.

Some horses, especially ponies, will take advantage of young novice riders by balking, grass cropping, or willfully going their own way regardless of the rider's direction. The formation of bad habits can be avoided when you have control of both horse and rider through the longe line.

Use of the longe line can be overdone. The child will be eager to manage his horse alone, and should be allowed to do so as soon as possible. The longe line may be used again periodically, whenever any difficulties tend to develop, or to introduce new exercises. For instance, when first starting the canter, your child can get the feeling of the gait while the horse is on the longe. Once confidence is gained from this successful experience, he can try to initiate the canter with his own aids. You will have control of the situation, however, if your child's aids are too vigorous or are inadequate.

The Older Horse

When purchasing or choosing a horse for your child, consider the age of both the horse and the child. The older horse is usually less spooky, more patient with his rider's mistakes, more sure-footed, balanced, and all-around more tractable. Of course, there are exceptions—sometimes the older horse knows all the tricks. Some of his tricks may be grass cropping, barn sourness, and balkiness. It will be up to you to test the horse for these vices.

A three- or four-year-old horse, even if well trained, will have his frisky or spooky times. If allowed to have his way, or if he should get into some precarious predicament, he could develop a bad or dangerous habit that would eventually result in making him a spoiled horse. Also, unhappy experiences when in the learning stage dampen a child's enthusiasm and may even spoil his love for the animal and the sport.

Some older or especially talented children are capable of managing a horse that would be too difficult for the average child. But avoid the temptation to overmount your child. He will be able to learn just as much, or more, on a quiet, experienced older horse, if he is properly instructed.

Part 2 · Therapeutic Riding and Hippotherapy

The term "therapeutic riding" is comprehensive and means many different things to the many instructors and clients involved.

The National Center for Therapeutic Riding (NCTR) is located in Washington, D.C. The basic program consists of an eight-week session with groups of handicapped students. The program has been formulated with an emphasis on the development of educational and social skills as well as basic riding skills. Horseback riding promotes the improvement in reflex muscle activity, eye-hand coordination, and balance and equilibrium reactions as well as instills self-confidence, and gives the student a real sense of accomplishment and personal success.

The North American Riding for the Handicapped Association (NARHA) headquartered in Denver, Colorado, operates centers across America. This is a service organization whose clients participate in more than 350 separate riding programs throughout the United States, Puerto Rico, and Canada. The purpose of the NARHA is to share information and provide educational programs to help centers do the best possible job of serving their clients.

Equine Facilitated Therapy—"hippotherapy"—is one of the newer branches in the field of rehabilitation therapy. Hippotherapy literally means "treatment with the help of the horse." Specially trained physical and occupational therapists use this medical treatment for patients with movement disorders, including children with developmental disabilities. The goal is to improve posture, balance, mobility, and function of the patient through the influence and movement of the horse. The horse is not controlled by the rider. The therapist positions the patient, analyzes the patient's responses to the therapy horse, and directs and controls the horse's movement.

Part 3 · What You Can Learn from Problem Horses

Nobody's perfect—if only for the simple reason that we all have a different idea of what constitutes perfection.

The same is true of horses. Despite your care in selecting a horse, it is likely that there will be one or more areas in which your horse is a problem. Even if the horse does seem perfect for your beginner needs, you will probably outgrow him. You will want a horse more responsive and more challenging to your improved abilities.

The perfect horse is an ideal. He's what we aim for in selection but seldom obtain. So is it hopeless to try to learn to ride on our less-than-perfect animal? Of course not! As one well-known horseman says, "You can learn something even from a wooden horse." You can learn to cope with your horse's bad habits, perhaps even retrain him, provided that these habits are not dangerous vices. And you will be a better horseman for doing so.

What Are Vices and Where Do They Come From?

Bad habits in horses vary in degree from humorous quirks, through frustrating mannerisms, to dangerous vices. Usually the habits may be considered vices when they become seriously annoying or dangerous to either the horse or his handler.

Most bad habits are caused by either fear or boredom. Generally, the poor training or mishandling that produces vices is the result of a lack of understanding or lack of skill on the part of the handler or rider. He might think that a horse is being stubborn or belligerent when the horse does not understand or is fearful. Thus he punishes the horse, and the animal develops defenses against this unexplained, and to him unwarranted, punishment.

If in bridling his horse, the handler bangs the bit against his teeth several times in a row, the horse learns that he is hurt by the bridle. He throws up his head to avoid taking the bit, and so develops head-shyness.

The horse's natural reaction to fear is to run. Wild horses take to flight as their natural defense against anything that frightens or worries them. Only if they are cornered will they resort to their other defenses—kicking, biting, or striking. Horses kept in stalls are more apt to develop such vices if they are frightened or mishandled.

The United States *Cavalry Manual* refers to bad habits as "defenses," thus serving to remind a rider of their man-made origin and the handler's responsibility to prevent them.

Horses crave exercise. They are not naturally sedentary creatures. Enforced lack of exercise is one of the gravest and most common misdeeds a novice horse owner will commit against his mount. This is often combined with overfeeding, which serves to aggravate the condition.

Confined to his stall for long periods, the horse may begin cribbing or weaving as a defense against boredom. Then, tacked up for a ride, he may be fractious, begin bucking, head tossing, or jigging in an excess of energy.

Understanding your horse's temperament and needs will help you to prevent the development of vices in him.

What Can You Do About Vices?

Preventing the development of vices is vitally important to you as an intelligent horse owner or rider. But what can be done about the horse that comes to you with his vices already well ingrained?

If you understand the cause of the defense, you are in a good position to correct it. Whenever you are with a horse, you are in effect training him. Your actions will either aggravate the problem or start toward its correction. Consistent corrective action as the problem occurs will eventually correct it.

Some defenses are very difficult to correct if they are deeply ingrained. You may learn to cope with them. If a horse is young and is experimenting, your corrective action will usually cure the vice quickly and easily.

Dangerous Vices

You should not attempt to cope with or correct the more dangerous vices unless you are an advanced horseman and an experienced trainer. Such horses require the handler to be sensitive, intuitive, and skilled to a degree that is beyond the experience of the beginner. It is not worth the chance of injuring yourself or ruining your horse to attempt correction of such dangerous vices as striking, kicking, bucking, and rearing. Your horse should be carefully screened for these vices when you buy him. If you find out later that your horse has one of these dangerous vices, you would be well advised to try again for a more suitable mount, or send the horse to an experienced, reputable trainer who will be able to judge if the horse can be safely re-trained. Every effort should be made by the novice horseman to avoid buying, riding, or stabling such an animal.

The following dangerous vices are listed here so that you can recognize them and have some idea of what to do about them if you have to.

Striking

When a horse strikes, he rears up and lashes out with his front feet, usually aiming at a specific object, whether person, thing, or another horse. This is most often found in stallions, and is a wild stallion's natural means of fighting to win or hold his band of mares. Also, horses will defend themselves against snakes and wild animals by striking.

This vice is extremely dangerous for two reasons. First, it is generally a well-aimed and lethal blow, administered with the cutting edge of the hoof. Second, it is generally unexpected; a novice may stay well clear of a horse's hind legs, but may never expect the front legs to be dangerous.

Kicking

Kicking is another natural defense. When around such a horse you should always be aware of his vice. A confirmed kicker should not be stabled in the pleasure-horse barn. Certainly any legitimate horse dealer or breeder should never sell a kicker or striker to a novice.

Some horses will kick at horses coming up behind them while they are being ridden. These horses may be valuable hunters or jumpers and so the vice is tolerated by their experienced riders. Such horses should wear red ribbons in their tails. The red ribbon identifies them as kickers and warns you to stay well away from them.

Remember also that any horse may kick if approached and surprised when he is asleep. Always observe safety rules, and teach your students or children to follow your example.

Bucking and Rearing

These actions may originally be caused by fear and then ripen into confirmed habits. Perhaps a young horse shies at an unfamiliar object, and because he is feeling frisky, he develops this into a buck or rear. A novice rider may involuntarily kick the horse, jerk the reins, or let out a war whoop, and away we go! With this sort of adverse encouragement, the horse may well be worse next time.

Bucking and rearing can be controlled with restraining devices such as martingales and checkreins, but these may not always be available or used correctly. Each confirmed rearer or bucker will try out his new rider for possibilities.

Occasionally a vice such as bucking or rearing will appear in an otherwise well-mannered horse under unusual circumstances. We know of an animal that will go to pieces in a hailstorm, become panicky, and begin rearing. If you find yourself suddenly in such a situation, you should know what to do.

In order to buck, a horse must have his head low. Try to keep his head up. Speak sharply to him, and *urge him on with your legs*. If his head is already down, you may be able to turn it to one side and urge him around in a circle. Sometimes a horse will buck if there is a burr under the saddle, if his tongue gets over the bit, or if there is some other discomfort. Check for this if your normally well-behaved horse seems to buck for no reason.

When a horse rears, he first throws his head up. A panicky rider will pull back on the reins, making matters worse and possibly pulling the horse over backward. Keep the horse's head down. Lean forward and bring your hands down as low as possible, alongside his shoulders, if reins permit. *Urge your horse forward and keep him turning*—he cannot rear if he is moving forward. If you are fearful that your horse will run away with you, urge him forward and turn him around in a tight circle (keeping your hands low). If needed, use the pulley rein to turn the horse effectively. But take care that you don't use so much strength that you throw your horse—in this position you probably would end up underneath!

Charging

Sometimes a horse may charge you—that is, race at you with his teeth bared. Charging usually occurs in a paddock or pasture. The charging horse has little respect for people; he may have been spoiled as a youngster by too many handouts. He may run into you or even over you, and will become more dangerous as he practices. This vice must be stopped immediately and forcefully by an expert. A sharp rap on the nose or a strong application of the whip should suffice. However, this treatment should be repeated whenever the vice recurs.

Bolting or Running Away

This is a dangerous vice for both horse and rider. Anything—a drop of rain, a bee buzzing by, a hand lifted to scratch your neck—can trigger a horse with this habit. A runaway horse generally raises his head, takes the bit in his teeth, and cares nothing for where he goes—through fences, into traffic, over ditches, under low-hanging branches.

You cannot stop him by force; he is stronger than you are. If possible, try to turn him in a large circle, gradually working down smaller until he must slow and stop. He may not respond to normal pressure on one rein. If not, use the pulley rein. Remember to apply pressure gradually so that you don't throw him.

Often a horse can be cured of bolting if you force him to continue running. This is not always possible, but if you have plenty of room, free from dangerous obstacles such as traffic or badger holes, and if you are secure in the saddle, let your horse run. Use whatever force is necessary to turn him away from the barn. When he begins to slow down, urge him forward, uphill if possible. Keep driving him on until he is laboring (but don't run him to death). You have captured the initiative, and he must decide that running isn't all the great game he thought it was.

A change of bit is often effective in controlling a bolt-prone horse. Sometimes a more severe bit is necessary. Sometimes a horse has been hurt by too severe a bit in the hands of a rough or clumsy rider—he learns to take the bit in his teeth and run as a defense. In this case you might use a mild jointed snaffle bit in combination with a running martingale to keep the bit in place and his head down.

Most important, don't panic if your horse bolts. Think. You are usually much safer staying on a runaway than trying to bail off.

Bad Habits in Pasture and Stable

Many of these vices, such as weaving, cribbing, pawing, and blanket chewing, are caused by insufficient exercise. Often the cure may be simply to turn the horse out on pasture, or to see that he gets consistent daily exercise. You may exercise your horse by riding him, of course, or by longeing him (often advisable if the weather is bad or the footing dangerous).

Hard to Catch

A horse that is hard to catch has usually been made that way through poor or infrequent handling. Or he may have been pastured with other hard-to-catch horses and learned the trick from them.

If the habit is not too confirmed, you can cure it by stabling or pasturing your horse by himself. You feed him, you groom him, you ride him—you alone. Make your experiences together pleasant. In this way your horse will feel secure around you and will look forward to seeing you. Knowing he will be rewarded by grain or pelleted feed on your arrival, he will come to you eagerly. This is all part of building the proper relationship with your horse.

Never run after a horse that is running from you. He will only go faster, aggravating and confirming the problem. Roping is inclined to make your horse head-shy, and if you are roping on foot, you may not be able to hold him (supposing you get close enough to catch him) if he is frightened and rears.

If you must keep your horse pastured with other hard-to-catch animals, one method of catching him is to drive or entice the whole herd into a large corral, then a smaller corral, until your horse is cornered and unable to run. If you water your horses in a trap corral, you may catch them all when they come in to drink. Get your horse alone, if possible, and be watchful of being kicked, especially by the other horses.

One method used successfully, especially by pleasure-horse owners, is to leave a safety halter on your horse during this training period. Entice the horse to you with grain. Take hold of the halter quietly, pet him, talk to him, and lead him a few steps. Then let him go. Do this often: sometimes three or more times a day at first. Even when he seems to be over the bad habit it would be a good idea to visit him occasionally, letting him go after a moment or two.

A horse that has a bad experience every time he is caught will make a point of avoiding capture. Your goal is to give him a pleasant experience when caught.

Vices While Being Led

A well-mannered horse should lead well. A horse that bites, crowds, pulls, or balks while being led cannot be called well mannered, even though he may be so when under saddle. Most good horsemen enjoy working with their horses on the ground as well as in the saddle. Bad manners while being led should be discouraged at once.

A horse that bites should be punished. Try leading him with a hackamore arranged with a chain under the jaw in such a way that you can tighten or loosen it at will. Each time he makes a grab for you, jerk your lead chain to punish him. It won't take long to cure him if you are consistent and faithful with the treatment. (Please—do not try this with young horses that nip because they are already fearful. The horse needs to gain confidence in you rather than become more afraid. Scold the horse sharply when he tries to bite and talk soothingly when he is being good. If this does not suffice, you may have to hold a sharp object in your lead hand. Hold it so that he will run into the point when he tries to bite—he will be punishing himself and will not become afraid of you since you have apparently done nothing at all to hurt him.)

A horse that crowds and walks all over you has little or no respect for you. Lead him with your right hand close to the halter (if too difficult to control, use a bridle). Carry a short whip in your left hand. Hold it in the center with the butt end toward the horse. As he crowds ahead, stop him by holding the whip across his chest. If he lunges back, touch him on the hindquarters by swinging your left arm behind you.

When going through gates, doors, and other narrow passages, make him wait for you to go first. Never let your horse barge out in front of you. Use a short lead. If you were to use a long lead, the horse could run by you and kick up as he passes you—an extremely dangerous situation.

As with children, good manners must be taught, and mistakes must be corrected. It is a pleasure to have well-mannered children and horses around; ill-mannered ones are not enjoyed.

Halter Pulling

If you have a few broken halters and ropes in your barn, you know how costly and frustrating halter pulling can be. If your horse has been able to break his halter or rope by pulling back—even if only once or twice—he may well become a confirmed halter puller. Fear is often the cause of a young horse's attempt to pull back. If nothing breaks, it is not likely to happen again.

Prevent this habit from ever developing by, first, gentle and proper halter breaking; second, by always tying your horses correctly and by using strong equipment. It is not practical to economize on equipment. Good-quality ropes, halters, and other equipment pay for themselves many times over.

See Figure 29 for "horse knots" that are both strong and easily released. Halters made from natural-fiber rope and nylon rope generally have more strength than those made of leather. Take good care of them and they will last longer.

An older, confirmed puller can be dangerous, and sometimes harsh methods must be used to break him of the habit. Under these circumstances it is best to get help from an experienced horseman.

You can discourage a horse that already has the habit, however, by always using extra-strong equipment. Snap links and other metal parts on halters and ropes will break; tie the rope through the halter. You may tie the horse to a rubber inner tube that is in turn secured to a post or a stout tree and encourage him to pull back. Eventually he'll tire of the useless effort. Tie the rope short, and at a level with his withers. If it is tied low, the horse has more leverage since he can brace his legs, and further, he may injure his neck and back. The resilience of the inner tube saves the horse from too much shock or stress. (See *Basic Training for Horses*, Part 1, Chapter 2, "Teaching to Stand Tied.")

Nipping

Many horses that are often handed tidbits develop the nipping habit because they become nosy and greedy about their treats. Some horses are materialistic enough to be unmoved by any praise that isn't edible. But generally it is best to reward your horse when he does a job well by a kind word and a pat on the neck. When you do give him a treat, put it in the feedbox.

To catch a shy horse in a large pasture, you may have to give him a handful of grain. There are other situations, such as training to load in a trailer, where a treat may be the best reward. But as a general rule, use restraint in feeding tidbits.

If the problem persists, follow the suggestions for a horse that bites.

Bolting Grain

Because a horse has no vomiting muscles, the effect of bolting grain can be very harmful to his digestive system. By feeding hay first, it will help to curb his appetite. A good preventive measure is to put several stones the size of your fist into his grain box. He will have to eat around them and will not be able to take large mouthfuls. Or you can buy metal feed tubs with partitions in the bottom that have the same effect.

A metal feed tub, designed to be mounted in the corner of a stall, with built-in partitions to discourage bolting grain.

Crowding

Crowding usually occurs when you enter a straight stall or when you are grooming a horse. The horse pushes you against the side of the stall, sometimes leaning on you with all of his weight. A crowder generally has little respect for people.

To cure this vice—and often one lesson is sufficient—take a pointed stick of wood with you; it should be about twelve inches long. As he crowds over against you, set the blunt end of the stick against the wall or partition, the sharp end toward the horse. You will be protected, and the horse will punish himself.

Any punishment that can be self-inflicted is more effective than your punishment after the act has been committed.

Chewing, Cribbing, and Wind Sucking

When a horse chews on the wood of his stall or manger, the cause can usually be discovered to be boredom or a lack of something in the diet. Supplying the deficiency or adequate exercise will usually correct the problem. However, with some horses the habit is so ingrained that they chew whenever and wherever they have the opportunity. Cure is difficult, if not impossible.

Chewing often leads to cribbing and wind sucking, and the two vices generally coincide. The predisposition toward cribbing is said to be inherited. The horse gets a grip on the edge of his manger or a partition (even his own joint, such as a knee), arches his neck, and swallows air. The air can bring on colic or other digestive disorders, and the cribbing itself can wear down the incisor teeth.

Wind sucking is cribbing in the air.

These habits can at least be discouraged, if not cured. Make fences, gates, and partitions unappetizing by painting them with an anticrib liquid. There are several commercial mixtures on the market. You may cover exposed edges of a stall with metal trim (be sure that the sharp edges are turned under), or in some cases an electric wire can be installed to give a mild shock.

Many horsemen believe that use of a cribbing strap is the best preventive measure. This is a broad strap (a stirrup strap will do) that is adjusted around the horse's neck snug enough to keep the horse from swelling his neck prior to swallowing air, but loose enough to be comfortable when he eats or otherwise behaves normally. Obviously, the adjustment is of paramount importance. Too loose it will be ineffective. We know of a youngster in a riding academy who adjusted the cribbing strap so tightly that the horse lost consciousness and fell, blinding one eye. If he hadn't been discovered at that point, he would have choked to death. Any such device should be checked by an experienced horseman.

Both cribbing and wind sucking (as well as the following vice, weaving) are often imitated by other horses in the near vicinity. This is another reason for not having horses with these vices in your stable.

Weaving

The weaver stands in one place and shifts his weight from side to side; he appears to be mesmerized by his own motion. Weaving usually is practiced by a nervous, high-strung horse or an excessively energetic one that is confined to a small stall. This horse should have a paddock, run, or small pasture, and he should receive regular, adequate exercise. Without proper exercise his disposition or nervous temperament will degenerate. It is difficult to keep a horse with this habit in good condition, especially if you wish to show him.

Blanket Chewing

This habit can be costly to the horse owner and should be stopped as soon as it is detected. Boredom is usually the cause, and again, exercise and freedom in a corral or pasture are the best preventive measures.

If exercise does not stop the blanket chewing, you will have to use a side stick. This is a stick long enough to be attached to the bit at one end, surcingle ring at the other. The horse can move his head up and down freely but cannot turn it. The side stick is useful also to keep him from chewing at a wound, biting when being doctored, and other such problems. A leather bib is another good alternative. (See *Basic Horse Care*, Chapter 4, p. 63).

Tail Rubbing

Tail rubbing can be unsightly and downright disastrous for a show animal. If this is due to worms (check under the tail for skin irritation), call the vet and proceed according to his recommendation. If due to an incomplete wash job, rinse thoroughly.

Tail rubbing can be unsightly.

Some horses, however, make tail rubbing a habit. Equip his stall with a wooden shelf twelve to eighteen inches wide, running all the way around at a height just below his point of buttock. His tail will be kept out and away from walls and partitions.

When trailering your horse, be sure to bandage his tail. Clean your trailer after every trip. Rump chains and their hose covers can become caked with manure, making the horse sore, as well as rubbing his hair and skin off in patches.

Touchy Feet

An owner has no excuse for neglecting his horse's feet. The feet should be trimmed and cared for regularly, and they should be checked with a hoof pick before and after every ride.

Regular handling of his feet should be an important part of every young horse's training. If your horse is an experienced riding horse but won't allow his feet to be handled, it is up to you to correct the situation.

You must consider the degree of your horse's resistance. If he is going to kick out violently whenever his feet are touched, ask an experienced horseman to help you begin retraining. He will be acquainted with the restraining devices necessary to insure safety in working with the horse.

In most cases, however, if you use care and common sense, the horse's resistance will not be dangerous. Work with his feet often at first until resistance is overcome. When you groom your horse, spend extra time brushing his lower legs and around his feet. Always work in the same way, so that your horse can anticipate which foot will be worked on next. It won't be long before he has each foot up and ready for you.

Pick up the forefoot as described in Chapter II. Then slide your hand under the pastern, and don't let him jerk his foot away from you. If you are braced against his shoulder you should be able to hold the foot up fairly easily. You don't have to hold it still if he jerks. Let your arm swing forward and back with the horse's foot. As soon as he quiets down, set his hoof down very gently on the toe. Repeat several times and move on to the next foot.

Work in the same way with the hind leg. Lean against the hip (if he wants to kick, he won't be able to get up much power if you're right next to him), and run your hand down the inside of the leg. As you lift the foot, it will be easier to pull the leg forward first, then bring it back into position.

Remember that a touchy-footed horse probably associates pain or some other unpleasant experience with having his feet handled. Have your veterinarian check the horse's feet for bruises, corns, cracks, or punctures that make a foot painfully sensitive. With either the touchy or inexperienced horse, be especially gentle when you handle his feet. Use the hoof pick very carefully and always set the foot down slowly. Dropping the foot will frighten or jar the horse and make it more difficult when you pick up his foot next time.

Hard to Bridle

Again, poor training or an unfortunate experience is usually the cause of this problem. As a general rule, the horse tries to avoid the bit by raising and turning his head. This is especially frustrating for short people.

If the horse is well halter trained, tie him fairly short in a straight stall and bridle him over the halter. Work slowly and talk gently to him. Make very sure that the bit fits properly in the mouth. If he clamps his teeth shut, place your fingers in the bar area behind his lower front teeth (reach under his jaw and use thumb on one side, fingers on the other), and pull down, which helps to open his mouth. If the horse is afraid of having his ears touched, unbuckle the headstall so that you can put the bit in his mouth first, then rebuckle the bridle.

Several sessions of bridling over the halter should be enough to give the

Unbuckle the headstall to bridle a horse that dislikes having his ears touched.

horse confidence in you and thus break the habit. Be especially gentle in haltering and bridling, groom him often and gently, and talk to him soothingly. Never bump the bit against his teeth or try to put a cold bit in his mouth.

Be sure that you can finish what you begin. Each time he keeps you from bridling him, the more confirmed the habit will become.

Swelling When Cinched or Girthed

It is usually the smart, older horses that try this. They inhale deeply and then hold their breath while you tighten the girth. When they expel the air, the girth will be dangerously loose.

Always walk your horse for several feet after saddling, then recheck the girth before mounting. Tighten it again, if necessary. Some horses need to be walked around more than others before they lose their swell.

This is an excellent practice to adopt whether your horse swells up or not. It is always wise to recheck the girth before mounting; remind yourself to do this by putting the near stirrup over the horn of the Western saddle or leaving the stirrup iron run up on the leather of the English saddle.

Also, by walking a few feet, any pinched skin under the girth (especially under a Western cinch) or other part of the saddle can smooth out. Or, lift a foreleg and pull it forward to release any pinched skin.

Some riders like to "knee" their horse in the cinch area to make him expel the air. This is likely to frighten the flighty, green, or timid horse, and if overdone can spark other retaliatory defenses such as kicking and biting.

Cinch-Bound (Girth-Bound)

Cinch-bound horses react by rearing or throwing themselves on the ground when the cinch is pulled tight (without having been led first and cinched gradually). Usually an unfortunate experience has precipitated or contributed to this violent and dangerous vice.

A cinch-bound horse is especially dangerous when tied and cinched roughly and tightly. Once this vice manifests itself, the horse should never be tied while being cinched. After rearing and pulling back, he will then jump forward as he feels the restriction of the leadrope, and may injure either himself or his handler.

To remedy this problem, hold the leadrope, rub the cinch area gently, lead the horse and cinch very lightly, again rub the area, lead and cinch, and continue in this very gradual manner until the cinch is tight enough for safety.

Few cinch-bound horses object to this method; however, they never forget the initial experience of pain. A horse with this vice should be monitored closely, and each rider always should be warned and taught how to saddle up.

Hard to Load into a Trailer

Usually this problem is presented by a horse that has either had no previous experience with a trailer or else has suffered some unfortunate experience. Occasionally a horse that has been well trained to load in a trailer will balk at loading, especially if the trailer is of a different kind than he is used to. In the latter case, if you are patient, introduce the horse to the trailer slowly, and avoid any excitement, he will usually load without difficulty. He will load even more readily the next time since he had no unpleasant experiences to associate with the trailer. On successful loadings, reward him with grain in the manger.

If you purchase a horse that has never been loaded in a trailer, it is generally best to ride him home or transport him by truck (using a loading chute). Once home, plan to begin trailer training him. Horses that load readily on the first try are rare. Most of them decide the entrance is too small and dark. A four-horse trailer or stock trailer is ideal for introducing the reluctant horse to loading.

A good method of trailer training your horse is to let him get used to it gradually. Park the trailer in a small corral where you keep your horse. Give him his daily grain on the tail gate, or at the rear edge of a step-up trailer. At each meal, creep the feed forward. Before he realizes it, he will have his front feet in the trailer and then be walking all the way in. The nice part of this method is that there is a substantial reward for any effort he makes. He is actually training himself—you need not spend hours a day at it. You can measure his progress by the fact that the grain has been eaten.

There are many other methods of training a horse to load—probably as many as there are horsemen. Most important in all methods is to use patience, take enough time, and give a reward. Avoid fear and excitement.

Vices and Problems While Mounted

Moving While Being Mounted

Usually an unpleasant experience associated with being mounted is the spark for this habit. Perhaps someone once dug the horse with his left toe while mounting, or let his right foot kick the horse's rump as he swung over. A noise or sudden movement may have startled the horse as he was being mounted. A young horse can easily associate a feeling or noise with what you are doing, and the next time you mount he may move forward or sideways. Go to work on this problem immediately. If you are not actively improving your horse's behavior, you are allowing it to get worse.

Keep your tack clean, pliable, and free from irritating burrs, caked sweat, foxtail heads, or other foreign matter. Check it frequently for needed adjustment. Carelessness can create problems and complicate training unnecessarily.

There are several methods of training your horse to stand still while being mounted. Your horse must learn what you want him to do before you can break the habit. Understanding, as always, is the key to training.

At first, work in a fence corner so that the horse cannot go forward or turn his hindquarters away from you. Say "whoa" and mount. (Your mounting should be easy, fluid, and quick, and of course be without jabs or knocks to the horse.) Mount and dismount several times, saying "whoa" each time he offers to move and praising him when he stands properly. If the horse is difficult, you may have to tie him in the corner and practice mounting frequently.

When the horse understands what is expected of him, gradually mount farther and farther from the corner. Mount and dismount several times each time you ride. Repetition of correct action erases the bad habit.

If it is necessary to mount in open country, without available fence corners, you may try shortening the off rein as you mount. This turns the horse's head slightly away from you and his hindquarters toward you. If he moves as you mount, he will, theoretically, be moving under you.

The old Western riders used to cheek cowhorses to teach them to circle around the rider as he mounted. The rider would hold the cheek piece of the bridle with his left hand so that the horse's head was turned toward him. This works well if you are quick and adept in mounting, and if you have long arms, but it will probably be useless for the novice. Nor does it teach the horse to stand quietly.

Barn Rat (Barn Sour)

The barn-sour horse will head for the barn whenever he figures he's been out long enough—sometimes at full gallop. Some barn rats won't leave the barn at all unless accompanied by other horses, and others refuse to pass a certain point on trail or bridle path. An inexperienced rider is nearly helpless on such a horse.

Ride the barn rat every day and give him some good hard workouts away from the barn. Whenever he turns toward the barn, reverse him and continue working him for fifteen minutes more. This happened once to us and we spent the entire day getting back to the barn. After several days of this treatment, we were almost ready to switch to motorcycles, but the horse was cured.

If you cannot get the horse to leave the corral or to pass a certain point on the trail, turn him in a small tight circle and try again. You may have to turn him around and around. Use your legs strongly and slap him with switch or crop. When he heads out properly, praise him.

Do not allow him to anticipate your commands at any time. He must learn to obey you.

Instructors should be careful when choosing riders for the barn rat. The wrong rider will help increase the horse's delinquency to the point where he can no longer be used for school riding.

Grass Cropping (Eating While Mounted)

A horse or pony with this habit usually has been ridden often by a child or novice. The rider is unable to anticipate the animal's moves, does not understand the importance of driving the horse forward in this circumstance, or does not have the strength to keep him from snatching to the side in tall grass.

Consistent alertness and correction are needed to cure the habit. You can't let the horse crop grass one day and expect that he won't do it the next. Use your legs to keep the forward impulsion. Use your hands to keep the horse up on the bit; the proper use of the rein and leg aids will preclude the opportunity for grass cropping.

Pulling on the reins to jerk up the horse's head is inadvisable because of the hardening or injurious effect on the horse's mouth. Also, it can develop into a contest of strength, which, considering his weight and yours, you should by all means avoid.

Instructors, watch carefully when a child is mounted on a grass cropper. When the horse reaches for grass, the child can easily become unseated. Teach the child to anticipate the horse's movements and to use leg pressure to move the horse forward, *before* he reaches for grass. When young children must ride such a horse, some mechanical device such as a checkrein should be used to prevent the horse from lowering his head.

It is not wise to allow your horse to graze while saddled and bridled. A saddle and bridle should mean work to him, not dinnertime.

Fig. 18   "When the horse reaches for grass, the child can easily become unseated. . . ."

Rolling

Rolling, whether in water, snow, or dirt, can be caused by fear, stubbornness, or lack of exercise. Often horses that are kept in stalls and do not have the opportunity to roll in a corral or pasture will suddenly decide to roll even when under saddle. Some horses can hardly resist rolling in a puddle or snowbank. Make sure your horse has the occasional freedom to lie down and roll, even if only in a small corral or paddock.

Longeing will help the horse that lies down because of fear. Longe your horse next to—and then through—rain puddles and snowdrifts. Make going through water or snow an everyday occurrence and the horse won't build up a mental block against them.

A horse that plans to roll will usually let his rider know by pawing, lowering his head, and then slowly (or sometimes quickly) stepping in place while folding his legs under him. Urge him forward with your legs (kick him vigorously if necessary), and lift his head. Alert riding, in which you keep contact with the horse's mouth, will prevent him from thinking about rolling to begin with.

Instructors, be sure to warn the student mounted on a horse that likes to roll. If the student is a beginner and doesn't recognize what is happening even though warned, speak sharply and it will startle the horse enough to make him momentarily forget his plans.

Balking

Balking is often synonymous with downright stubbornness. If your horse won't move forward or back when you give the correct aids (if he is an experienced horse), he is probably used to having his own way. As with the barn rat, you must show him who's boss. Carry a crop and use it behind the cinch (unless he is inclined to "crow hop," in which case it may be better to use it on his shoulder). Turn him in small circles to break his train of thought and perhaps forget his objective. If absolutely necessary you may even have to dismount and lead him. The important thing is to win every round with him.

Always, in problems of this kind, remember to control your temper. Firmness, persistence, and the correct use of the aids will accomplish what frantic loss of control will not. Most important, always analyze the problem to be sure the balking stems from stubbornness instead of fear. If you were to add the fear of punishment to the fears your horse already has, the problem would be seriously compounded, and you would be destroying his confidence in you.

Conflicting aids (for instance, kicking the horse while pulling back on the reins) can also lead to balking. Since the horse doesn't know what you want him to do, the easiest thing for him to do is balk.

Sometimes you may be faced with a serious problem in balking, in which the horse will even lie down to prevent entering a trailer, crossing water, or otherwise going forward. Of course, the problem is best solved by preventing it from ever happening to begin with through proper training and preparation ahead of time, as well as quiet patience at the time. If it's too late for this, however, you must win the battle however you can or face an increasingly spoiled and eventually useless horse. You may have to use harsh methods, including a whip, to get the horse up off the ground. Or you can try sitting on his head so that he *can't* get up for a few minutes. This may panic him enough so that he'll jump up as soon as he gets the chance.

Under such circumstances you may consider the situation to be getting dangerous, and it may be wise to call an experienced horseman for advice and assistance. Because extreme balking can lead to rearing and bucking, it is better to be sure of your method than to guess.

Refusing to Cross Water

A horse may refuse to cross water because of fear or because he dislikes getting wet. Your horse should be trained to cross water readily before you go on a long trail ride.

If the horse refuses to cross water because of dislike or stubbornness, he will have to learn that balking, rearing, or lying down will not win him his way. One method of combating this problem is to use another horse to lead the troublemaker. Lead him across and back without a rider until he walks across calmly without lunging or jumping. Then lead him across mounted, and finally have him follow the lead horse. After several trips he will probably cross willingly enough. Try to repeat the leading exercise across several different kinds of water—swift, deep, muddy—if you can; otherwise he may cross one puddle but present the same problem at a stream or ditch.

You can prepare him at home by longeing him through puddles and across small ditches.

Refusing to Back

Most horses dislike backing and avoid it unless trained to do so. To teach your horse to back, begin training from the ground. Take the reins in your left hand close to the bit, and move them with give-and-take pressure toward his chest. Simultaneously prod him with the three middle fingers of your right hand in the center of his chest. Say "back" as you tap and work your rein hand. Praise him for a step backward; a few steps, or even one, are sufficient at first. Praise him generously and lead him forward again.

When he understands this, say "back" and give short pulls toward his chest with your left hand on the reins. Eventually the pressure on the bit given with the voice command will suffice, then pressure alone.

Next, mount and ask a helper to stand by to tap your horse's chest if he does not respond to your intermittent pressure on the reins and voice command to back. Be sure that the rider gives the command; the horse's attention should be directed toward the rider. Again, be satisfied with only a few steps at first, praise the horse generously, and ride forward to maintain the forward impulsion.

There are many other methods of training to back. The above method is quiet yet can be used effectively with the problem horse. Probably it is similar to the method by which the horse was originally trained. The advanced trainer, however, who values a solid foundation and is not pressed for time will probably want to use more refined concepts in his training.

Tail Wringing

When a horse wrings his tail (the tail goes around in a circle or back and forth), it may seem a minor vice, but the problem has deep roots that make it difficult to diagnose and correct. It is frustrating to the showman as it gives the judge reason to discredit your horse regardless of his performance.

The horse is rebelling over something—perhaps his tack does not fit him correctly or he has become bored with ring work. It may be that your aids are more strenuous than necessary or you are asking more of your horse than his training or conformation will permit. When you find the cause of his discomfort or rebellion, you may then work on eradicating the vice.

Shying; Fear of Vehicles, Loud Noises, or Storms

Any unknown object, experience, or noise can be frightening to a horse. The cure is often familiarity—encountering as many situations as possible, under controlled conditions. For instance, if your horse is afraid of vehicles or trains, pasture him for a while where he'll be able to see, hear, and smell them often. He will soon ignore them because familiarity has eliminated fear. By having the horse repeatedly confront—without harm—a situation that may be frightening to him, you are in effect desensitizing him to that situation.

Horses often react to frightening conditions by shying. This is a normal reflex, but some horses carry it to absurd extremes. There are different theories in regard to handling the shying horse; many horsemen believe that time and patience are the best cure. Fear is the cause, and therefore the horse should not be punished, but rather given confidence. Allow him to take his time, look an object over carefully, smell it, and perhaps touch it with his nose. Talk to him reassuringly. If he is a very timid horse, you will probably have to take time with a dozen or more objects on a ride, and perhaps the same object over and over again. It will require much patience on your part but will bear twofold results. For one, eventually your horse will overcome his fears. More important, his confidence in you will have grown to the point where he will willingly accept your direction because he knows you have never led him into harm.

If your horse has weathered storms when running free in pasture or paddock, he is not likely to be bothered in hail, wind, or rain. However, be especially careful when riding an animal that is continually stabled. If he shows increasing nervousness when you are caught out riding in unusual weather conditions, you should be alert to a possible tendency to rear or bolt. Turn the horse away from the wind, soothe him with your voice, and try to get under cover as soon as possible. You may feel safer if you dismount and lead him. Be careful not to get trampled, however, if he should panic. Hold him by the reins close to the bit. If you have closed reins, don't bring them forward over your horse's head; if he were to break away from you, he could catch a foreleg in the reins.

As mentioned above, when your horse is faced with a frightening situation, your attitude will do much to alleviate or aggravate his fear. Keep calm and talk to him reassuringly. If he has learned to have confidence in you through your daily relationship, he will usually rely on your judgment.

Electrical storms are special situations that are potentially very dangerous. If an electrical storm is coming close, dismount and get away from your horse. A horse, with four feet on the ground, especially if shod, is very susceptible to lightning. It would be heartbreaking to lose your horse, but there's no point in deliberately going down with the ship. Riders are killed by lightning every year.

Electrical storms can also mean trouble if you are riding in an inside riding arena. Keep away from entrances and windows, as lightning tends to gravitate toward them. The noise of hail on metal roofs and walls can be frightening to horses. Lead your horse and talk to him quietly. In a class situation, if the horses are tied, have students stay clear—the horses' uneasiness or struggles can be dangerous for inexperienced students.

As always, prevention of the problem is well worth the inconvenience of a change in plans. If an electrical storm seems likely, why not work in the corral or ring instead of going out on a trail ride, and finish before the storm comes close? (See also Chapter VIII on "Manners and Safety," number 14.)

Uneven Cadence in Gait

There is little enjoyment in riding a horse that will not hold a gait. He moves in fits and starts, and is lacking in forward impulsion.

Make sure before beginning corrective work that the problem does not stem from improper shoeing, lameness, or nervousness. Be aware that a green horse is not used to balancing the weight of a rider. It is through proper training, experience, and the development of muscling and coordination that he becomes cadenced.

Plenty of proper work in the ring is one good cure for uneven gaits. Generally speaking, it is not advisable to take the horse on trail rides during this period since the uneven ground works against you for this purpose. If you have ridden your horse by applying the increasing aids properly, he will be responsive to your aids. If you are able to anticipate his hesitations and surges forward, it will be easier for you to stabilize him.

Begin work at a trot. (The walk is the most difficult gait to regulate.) Usually it is best not to ask for much (or any) collection at first. Set your horse into the speed you desire and either check or increase his rhythm at each break he makes. This is hard riding, since you must constantly be working with hands, legs, back, and weight to keep your horse in an even rhythm. Try to keep him in the trot *as you want it* for five minutes. This is work for the horse, too, so after five minutes just stand for a minute, lead him around on foot, or do some other maneuver that he knows well. When he goes well at an ordinary trot, try a slower or more extended trot and keep him even and in rhythm for five minutes. With each gait, gradually increase the time until he can hold the gait steadily for ten minutes or more. Do not begin the canter or lope until a reasonable stabilization has been achieved at the slower gaits.

Longeing and long-reining can also help in correcting uneven cadence in gaits, especially when used in conjunction with mounted training. Use the longe whip to keep him in the gait. (Point the whip below his hocks and snap it to drive the horse forward—there should be no need to hit the horse with the whip.) It will also be beneficial to work your horse in the same ring with a trained, cadenced horse.

The achievement of success will take many hours of consistent work.

Stumbling

Repeated stumbling in a mature, experienced horse is less often due to a physical defect than to a mental attitude caused by laziness and boredom. You should be able to tell if your horse is stumbling because of lameness, a sore foot, or defective shoeing, and correct this immediately. But if you have an older horse that continually stumbles while gazing into the blue, even when there's nothing to hinder him, you'll have to wake him up.

To cure repeated stumbling, work your horse. A lazy rider produces a lazy horse. Let him know that when you are riding him there are things to accomplish. Take him over very uneven ground at a fast, even walk. Turn him, make figure-eights, and later work at a slow trot or jog. Carry a crop or willow switch; give him a slap on the neck and scold him briefly each time he stumbles. He must learn that you dislike the habit and that he will be punished when he forgets to pick up his feet. If this seems harsh, remember that you are saving your horse from broken knees and yourself from a bad fall.

Sometimes stallions will stumble often because they are always looking around for other horses. Use the same corrective measures. Use the crop also when they whinny or act up. While under saddle, they must attend to business.

When training a young, inexperienced horse, expect him to stumble and do not punish him. He has not yet learned to adjust his movements while compensating for your weight. However, keep him alert by varying the work, and avoid overreaching his physical capabilities. Patience and understanding are necessary.

Head Tossing

If you've ever had your nose flattened by a head-tossing horse, you know how miserable this habit can be. Among the causes of this vice are ill-fitting and poorly adjusted bits and bridles, keeping a horse "high" without enough exercise, too much jingling tack, incorrect use of a hackamore or martingale, and rough or fussy hands. Some Western-trained horses have been taught to respond to a loose rein and toss their heads when contact is too heavy.

Make sure your bit and bridle fit the horse properly and that all tack is nonirritating. Perhaps the bit itself is irritating to the horse. You might try a different style of bit, or use a hackamore.

Longe the "high" horse before riding him to let him work off excess energy. Use a running martingale when riding him, and don't give with your hands when he tosses his head. He will punish himself by coming hard against the bit. When he realizes that he's more comfortable with a quiet head, the habit will be overcome, but it does take time and patience.

Occasionally a standing martingale is used on the head-tossing or star-gazing horse. The standing martingale has its place for advanced horsemen. However, it does nothing to correct a habit, but it does have its place: It saves your nose!

Some horses habitually evade the bit. If the above suggestions do not help, you may wish to refer to *Basic Training for Horses*, Part 5, Chapter 2, "Problems in Position of Head, Refusal to Accept Contact, Tossing the Head, or Leaning on the Bit."

Stargazing

A stargazer raises his nose to the sky and usually takes the bit in his teeth. He is generally very difficult to direct. The cause of this habit is usually attributed to hard hands or poorly adjusted equipment. The horse raises his head to evade the bit that has been punishing his mouth.

Check your tack for proper fit. You might try a different bit, especially one that is less severe. Longe the horse with side reins, adjusted so that the horse has some free movement of his head, but cannot stargaze. When you ride, be very light with your hands.

An older horse in which the habit has become ingrained presents more of a problem. His neck muscles are often unusually well developed, and they have been allowed to become stiff and unyielding. He must be taught, through more advanced training techniques, to flex his head and neck laterally as well as vertically. These may include use of side reins, running martingale, or other mechanical aids. The horse must learn to give to your hand with confidence, knowing he will not be unexpectedly jabbed. Generally, the best plan is to go right back to the basics in retraining.

Summary

Remember that most vices are defenses. They are caused by neglect, boredom, poor handling, unfortunate experiences, or fear. Lack of exercise causes most of the troublesome barn vices. Ride or longe your horse often if he is not allowed to run free in a pasture.

Usually a horse is more contented in his home surroundings if he has one or more stable companions—if not another horse or pony, even a goat, dog, or cat will help. The famous Hungarian race horse Kincsem refused to travel to races without her friend, a disheveled cat. The Godolphin Arabian was so fond of a particular cat that an old print shows the horse nuzzling the ugly tom.

If he must be kept in a stall the greater part of each day, a Dutch door is better than a solid one; then he can watch whatever is going on in the stable area. Try imagining yourself in his place; you'll be able to come up with several sensible arrangements for his comfort and relief from boredom.

Our horses are dependent upon us to fulfill their needs, whether for care, comfort, or companionship. It is our duty and should be our joy to provide for them well.

There are no pat answers when working with horses. Each horse is a distinct personality. While the above suggestions may work with some horses, your horse may be the one that's different. Each horse you work with gives you the opportunity to expand and improve your understanding of his mentality and personality. By working with him, riding him, and studying him, you learn his ways, his reactions, his temperament. As a thinking horseman you apply imagination to find just the right way of handling this particular horse in this particular situation. As your understanding grows, your ability grows also, and together you and your horse manifest in increasing proportion the close relationship that is necessary for harmonious horsemanship.

Part 4 · Your Horse's Feet

One of the most common omissions of the new horse owner is to neglect his horse's feet. Obviously, the new owner must feed his horse something, he must keep his horse somewhere—but until the horse suddenly goes lame, the owner might not realize that hoofs don't naturally take care of themselves.

Wild horses have practically no leg or hoof trouble. But once out of a completely natural environment, care of the hoof is essential.

Purpose of Shoeing

Actually your horse is better off if he can get by without being shod. If you ride your horse regularly, but on ground that is neither paved nor overly rocky, he may not need shoes. Or if your horse spends most of his time on the range or on pasture, with only light or occasional work, he probably won't need them either. In any case, however, his feet must be trimmed regularly and properly cared for.

Shoeing interferes somewhat with the natural functions of the foot structures. It limits the amount of expansion and contraction in the foot structures as weight is thrown onto and released from the hoof. It adds weight to the horse's foot and therefore increases fatigue. It also increases the amount of shock received by the leg and weakens the hoof wall with nail holes. Wearing one set of shoes for too long a time, or a poor job of shoeing to begin with, can seriously injure the horse.

So why shoe him?

Shoes protect the horse's hoof from becoming overly worn. Deficiencies in gait, stance, or the hoof itself can often be overcome by corrective shoeing. Shoes may be used to relieve injured parts of the hoof. They provide better traction. Shoes for harness-racing horses, flat racers, American Saddle horses, Hackney ponies, and others help the horses to perform under their own special conditions.

Finding a Reliable and Reputable Farrier

It is better for your horse to go unshod than to be poorly shod. But how can you find a horseshoer who will really do a good job?

Horseshoeing was in danger of becoming a lost art when the U.S. Army closed its farriery school in 1939. Horses were no longer being used for work or war, and farriery seemed a very unpromising profession. It has been saved from extinction, for the most part, by the horseshoeing schools such as those at Michigan State College and California State Polytechnic College. Even so, expert farriers are hard to find today, and they are in great demand. Unfortunately, there are less expert and distinctly inexpert farriers at work also, and they are busy because the demand is so great and because many horse owners are not aware of what constitutes good shoeing.

Ask your veterinarian to recommend a good horseshoer, or check with an established horse breeder or trainer. If you live near a large university, you may find out who does the shoeing for their veterinary clinics.

Even so, you can't always rely on recommendations. You should know what you want done and what the job should look like after it has been done. You'll have to judge your farrier by the job he does. And this is no small task if you don't know which end of the horseshoe is up.

What to Look For in Proper Shoeing

Remember that, as in anything else, proper shoeing involves common sense. After the horse has been shod, stand him squarely and make sure that he is standing properly on all four feet. Look at him from both front and side. Do his legs stand straight? Is his hoof in line with the pastern? Walk him around. Does he walk squarely without favoring any of his feet? If the horse has not been shod for a long time, if his feet needed a lot of trimming due to previous neglect, or if he is wearing a different kind of shoe, such as ice calks, he may walk a little uncertainly until he becomes used to the new shoes. His leg and shoulder muscles also might be sore for a day or two, but rarely longer. Lead him in a trot: Does he overreach or travel crab-fashion? Any lameness, prolonged uncertainty in walking, or other disturbances of gait may be a sign of poor shoeing.

Now look closely at the hoof itself. The hoof must be trimmed before it is shod and the proper shoe selected to fit the hoof. Hot shoeing used to be the best method of shoeing, but this is no longer necessarily true. For one thing, inexpert farriers sometimes "cheat" by burning shoes into poorly trimmed hoofs. Further, the wide selection of shoes available today makes it possible for cold shoes to do an excellent job.

What you should watch for is that the shoe has been selected to fit the hoof. The most common problem today among inexpert farriers is that the hoof is trimmed down to fit the shoe.

Make sure that the shoe is fitting solidly against the hoof. If the shoe is not flush with the hoof, the shoe will not seat properly; it will soon become loose and be lost.

Look also at the heels. The heel of the shoe should not be longer or shorter than the heel of the hoof under ordinary circumstances.

The frog is the cushioning part of the hoof, and it absorbs the shock of concussion. If it has been trimmed too severely it will not be able to function as it should.

It is well worth your time to find a good farrier even if you must try several times, and even if you must pay more. Your horse, especially, will appreciate it.

Some farriers, while well able to do ordinary work, may not be capable of certain kinds of corrective shoeing or other specialized shoeing situations. They will probably recommend an expert in the particular field you need. If they do not, check with your veterinarian. Attempted corrective shoeing by an inexperienced person can ruin your horse.

Helping Your Farrier

Having found your farrier, how do you keep him?

Make appointments well in advance—and keep them. If he's good, he's going to be busy and won't appreciate last-minute changes (nor be able to make them). Set up a regular schedule with your farrier as soon as you are assured that he's reliable. Many horses should have their hoofs trimmed and be reshod every four weeks. A few need it more often. Many can go six to eight weeks, some even ten or more. Take your farrier's word for how often he should come. He's too busy to come more often than necessary. You'll be well rewarded for keeping your horse's feet in good condition.

Always be there when your farrier comes. Have your horse ready and at a good place to work—perhaps at the crosstie in the barn where there are few distractions, and where the floor is level and smooth. His feet and legs should be clean, that is, with no caked-on mud. Stand at your horse's head and quiet him. Even if they are quiet and experienced, most horses appreciate the assurance of your presence.

Tell your farrier what you want and discuss any problems with him. But don't argue, correct, or otherwise jabber when he's working. If you won't be using your horse for a while and he's going out on pasture or on the range, tell the farrier so that he can remove the shoes and make an appointment for trimming the hoofs.

Naturally, you don't want to have a farrier that will abuse your horse. But if the horse begins acting up, don't complain if your farrier reprimands him. This brings us around again to the point that you are responsible for the behavior of your horse. If he has touchy feet, get to work right away on correcting the vice. If the horse is still difficult when the time comes to shoe him, tell your farrier, and comply with his request for use of restraining devices.

Young horses should be trained to be mannerly about their feet from the time they are foals.

Proper Hoof Care

Your horse should have regular day-by-day hoof care while you are using him. Always clean your horse's feet before and after each ride. Check for pebbles, nails, punctures, or other wounds. Make sure that the shoes are on securely and that the nails are smoothly clinched, not loosening. Check around the frog for evidence of thrush and the feet above the hoof for evidence of interfering.

Keep your stable dry and clean. Don't allow your horse to stand for long periods in urine and manure. Wood or earth floors are better than cement for your horse's feet and legs.

If your horse is stabled or if his pasture is dry, his hoofs may become dry and brittle. Normal functioning of the hoof structures requires a certain elasticity. Because elasticity is impaired in the brittle hoof, chipping and cracking may result. The horny frog should be soft and elastic, and all the horny parts of the hoof should be kept moist. Use a hoof dressing to keep the hoof wall from drying. See "Hoof Dressing" in Chapter II, Part 2, for ingredients, or use any commercial brand. This may also be applied to the frog. Other methods for supplying moisture to the hoof (as recommended by the *U.S. Cavalry Manual*) include: Stand the horse in water or moist clay; pack the feet with white rock or moist clay; or apply cold-water packs to the feet.

Feet should be trimmed on a regular schedule even when the horse stays out on pasture. They are not trimmed as short as the hoof that is to be shod, because they will need the extra length of wall for protection. If the hoofs are kept properly trimmed, the feet will maintain the correct angle and this in turn helps the horse to develop and maintain strong, straight legs. Leg muscles will be kept in proper shape and condition, and will not become pulled or stiff when the horse is shod.

Give your horse a chance to get used to new shoes, especially if they are different from those he's been wearing or if he's been unshod. Longe him or let him run in pasture or paddock for a while before riding him. He may have to rebalance his own weight, and should have a chance to do so before he must balance your weight also. Many accidents could be prevented by observance of this simple rule.

CHAPTER ELEVEN

Advancing in Horsemanship

Part 1 · Specialization or Liberal Education?

Why Advance in Horsemanship?

You have come a long way from the day you first scrambled onto your horse's back with aid of a leg up. You now handle your horse capably, you enjoy riding him on the trail and in the ring—perhaps you are even bringing home ribbons from shows or contests. Most important, you and your horse enjoy each other's company.

So why push it? Why learn more?

Because forward impulsion is as important in life as it is in horsemanship. A horse that lacks forward impulsion also lacks balance; he cannot obey commands; he is incapable of obtaining either extension or collection. He lacks fulfillment of purpose. In life we find that if we are not moving forward, we are stagnating and becoming increasingly dissatisfied.

Have you ever ridden a horse that was better trained than yourself? Then you know what it is to think: "We're on the brink of something. Together this horse and I could do just what I have always dreamed of doing. But I don't know how to tell him to do it."

Proficiency brings enjoyment in any endeavor. Continued advancement in horsemanship develops deeper harmony between you and your horse. As you reach toward the goal of harmonious horsemanship, you experience the pleasure and ease of performance that once lived for you only as starry-eyed hopes.

Advanced training is necessary if you are to continue to compete successfully in shows, tests, or contests. You can't remain in the novice class forever.

While a well-trained horse is a pleasure to ride, is advanced training really good for the horse? Most emphatically, yes! A person with a trim and vigorous body, toned by regular exercise, mental challenge, and emotional fulfillment, is a person in top mental and physical health. He is apt to be longer-lived, more intellectually alive, and more physically attractive than his lumpier, in-a-rut confreres. There is no question but that this holds true for horses also—when the advanced training is accomplished correctly, neither rushed nor forced.

Colonel Alois Podhajsky, former director of the Spanish Riding School of Vienna, said: "Like any other gymnastics, riding should strengthen the horse and prolong his life. . . . Constant and serious work may improve the outward appearance of a horse. . . . Correct training renders the horse more beautiful, the great Greek riding master and philosopher Xenophon said four hundred years before Christ. The improvement of the physical form is the result of any intelligent and well-developed gymnastics."*

How Do I Advance in Horsemanship?

To advance in horsemanship, you increase your understanding as you train yourself and your horse toward the goal of harmony. Even if you don't think of yourself as a trainer, every rider, once he has passed the beginner stage, is training his horse (however unconsciously) whenever he rides him.

Training your horse in a basic foundation (or continuing to work understandingly with a trained horse, if you prefer) is the equivalent of giving him a liberal education. Like any athlete, your horse may have a definite talent toward one or more aspects of advanced training. But this cannot be developed by either you or him until the basic foundation—the liberal education or balanced curriculum—is broad and solid enough to allow for profitable selectivity.

Until your horse is so expert in a specialized field that he is actually priceless—and sometimes even then—varied training in several or many different fields is almost always beneficial. For instance, a dressage horse can benefit from a hunt or trail ride by renewal of enthusiasm and impulsion. The

* *My Horses, My Teachers*, Doubleday, 1969.

hunter will benefit from ring work by increasing in suppleness, obedience, and balance. The Western-trained reining horse will keep from going sour when his work is varied occasionally with English ring work or a bit of low jumping in English tack. Variety and new challenges keep interest, impulsion, and enthusiasm alive for both horse and rider, and they promote physical agility and versatility.

There are many doors open to the horseman, from show jumping, hunting, polo, drills, or dressage, to gymkhana events, reining, roping, cutting, or racing. Knowledge of several different fields allows you to make an intelligent choice for specialization, according to your temperament, interests, physique, availability of friends with the same interests, availability of facilities, and capabilities of your horse. Or you may find that both you and your horse prefer a well-rounded training in several fields, without specific specialization.

Incidentally, availability of friends with the same interests may be a more important consideration than you would at first suppose. If you and your friends are interested in barrel racing, pole bending, and other gymkhana events, you'll work together to improve your techniques. You'll find proper equipment and a suitable area in which to practice and train. You'll gather reading material and study successful techniques, and you'll be able to act as checks on each other, constructively criticizing each other's strengths and weaknesses. You will have the impetus to compete, at first within your own group, and later in local or regional events. Finally, you'll make the right contacts and acquaintances to help you find a mount with the conformation, temperament, and experience to perform well in the field of your choice.

Part 2 · Advanced Equitation

Harmonious horsemanship stands as the foremost goal in riding of any kind. As we continue to advance in horsemanship, we look deeper into what we do, how we do it, and most important, why. Important to this quest is the understanding of what is meant by impulsion, obedience, balance, good hands, collection and extension, and bending and flexing; what is required in proper performance of the gaits; and how the proper execution of schooling exercises or reining pattern maneuvers leads toward this harmony of communication, rather than being an end in itself.

Impulsion

Impulsion is the urge, the thrust, the inner drive to move forward. Some horses have it naturally; others must be trained to it (or perhaps retrained; poor or abusive training is usually the cause for lack of impulsion in a horse). Impulsion is vital; without it, a horse may be difficult or impossible to train at all. Lack of forward impulsion may be said to be the foremost cause of most vices under saddle. The correct use of the rider's legs activates the horse forward; the correct use of his hands controls and directs him.

Without forward impulsion, a horse cannot achieve balance. (Try to stand on your heels; now lean forward and stand on your toes. What a difference in balance!) When unbalanced, a horse is unable to obey commands. In the higher concepts of training, even backing must be obtained with forward impulsion.

The forward impulse can readily be seen in the extended gaits and is just as important in collection. Forward impulsion, when restrained, results in higher action. If the horse cannot move forward freely, he must transfer his movement upward. The piaffe, where the horse performs a highly stylized trot in place, is the result of restrained forward impulsion. Observe the difference between a horse performing the levade and a horse rearing. The extreme forward impulsion of the horse, restrained absolutely from moving either forward or back, has lifted his whole forehand off the ground through the action and suppleness of the hindquarters. The rearing horse, on the contrary, is lacking in forward impulsion. He is stretched out rather than collected. He is thrown onto his hind legs by the reverse action of the forehand—and therefore he is out of balance. He may go on over backward or come down to either side, out of control.

Impulsion, then, must be one of our goals, no matter whether we are interested in calf roping or cross-country riding, pole bending or polo, drill teams or dressage.

Balance

Balance implies impulsion combined with suppleness and flexibility. A horse and a rider are said to be balanced when their weight distribution allows them to perform with ease and efficiency. No matter how great the urge to go forward, it cannot be properly controlled if there is stiffness or lack of flexibility. Muscles must be trained and conditioned to suppleness in any athletic endeavor.

Why must balance be one of our goals? Because it is absolutely necessary for obedience. The balanced horse is ready to respond instantly to commands. He does not have to gather himself to perform an exercise—he is already prepared, already on the bit, already in hand: impulsion in harmony with collection.

Obedience

We've seen that obedience is impossible without balance and impulsion. But all the balance and impulsion in the world are completely useless if not impelled by willing obedience.

And here is the crux of the whole theory of horsemanship. Without *willing* obedience, your horse is not your partner—he is your antagonist. Or to put it another way, you are not your horse's friend and companion—you are his enemy.

How is willing obedience achieved? Through understanding. Proper training cannot be rushed or forced. Through understanding you avoid overreaching your horse. You build step on step, never asking for more than he is able to give. You build confidence, and love, and the desire to please— willing obedience.

Of course, results can be obtained by quick methods, as every trainer knows. (Owners, watching over the trainer's shoulder, often expect to see spectacular results—like taking a sputtering car to the repair shop and driving it away, an hour later, purring smoothly.) So can most anyone, at gunpoint, perform leaps and gyrations. But the effect is quite different from the ballet dancer who is beautifully responding to the music and rhythm of the dance. The effect of rushed training is rarely lasting, and it often produces more problems than it overcomes.

Willing obedience should stand as the beacon light to harmonious horsemanship.

Good Hands

Good hands are light, sensitive, and understanding. They are developed through a combination of experience and knowledge—neither one alone is sufficient.

The first prerequisite of good hands is a good seat. Your seat must be independent of the hands. You should be able to sit the saddle in balance throughout all gaits and any maneuvers whether your hands are on the reins, over your head, or behind your back. Only then will your hands be capable of becoming first steady and considerate and finally a highly sensitive means of communication. Your hands do not pull and give—that is, exert forward release and backward pressure. Sensitive communication comes through the fingers. By pressing, relaxing, or not acting, the fingers keep delicate contact with the horse's mouth, yielding as the horse yields, maintaining a fine line of constant communication.

Proper coordination of the aids is another prerequisite of good hands. Your legs and back push the horse up to the bit (keep him on the bit), where the hands keep contact with the horse's mouth. Overaction of the hands may be caused by too little use of the legs and back. The rider obtains little impulsion, balance, and precision, and his horse shows short, choppy gaits.

What happens when a rider does not have good hands? Heavy hands are used inconsiderately and inconsistently. If the seat is insecure, the hands are often used to help maintain balance. Their overaction or heavy action on the bit hurts and eventually numbs the horse's mouth. Seeking relief from the bit, he stargazes, bores, or habitually works behind the bit. Or he develops a hard mouth that is no longer capable of receiving or transmitting signals.

The opposite of heavy hands is no hands at all. Riding with a very long rein, the rider maintains no contact whatsoever with the horse's mouth except for an occasional jerk indicating direction or halt. This generally must be compensated for in overaction of the legs or spurs to prevent the horse from falling asleep. This problem appears more often in Western riding than in English, perhaps because it develops through misunderstanding and mis-use of the Western horseman's severe bit and loose rein—a combination which requires extremely light, sensitive hands.

Improving Your Hands

There is an exercise the rider can use to develop and increase the sensitivity of his hands. It benefits both horse and rider. We suggest riding in an enclosed area using the rail or wall for stability. As always, begin at a walk before performing the exercise at the faster gaits. You may be surprised to learn just how sensitive or insensitive your hands can be.

Ride through the many school figures—such as reverse, volte, serpen-tine—with only *one* rein.

When guiding with one rein (let's say the left), there are times when it will be an opening or direct rein (turning into a left reverse) and times when it will be a neck or bearing rein (turning a right corner). If you overreact with your left rein, your horse might tilt his head when he bends, he might execute the movement incorrectly, or he might not perform it at all.

You will discover that most horses have a "soft" (flexible) and "hard" (stiff) side. Horses that are too soft on one side will "rubber neck" (turn head and neck excessively). On the stiff side, the horse will not bend enough. Using your one rein very judiciously, and working in both directions, you will discover how to use the rein sensitively—whether to touch higher or lower on the neck, whether to "open" the rein slightly to get a better bend, or whether you need more or less contact.

Making downward transitions with the one rein to the halt will also increase sensitivity. This is a more advanced exercise.

Work with each hand (rein) separately in both directions, and practice to perfect your sensitivity and your horse's responses.

The Pulley Rein

The pulley-hand is an emergency rein effect that can effectively stop or circle a runaway. It can also bring a rearing horse under control.

The rider braces (pushes) with one hand (holding the rein) against the horse's neck, near the crest. The other hand uses the leading (opening) rein slightly higher than normal, overbending the horse's neck and muzzle in the desired direction. The horse will become slightly off balance, while the rider is well stabilized with seat and legs.

This is a powerful rein effect and should be performed gradually. Take care that the horse is not pulled so sharply with this increased leverage that he could fall. Circling the horse, slowing, and finally stopping is the desired result.

Intermediate/advanced and advanced riders should be able to use this technique. The horse with a vice requiring use of the pulley rein should go back to basic training.

Extension and Collection

Extension and collection have to do with the placement of a horse's center of gravity. A good riding horse must be able to propel himself (extension) as well as carry himself (collection). An example of extreme collection would be a horse performing the piaffe. An example of extreme extension would be a horse racing.

A collected horse is a shortened horse, one that is gathered together; he has his haunches well under him; his hindquarters are actually lowered while his forehand becomes more elevated. His center of gravity moves toward the hindquarters, and his stride will shorten and elevate. His back is arched, and his hind legs bend more in the joints. However, the horse cannot be pulled back into collection. He must be pushed up into it. To produce a thought picture of collection (exaggerated though it may be), imagine a horse being urged into a stone wall. He cannot proceed, and instead of taking forward strides his body must bunch up. His strides become more elevated the more he is urged forward. If his energy cannot move forward it must move up.

To obtain collection, the rider drives the horse forward (impulsion) while restraining the forehand from lengthening its stride or making it faster. The horse should have a relaxed jaw and be on a light rein, with increased bending of the joints in the hindquarters. The Western horseman says his horse is "up in the bridle." While extreme collection is beyond the scope or abilities of most horses and riders, a good riding horse should be capable of a fair degree of collection in order to perform capably. Collection must be obtained slowly, through consistent and considerate training. The horse's muscles must gradually become strengthened, as in the training of any athlete. Rushing the process will be self-destructive because the horse becomes sore or even injured. Before the training to collection is undertaken, your horse should go eagerly forward, have even rhythm at all paces, and be well balanced.

Extension, on the other hand, lengthens the horse rather than bunching him up. His center of gravity moves forward and his stride lengthens and has more reach. Energy is transferred forward rather than upward. In an extended walk, for example, the track of the hind foot is made several inches ahead of where the track is made at a normal walk (and several inches in front of the track made by the forefoot).

Extension, too, must be obtained through careful, scheduled training. A rider should thoroughly understand the theory of extension and collection before he tries to ask his horse for their execution. Otherwise he may be fooled by increase or decrease of tempo. Tempo involves the amount of ground traveled in a given time. Extension is not synonymous with speed. It is a lengthening of stride, as opposed to the heightened stride of collection.

Ride a well-trained horse at a normal trot. Close your eyes and listen to the rhythm (even regularity of stride) of his hoofbeats. Collect your horse and you cover much less ground though the rhythm of his hoofbeats remains the same. With a smooth transition you extend the trot until the horse is covering much more ground with each stride—the rhythm of his hoofbeats is still the same.

Dressage tests require horse and rider to perform the walk, trot, and canter with various degrees of collection and extension and with a definite cadence. A cadenced horse moves with a steady, noticeable beat which is rhythmical and consistent.

Bending and Flexing

Bending and flexing are directly related to suppleness. They are an inherent ingredient of collection. It is impossible to collect a horse without proper flexion.

A horse flexes at the jaw and at the poll. That is, he yields to the pressure of the rein by relaxing his jaw and by flexing vertically and/or laterally at the poll. As the leg aids impel the horse, he moves up into the bit, accepting it through proper flexion. When flexion is incorrectly asked or trained, it will produce exactly the wrong effect, inducing the horse to go behind the bit.

Bending acts through the body. It is a supple horse's response to the aids in order to maintain a state of balance and ready communication. A lateral bend curves the horse evenly from poll to tail. It may be very slight or considerable, depending on the maneuver or degree of turn. If the horse is asked to bend before he is physically able to do so, the results will be

Vertical flexion, demonstrated by Fortte, an 8-year-old Holsteiner gelding, in a second-level dressage test, Teri Hallman up. For examples of lateral bending, see photos on p. 103. (Photo by Liz Cline, courtesy of Teri Hallman)

incomplete—the head and neck will turn without completing the action through the spinal column.

The advanced rider works to supple his horse evenly on both sides. But, as with anything else, it can be overdone; overbending and overflexing are pitfalls to watch for in training.

English or Western?

The following sections on Advanced Equitation have been divided into English and Western on the basis of common usage. However, the advanced rider may benefit from the study of both styles of riding, even though he prefers to specialize in one or the other. By reading both sections you may discover why your reining horse would benefit from a little practice with English school figures, or why your dressage horse would renew enthusiasm and impulsion with some stock work or trail rides.

Part 3 · Advanced English Equitation

The Gaits

In earlier lessons we were concerned mainly with properly sitting the gait as it was offered by our horse and properly managing our mount to tell him which gait we wanted and where we wanted to go. Now we are going beyond our beginning goals into more sensitive riding of these gaits. *How* do we want our horse to walk, trot, or canter? How can we best communicate with him to execute the gait to the best of his ability?

The Walk

The AHSA *Rule Book* recognizes the working walk, collected walk, medium walk, extended walk, and free walk. Throughout any variation of the gait, the horse should take cadenced, rhythmic steps, moving forward in a straight line. A normal walk has an approximate speed of four miles per hour.

The walk should be calm and energetic—brisk—at any tempo. Laziness is unacceptable even when the walk is used for relaxation, resting horse and rider. The horse should lift his feet, move them forward in full stride, and set them down flat.

Collection at the walk should be one of the later lessons in training because it is more difficult to achieve properly—without loss of impulsion—than collection at the trot.

The Trot

As with the walk, the advanced rider is concerned with obtaining the best possible performance from his horse at a trot. The trot—whether collected, working, medium, or extended—must be regular and rhythmic, with the diagonal feet striking the ground at exactly the same instant and with the same length of stride. If either fore or hind hoof should strike the ground a bit ahead of the other—so that two beats or even a slurred beat can be heard—the trot is incorrect and needs improvement.

A normal trot has a speed of six to eight miles per hour. Here again, while the extended trot is somewhat faster and the collected trot slower, the speed is not taken up by an increase or decrease of pace but rather by a lengthening or shortening of the stride.

The trot is the most important gait in training the horse. The collected trot improves balance and strengthens the hindquarters. The extended trot improves and controls impulsion. (It should not be used on hard surfaces since it may be injurious to the horse's legs.)

The Canter

Again, rhythm is one of the first concerns of the advanced rider in any variation of the gait—collected, working, medium, or extended. Remember that the canter is a three-beat gait—the gallop has four beats. To hear four beats during the canter means that it is being incorrectly executed. When the diagonal pair of legs (depending on the lead) strikes the ground, only one beat should be heard.

The speed of the normal canter is nine to twelve miles per hour. Extension is increased through length of stride, not hurried steps. In a well-executed collected canter, the horse appears to be moving effortlessly, almost floating across the ground. In a disunited canter, the horse leads with one leg in front but has a different lead behind. A disunited canter usually feels very rough to the rider, and the horse can fall easily because of his lack of balance.

Simple and Flying Lead Changes

The advanced rider works for a smooth and accurate change of lead (or change of leg). When working on a figure-eight, he takes the correct lead on one circle, then takes several trotting or well-defined walking steps at the juncture of the eight before asking for the other lead. This is the simple change of lead.

In the flying change, the horse changes leads at the moment of suspension during the canter. This is done smoothly, without altering speed, direction, or tempo on the part of the horse and without excessive throwing of the rider's weight or overemphasizing the aids on the part of the rider.

Proper execution of the flying change requires a high degree of training for both horse and rider. Before starting this exercise, the horse must be able to strike off on either leg on a straight line. Insufficient training results in the horse throwing his quarters in when going into the canter. Faults in head carriage and rhythm will also be apparent. When the flying change is attempted before the horse is fully balanced and has attained sufficient strength and stability, or before the rider has refined his aids properly, the result may be a disunited canter.

The Counter-Canter (False Canter)

In the counter-canter, the horse takes the wrong lead; that is, tracking to the left, he is on a right lead. Do not confuse this with the disunited canter. The counter-canter is performed intentionally and is an excellent exercise for developing suppleness, balance, and obedience. It is necessary preparatory work for the flying change. It should be as smooth and elastic as the canter. The horse's body is evenly arched *away* from the direction of movement— that is, his body is flexed toward the lead he has taken, as in the correct canter. His conformation will not allow him to be bent to the line of the circle. The horse is still working on a single track, that is, his hind legs track his forelegs. (Counter-canter to the left: horse takes right lead, flexes to the right, moves to the left.) Do not attempt to make sharp curves and do not try to keep the counter-canter up for any more than short periods, especially at first, since it is very tiring for the horse.

The Halt and Half-Halt

Use of the halt and half-halt provides a valuable exercise in collection. In the halt, the horse is directed to stop through your use of a deep seat, active legs, and fixed hands. Your legs push the horse forward, ready to maintain impulsion. Your hands remain fixed and thus restrain forward movement. They do not pull backward. When asked to stop in this way—that is, pushed forward but restrained from moving forward—the horse will stop with his hindquarters well under him and his head and neck flexed. He is supple on all four legs, balanced, and perfectly straight. The halt should be complete—that is, the horse stands still and square—but he remains on the bit, ready to move off immediately into any maneuver.

The half-halt is obtained by using the aids to prepare for a full halt, but the restraint of the hands is eased so that forward momentum is not lost. The action is almost imperceptible to an onlooker. The hindquarters come under the body in a position that will make the horse balanced and ready to perform. Through this action the horse may be brought down to a slower gait, he may be prepared for a transition in maneuvers, or he may simply be called to attention—that is, his position and balance improved without slackening speed. The half-halt may be said to be a rebalancing of the horse, preparing him for any movement.

The Rein-Back or Backing

When the horse backs, he raises and moves his legs in diagonal pairs—a movement of two-time as at the trot. His steps should be clean, with his balance mostly on his hindquarters. He should back in a straight line.

The rein-back is, actually, a reinforced halt. Equal leg pressure and applied weight aids push the horse forward into a fixed hand, and the horse halts. If pressure continues, he backs. Careful use of the aids, including yielding and reapplying the rein at each step, produces a smooth and cadenced movement. Sit deep in the saddle and look forward and up. Do not lean forward as the horse will be permitted to escape the driving aids of legs and seat. Your legs remain ready to keep the horse straight.

Move forward immediately after the rein-back to maintain the forward impulsion and keep the horse alert with his weight properly distributed so as to be ready to perform his next maneuver.

As in all advanced work, the rein-back should not be attempted until the horse is prepared, through physical conditioning and proper training, to perform it correctly. Rushing the training creates problems that are difficult to correct.

Transitions in Gait

The execution of smooth, rhythmical transitions in gait is the mark of a well-trained horse and self-disciplined rider. Transitions are changes from one gait to another (walk to canter, canter to trot, and so on) or from one phase of a gait to another (such as from a collected trot to an extended trot). They may also refer to a change of direction, such as from posting on the left diagonal to the right, or from the right lead in a canter to the left.

To execute transitions smoothly, rhythmically (without loss of impulsion), and at the exact geographical point where desired is difficult. You must use your aids skillfully and teach your horse to respond as though at one with your thoughts.

School Figures

The purpose of schooling movements is threefold. First, to develop the horse physically. The execution of school figures improves his suppleness, flexibility, and balance. It keeps him physically fit, limber, and in condition. In other words, it improves his athletic abilities.

Second, to develop the horse mentally—to encourage and maintain an attitude of alert interest and, therefore, willingness to move forward (impulsion). Obviously, then, overdoing school figures, or rushing them, is tiring and therefore defeats their purpose. Repetition of exercises, though necessary for both horse and rider, can become boring if always performed in the same way. School figures offer a variety of exercises that use the same components.

And third, to develop sensitivity, responsiveness, and obedience. Immediate and perfect response to the aids is one of the advanced rider's goals. Schooling maneuvers help the rider to refine and coordinate his aids—legs, back, hands—to such a degree that harmonious communication with his horse is continuous.

School figures are beneficial to hunters, jumpers, dressage horses, polo ponies, cowhorses, pleasure horses, or any other horse, because they help him to achieve the impulsion, balance, and obedience necessary for outstanding performance in any field.

School movements are exercises that can best be performed in a ring,

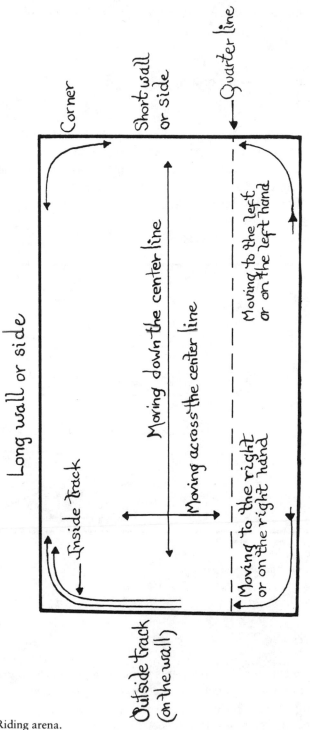

Fig. 19   Riding arena.

arena, or "school." Generally the area is a rectangle and the following terms apply.

Change of Hand or Change of Rein

The change of hand is a change in direction, usually performed through the center of the ring. When the change of hand is performed on the diagonal, ride the short side of the ring, turn the corner, and ride for one or two horse lengths before crossing the arena. Return to the opposite wall one or two horse lengths from the corner. If you change hands at a trot, change diagonals as you pass through the center. If in a canter, change leads through the center.

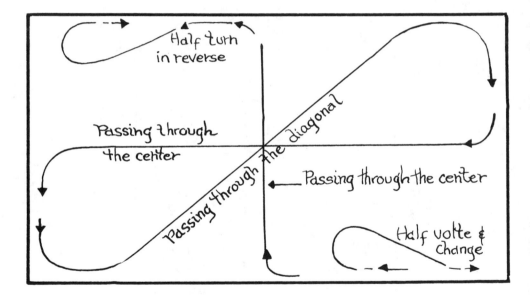

Fig. 20   Change of hand or change of rein

Circular Figures and Work on One Track

Any movement where the horse bends his spine from poll to tail and learns to balance himself on the turns helps to develop lateral flexion. The rider uses his aids—specifically his back, weight, and legs—to help his horse execute the movements correctly. Use the direct rein for direction, weight on the inside stirrup, and pressure with the outside leg behind the girth. (Inside here refers to the inside of the curve of the horse's spine—that is, the horse bends around the inside leg.) The horse's hind legs must follow directly in the same track as the forelegs. The rider's shoulders should be square to the horse's shoulders, not twisting to one side or the other.

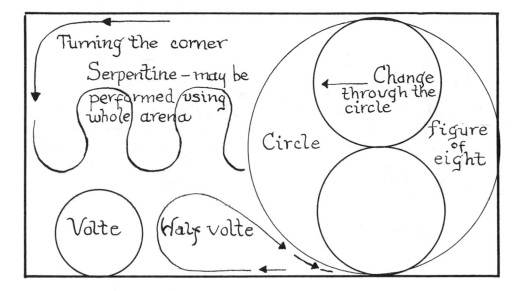

Fig. 21   Circular figures.

Volte. The volte is a small circle (twenty feet in diameter, or six meters). The figure should be exactly round and tangent to the track. The rider returns to the rail at the same point he left it. As in all the circular figures, the horse must bend evenly along the curve of the figure, performing willingly and fluidly on the rider's aids without loss of cadence.

Half-volte. The half-volte is performed at the beginning exactly as the volte. Halfway through the figure the rider returns with a straight, oblique movement back to the track (in the opposite direction). The half-volte in reverse describes the same figure in the opposite direction.

Turning the corners. The corners of the ring should be ridden exactly on the track of a quarter-volte. Correctly, the horse bends to the inside and his hind legs must track his forelegs.

Circle. The circle is the foundation for all turn exercises. It is valuable in promoting collection and balance. In dressage rules, a diameter of sixty-six feet is usual (one-half of the arena). The circle should be ridden in as smooth and cadenced a manner as the volte. You will find it more difficult to describe a perfectly round circle than the smaller volte, but it is easier for the inexperienced horse since the curve is more gradual.

Figure-eight (figure of eight). The figure-eight should be ridden as two opposite circles with X as the tangent. At the center of the eight (X), the horse's body is exactly straight for one horse's length before passing from one circle to the other. Diagonals or leads are changed at that point. A half figure-eight (see Figure 21) is used to change hands within a circle.

Serpentine. The serpentine should be ridden as a succession of equal curves bending to the left and right, separated by a few straight strides between loops. The series of curves should be performed by moving away from the center of a short side of the ring and finished by moving to the opposite short side. It is important to maintain rhythm, keep the correct bend, and execute prompt transitions while describing the curves accurately. A dressage-movement serpentine consists of three half-circles using the entire arena. As you cross the center line, straighten your horse for a stride and proceed with the appropriate bend in the opposite direction.

The Pivots or Turns

The pivots or turns may be considered circular figures, but they are valuable as an exercise to help teach the lateral movements. Whether or not the horse and rider go on with lateral work, they should be able to perform a turn on the forehand or on the haunches. One place where this training is helpful to the pleasure horse is in opening and closing gates.

Pivot around the forehand (turn on the forehand). Turns on the forehand may be 90, 180, or 360 degrees. Preparatory to learning the lateral movements, the horse must learn to yield readily to the leg—that is, move away from leg pressure. This means that he must move his hindquarters sideways as directed by the rider's legs. The exercise is performed from a half-halt.

To turn on the forehand, the horse moves his hindquarters around his forelegs. The inner foreleg acts as a pivot. This does not mean that the pivot leg is rooted to the ground, however. In performing the turn correctly, the horse takes even, regular steps in the sequence of the walk. The pivot leg steps in place and the other foreleg makes a small circle around it. The inside hind leg passes in front of the outside leg as it would in a normal walk—if the inside leg were to move behind the outside leg, the effect would be as though the horse were backing up. This, of course, would be incorrect. As always, forward impulsion is the key word.

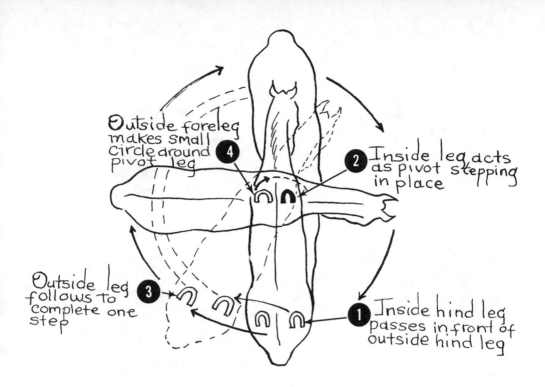

Fig. 22   Pivot around the forehand (haunches to the left).

Begin with a half-halt parallel to the wall or any solid barrier. To pivot to the left around the forehand, your right leg acts behind the girth both to arch the horse slightly and ask him for a step to the left with his hindquarters. Your left leg acts on the girth to keep the horse from backing. As he takes the step, relax the aids slightly and reapply them to ask for another step. The left rein remains ready to keep the shoulders from moving to the left, and the left leg remains ready to prevent him from backing up.

In elementary pivots, the horse's head is turned slightly to the outside (or away from the direction he is moving). In this way it is generally easier to keep the horse from moving sideways or backward. When the horse understands the exercise, he may be bent toward the direction he is moving.

As with any phase of training, do not hurry or confuse your horse. If this is a new exercise for him, it will be tiring. One or two steps will be enough. Praise him well when he responds correctly and go on to something else. Too much of one exercise can sour a horse enough to cause resistance.

Pivot around the haunches (turn on the haunches). This exercise, in which the forehand circles around the haunches, is performed at a walk, and prepared for by a half-halt. Again, it is important for the horse to step in the regular rhythm of the walk, stepping in place with the inside hind leg, rather

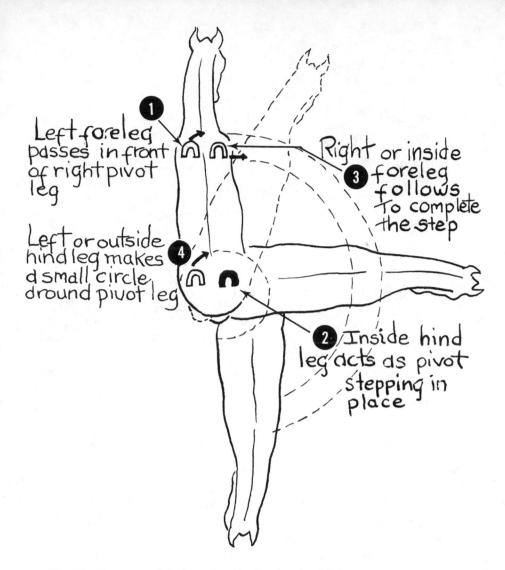

Left foreleg passes in front of right pivot leg

Left or outside hind leg makes a small circle around pivot leg

Right or inside foreleg follows to complete the step

Inside hind leg acts as pivot stepping in place

Fig. 23   Pivot around the haunches (forehand to the right).

than leaving it on the ground. It is better for the hind legs to describe a small circle than for them to pivot and thereby lose the rhythm of the walk.

In turning on the haunches to the right, the horse is flexed to the right. The right rein indicates the turn and the left rein supports it lightly. The left leg behind the girth asks for the turn around the inside leg, which remains on the girth. Both legs must be used to prevent the horse from stepping backward. Forward impulsion is maintained as evidenced by the outside foreleg crossing in front of the inside foreleg.

Lateral Movements or Work on Two Tracks

The lateral movements are two-track exercises in which the hind legs do not follow in the track of the forelegs but make a separate track of their own. The forehand is always slightly in advance of the hindquarters. Lateral work supples the horse, improving his balance and increasing the engagement of the hindquarters, as well as making him more obedient to his rider.

The lateral movements are difficult and tiring for the horse. They should not be attempted until the horse is proficient in the circular and one-track figures, nor should they be practiced for more than a short time. Training should proceed slowly, step by step. One correct movement is worth more than twenty poor ones.

Leg yielding is the foundation of all other two-track figures. In this exercise the horse travels at an angle in relation to his forward movement. His inside fore and hind legs cross in front of his outside lateral pair of legs. The horse's body is straight.

Leg yielding is intended as a suppling exercise.

Shoulder-in. This is perhaps the most important two-track exercise. The horse's forehand comes in from the track about thirty degrees (no more than forty-five degrees), and the forehand and hindquarters describe three separate parallel tracks—inside fore; right fore and left hind; and right hind (shoulder-in on the left track). The horse's head (and the entire curve of the spine) is bent away from the direction of movement. The inside legs step over and in front of the outside legs. The shoulder-in is distinguished from leg yielding in that the horse's spine is curved away from the direction of movement; in leg yielding the horse's spine remains straight.

The purpose of the exercise is to increase engagement of the hindquarters (including bending the three joints of the hind legs), encourage freer movement of the shoulders, improve light contact with the bit, increase suppleness and obedience, and improve the gaits.

Travers or haunches-in. In this exercise the forehand remains on the track, the hindquarters are displaced to the inside about thirty degrees, and the horse is bent toward the direction of the movement. The purpose is to improve suppleness and engagement of the hindquarters, but the exercise is not generally as much used by dressage riders as the shoulder-in and renvers.

Renvers or haunches-out. In this exercise the hindquarters remain on the track and the forehand moves in about thirty degrees (not more than forty-five degrees) to describe a separate track, as in the shoulder-in. However, the horse is bent toward the direction of movement instead of away

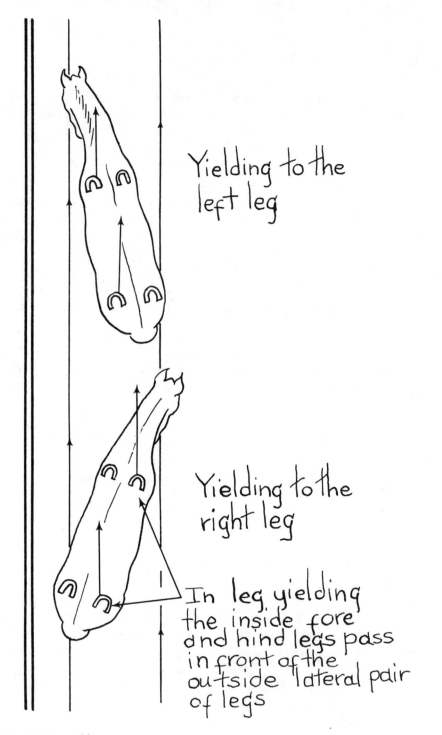

Yielding to the left leg

Yielding to the right leg

In leg yielding the inside fore and hind legs pass in front of the outside lateral pair of legs

Fig. 24   Leg yielding.

from it. Again, the purpose of the exercise is to increase obedience, suppleness, and the engagement of the hindquarters.

Half-pass. In this two-track movement the horse moves in a diagonal
line while his body remains parallel to the wall. The outside legs cross in front
of the inside legs, and the horse's body is bent *slightly* in the direction he is
going. As in all these exercises, the rhythm of the steps should remain even
and regular, and the tempo of the gait should remain steady and uninterrupted. The half-pass clearly demonstrates the combination of forward and
sideways movements that make up the two-track exercises.

Side step (full travers or full pass). In this exercise the horse moves
sideways, his outside legs stepping over and crossing in front of his inside
legs. A pleasure horse should know how to side step because it is necessary in
opening and closing gates and is helpful in lining up horses evenly and easily
in shows.

This exercise again begins from a half-halt. Give the aids for the walk,
but as the horse lifts his feet to move forward, use the right rein (if stepping to
the right) to show direction of movement, and the left rein to prevent
forward movement. The left leg is used behind the girth to move the hindquarters to the right. The right leg, on the girth, keeps the horse from
stepping back. Properly executed, the horse is bent slightly around your right
leg, with his head turned slightly toward the direction of movement.

Hunting, Polo, and Combined Training Events

Hunting

Probably more has been written in praise of hunting than of any other
equestrian sport. Although more exclusive and less available to the riding
public than other phases of riding activity, hunting offers a combination of
pleasure and challenge to those who can participate in it that is hard to match
elsewhere.

Hunting as a sport is part of our English heritage. It is steeped in
tradition, and the rules of dress, manners, and speech are defined down to the
finest hair.

A hunter should be well mannered, sure-footed, and love to jump. And
any rider, before "riding to the hounds" as a guest, should be thoroughly
familiar with the hunting rules and be able to ride and direct his mount at all
times, especially during the exciting heat of the chase.

Polo

The "sport of princes" used to be exclusive, expensive, and generally only a spectator sport as far as the average rider was concerned. Today, however, polo is becoming a popular sport, especially in the West. Groups of enthusiasts may organize a club and get together for a Sunday or holiday afternoon of polo. Information concerning the game may be obtained from the United States Polo Association.

The polo mount must have plenty of heart, intelligence, and that something akin to cow sense that makes him as avid to follow the polo ball as his rider. He should be quiet and responsive with a good mouth, yet not timid in horse-to-horse contact or with the mallet swinging past his head. In this sport the horses are trained to respond primarily to the reins since their riders are all over the saddle in their strenuous efforts to make a difficult shot.

Polo is a team sport combining danger and excitement with a high degree of training and cooperation for both horse and rider.

Combined Training Events

A combined training event includes two or three tests involving dressage, endurance, and jumping. Categories of combined training events include three-day events, two-day events, horse trials, and combined tests.

One of the ultimate tests of horse and rider is the Three-Day Event. It is a spectacular event, and its popularity is growing at horse shows throughout Europe, Australia, and the United States. This equestrian supercontest includes a dressage test, competition in the open (including speed, endurance, and steeplechase contests), and show jumping. Horses receiving combined training for the Three-Day Event become proficient in dressage, jumping, and cross-country traveling.

Equestrian events were first included in the Olympic Games in 1912 at Stockholm. Eleven nations participated. Today these events have three phases: the Three-Day Event, the Prix des Nations show jumping competition, and the Grand Prix de Dressage. Each event is open to both individual and team competitors.

The dressage test is held on the first day of the Three-Day Event. Although not as complex as the Grand Prix, it tests a horse's obedience and responsiveness as well as the rider's skill.

On the second day are the endurance, speed, cross-country, and steeplechase trials. The total course covers about twenty miles. The steeplechase course covers about two and one-quarter miles; it is judged mainly on time and general performance. (The steeplechase originated when country gentlemen raced each other across the fields of England, often using church steeples as finish lines or rallying points.) The cross-country route (about four and one-half miles) is more difficult, testing both horse and rider over open terrain. The competition-in-the-open may be called the practical use of dressage principles.

Third is the moderate stadium jumping event that proves the mettle, boldness, courage, and stamina of both horse and rider. The twelve obstacles are imposing, laid out over an irregular course over one-half mile long, and the contestants are timed.

Naturally, the Three-Day Event horse and rider are not specialists in any one event, and in scoring, this is taken into consideration. They are, however, outstanding all-around athletes.

The televising of the Olympic Games has popularized the equestrian sports, particularly the dressage competitions. Interest has also been promoted through the widely acclaimed performances of the Spanish Riding School as well as through dressage competition in many horse shows. The conception that dressage means only the "haute école" movements (passage, piaffe, and above-the-ground movements) is rapidly disappearing.

Part 4 · Advanced Western Equitation

The Western horse is a utility animal as well as a pleasure and sporting animal. If the Western horse can rein well and if he has cow sense, he can be easily trained for specialized work such as cutting, calf roping, steer roping, or gymkhana events, as well as for all-round ranch work and pleasure riding on the trail. Therefore, basic training for the Western horse emphasizes reining and overall handling ability.

The Gaits

The advanced Western rider has passed the stage where he must concentrate on his own performance. He is concerned now mainly with the performance of his horse. The proper development of the gaits not only is important in the show or contest ring, but has practical application for ranch work.

A horse that remains well balanced and conserves his energy throughout the various gaits will do his best work during the day and come in less tired and in better condition at night than the horse whose training is haphazard. In shows, equitation classes emphasize performance of the rider, and pleasure classes emphasize performance of the horse. A harmonious relationship must be maintained between horse and rider to perform well in any show class or to work efficiently on the range.

The Walk

The Western horse should walk briskly, rhythmically, and in a free-moving manner. This is important in the show ring and stems from the practical necessity of covering the ground quickly and in a relaxed manner on the trail and in range work.

As with the English gaits, a good Western walk must be trained into a horse. Usually the inexperienced rider considers the walk easy and neglects this gait, perhaps to concentrate instead on the leads of the lope. Lazy riding permits an uncadenced walk with short, choppy strides and hind toes trailing in the dirt.

In the walk, regular, rhythmic steps are of basic importance. The horse must be straight and well impulsed. His hind legs should work well under him with good length of stride. The track of the hind legs should overreach the track of the forelegs.

The Jog (Jog Trot) and Trot

The jog should be square, slow, cadenced, smooth, free, and easy. The horse should be alert and well balanced, giving the impression of being a pleasure to ride. The development of a well-executed, ground-covering jog that is smooth and relaxing to both horse and rider is as necessary for efficient ranch work as it is for a winning performance in the show ring or comfort on the trail.

Smoothness is of paramount importance in the Western jog. It is perhaps the main point looked for by the Western pleasure judge. Smoothness is the result of willing forward movement with good length of stride, with the hind legs working well under the horse, and with regular, rhythmical steps in which the diagonal pairs of legs strike the ground solidly and simultaneously. Check for smoothness by asking someone to take videotapes of you as you ride. The result of studying those tapes is often revealing.

The Lope

The Western lope—the pleasurable "rockin' horse" gait—should be smooth, slow, easy, and lightly collected with the hind legs working well under the horse. Collection in the Western lope is used to maintain the purity of the three-beat gait, to maintain alert readiness for change of gait, speed, direction, or maneuver, and to keep the hindquarters properly engaged. Height of action is not emphasized, and overaction is a fault.

In the Western lope it is important to maintain a straight, true stride. The horse should not be traveling on two tracks. Under working conditions, the horse should be prepared to accelerate suddenly and rapidly to catch a calf or turn back a cow or steer.

Incidentally, it bears repeating here that the advanced rider uses his aids subtly. There is a tendency for Western riders to "throw" their horses into the leads. Train your horse to take his leads easily and willingly, and ride enough yourself to become aware of the feel of the leads. You should not have to look down obviously at the horse's shoulder to check which lead he has taken. In many Western classes the judge sees a large group of riders bowing their heads as if in prayer whenever he asks for a lope.

Lead Changes

Reining patterns, Western riding events, and working conditions require lead changes. These should be performed smoothly, easily, and without obvious cues (see "Simple and Flying Lead Changes"). As with English lead changes, emphasis should be on timing, rhythm, and step-by-step progression rather than on throwing your weight and pushing your horse into spurts of speed to achieve the desired lead.

Working in circles and figure-eights promotes natural selection of the correct lead, and therefore helps you and your mount to coordinate the aids. Vary the eights and circles, however, to keep your horse from anticipating lead changes. When working an inexperienced horse in circles and figure-eights, be sure that your riding arena or area is level and that your figures are large. A horse inexperienced in balancing a rider can easily stumble on rough inclined ground or when the figures are too small.

Many Western horsemen believe that too much emphasis has been placed on leads, especially in shows. Under working conditions a horse should change leads naturally, both to maintain his natural balance and ease and to place himself in the most advantageous position. Overemphasis on taking leads only on signal interferes with this natural selection.

The Stop

Essentially, the normal Western stop—in advanced equitation—may be asked for in the same way as the English halt. By bracing your back and pressing your horse forward with your legs into a fixed hand, you obtain a square, well-balanced stop. Your hand maintains a lighter contact with the horse's mouth than in English equitation. The Western horse is also asked to do a smooth, square, sliding stop—that is, "put his number eleven down" or "stick his tail in the ground and die right there." Calf-roping and reining patterns require sliding stops. You will often see a sliding stop obtained through a heavy hand and great shift of weight, forcing the horse to throw up his head and open his mouth. Overcuing is unnecessary when the horse is properly trained—a sliding stop may be obtained even on a light rein.

When properly executing a sliding stop, the horse gets his hindquarters under him, sliding his hind feet. He stops straight and square without bouncing on his front legs. Begin the training of the stop from a walk and work up through jog and lope to the gallop. Sit well down in the saddle and close both legs strongly. You may also lift the reins slightly to signal the stop in the stride before the actual stop is asked.

With good basic work of stopping from the slower gaits, the sliding stop will develop without a great shift of weight. You should remain in a balanced position in the saddle. When you sit back on the cantle or lean back, you are more likely to burn your horse's fetlocks as the added weight makes them slide on the ground. Skinning or bruising your horse's legs will quickly undo all the work you have done in training him for the sliding stop. Therefore, use skid boots made expressly for the purpose of protecting the horse's fetlocks, or practice the stop only on soft, stone-free footing. The protection of skid boots is well worth their use, and it is wise to use them whenever training for or performing the sliding stop.

Backing

As in the forward gaits, straightness and regularity of steps are important. Keep light contact with your horse's mouth (that is, you want him to work up into the bit) and strive to put his hocks well under him. An unprepared, uncollected horse, one not on the bit, cannot work his hindquarters in a smooth, balanced way.

A good sliding stop: The horse's head is down and the rider remains upright in the saddle. (Photo by June Fallaw)

Well-trained horses are usually first taught to back from the ground. In some cases, preliminary lessons in backing may be effectively taught to a foal. If the horse first learns to back without a rider, he knows the word commands and is psychologically prepared for the movement by the time he must perform it with a rider. Because most horses dislike to back, it is best to work slowly and make backing lessons brief. Avoid overdoing the back and thereby prevent your horse from souring to it. When training the horse to back, select level terrain with good footing.

As in the English rein-back, proper use of the aids (the yielded and reapplied fixed hand, combined with equal leg pressure at each step) will produce a smooth, cadenced back. Using this method (as opposed to the commonly seen misuse of aids in which the rider shoves his legs forward, leans back, and pulls or jerks on the reins) keeps your horse's nose down, his neck well flexed, and his mouth closed. He remains on the bit instead of fighting it.

Until specialization is required, speed in backing is not as important for the advanced rider as cadence, balance, straightness, and smoothness. Roping horses learn to back at speed without their rider.

Reining Pattern Work

Pivots

A well-executed pivot is a joy to watch. It demonstrates the agility and obedience of the Western reining horse. The Western pivot is an entirely different maneuver from the English pivot on the haunches or on the forehand. It is a quarter turn (ninety degrees) from a standing position, made either to the right or left, with the horse rocking back on his haunches. In the ninety-degree pivots the hind feet stay in position while the front feet leave the ground and do not touch it again until the pivot is complete.

The pivot should be a light, fluid movement obtained with a light rein and with the horse's weight on his hindquarters. The rider should not have to heave his horse around, using a heavy hand and throwing his weight. As with other maneuvers, step-by-step, take-your-time progress is the only way to achieve lasting results in training. Rushing, gimmicks, and overdoing accomplish little more than confusing, tiring, and eventually souring your horse.

Your horse's position at the beginning of the pivot is important. He should be settled with his hind feet together and well under him (as in a half-halt, ready and alert for the next signal). Sit straight and balanced in the saddle. For a pivot to the right, rein lightly to the right; keep your hand low or lift just slightly to indicate direction and to prevent your horse from moving forward. Keep your left leg on the girth to indicate the movement and your right leg behind the girth to hold the haunches placed. When training, be satisfied with a slight turn and lift of the forehand—the ninety-degree pivot comes with practice.

Troubles to watch for:

- The horse walking around the pivot instead of carrying his weight back on his haunches and swinging his forehand.
- The horse throwing his head, pointing his nose away from the direction in which he is pivoting, yawing at the bit, or otherwise indicating that the rider has too heavy a hand. This may indicate not only that

you are using your hand too heavily or incorrectly, but also that the horse is not yet physically or mentally developed and ready for the maneuver.

- The horse wringing his tail, due to too much spurring, overdoing, or otherwise trying to rush training.

Spins

A spin is a 360-degree turn on the hindquarters (or four pivots in fluid succession). The spin is occasionally asked for in reining contests. Usually the horse must gallop, go into a sliding stop, spin, and come out of the spin into a gallop on the opposite lead. The horse should spin to the left if he is expected to come out of the spin on the left lead.

The Rollback

A horse performs a rollback when he is going east at a fast lope, slides to a stop, rolls over his hocks (180 degrees) to go west, and comes down in his own tracks at a fast lope on the opposite lead. Turning a small circle is not a rollback. Before attempting a rollback, your horse should have a light, well-developed mouth, a good square stop, and willing response to the aids for the leads.

The horse must complete his stop before beginning the rollback. When the stop is completed, the rollback is asked while the horse is still up in the bridle (still collected from the stop), alert, and ready for the next move. As with the pivots, avoid the heavy, upward-hauling rein hand (such poor horsemanship can cause rearing), overspurring, throwing your weight, and rushing training.

Most working horses enjoy this fast work. But a horse can be easily soured by overdoing it, or he may anticipate your commands. Instead of running through a whole reining pattern several times, vary the work by performing the maneuvers in varied sequence, working in different parts of the arena, or switching to English tack for some English schooling or jumping. Make training and practice sessions enjoyable for your horse by praising him generously and finishing on a positive note. (Always stop when you are ahead.) Most important, keep up interest by leaving intensive training behind occasionally for a trail ride or range work.

Turns on the Haunches and Forehand

The Western reining horse should also be capable of performing a pivot around the forehand, a pivot around the haunches, and the sidestep as described under English equitation, even though these may not be asked for in the reining patterns.

Contest Work

Gymkhana Events

Barrel racing. This is a race against time around three barrels arranged in a triangular pattern. The barrel horse must have speed, be good on his leads, have a responsive mouth, rein well, and be able to make small turns at speed.

Barrel racing.

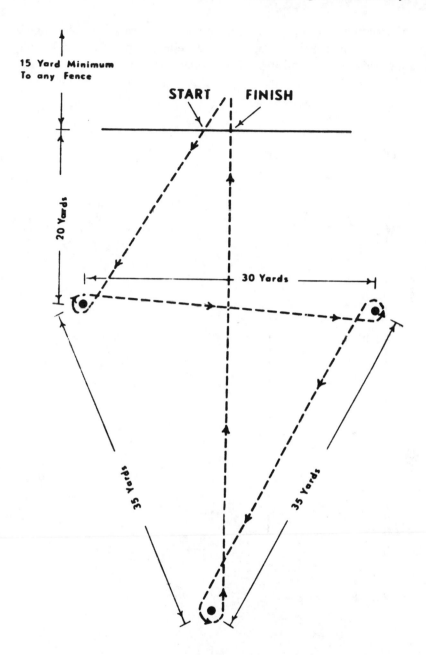

Fig. 25   A barrel-racing pattern. The pattern may also be run in the opposite direction. From Intermountain Regional Publication 3, "Western Horses," by John A. Gorman and John Ryff (an agricultural extension publication).

Pole bending. In this timed race the horse must weave between a line of poles without touching them. Again, speed, reining proficiency, and ability to change leads are prerequisites for the pole-bending horse.

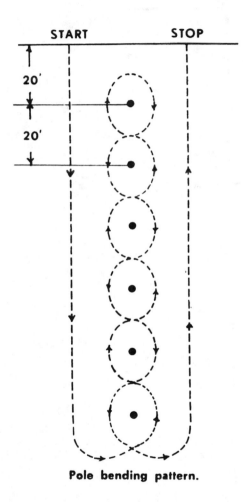

Pole bending pattern.

Fig. 26 A pole-bending pattern. The pattern may be run in either direction. From Intermountain Regional Publication 3, "Western Horses," by John A. Gorman and John Ryff (an agricultural extension publication).

Keyhole racing. A keyhole pattern is laid out on the ground for this timed event. The horse must race into the keyhole, turn around without touching the boundaries, and return to the starting line. To perform well in this race, a horse should have speed and a good sliding stop, be able to rollback or pivot, and respond quickly and accurately to the aids.

Besides the qualifications mentioned above, other gymkhana events may require horses to drag ropes and objects, to be unafraid of flapping clothing or dangling objects, to lead well, or to allow a second rider behind the saddle. Overall, the gymkhana horse should be speedy, smooth, responsive to rein and leg, and good on his leads.

Stock Work

Everyday stock work acts as a basic training course for contest horses. A year or more of experience in ordinary stock work gives a horse the cow sense he needs to perform well in cutting or roping. In addition, it gives his trainer the opportunity to watch the horse in action and determine where his natural ability lies.

Roping Events

Roping horses must have speed, agility, rating ability, a good sliding stop, and cow sense. They should rein well and be accustomed to ropes. In addition, they should stand quietly and alertly when in the box before the calf or steer is let out.

Calf roping. The calf-roping horse should stand quietly in the box until cued to follow the calf. He then speeds out to the calf (scoring) and follows the calf at the proper distance to put his rider in the best position for roping (rating). When signaled, the horse does a fast sliding stop and then works the

Calf roping. (Photo courtesy of Cheyenne Frontier Days)

rope by facing the calf and backing to keep the rope taut but not to drag the calf. There's a lot of training involved here, and it is a thrill to watch a good roping horse perform.

In *team roping* the header ropes the steer and turns him at right angles to the direction in which he was traveling, thereby setting the steer in proper position for the heeler to rope one or both hind feet. Both horses then face the steer, stretching him between them just enough to hold him immobile. Precision, training, and ability combine to make an impressive performance.

Cutting Contests

The cutting horse quietly enters a herd of cows, cuts out one the rider designates, moves her away from the herd, and then prevents her from returning to it by facing her and staying between her and the herd. The cutting horse should be experienced in stock work, have cow sense, and enjoy moving cattle around. He should possess stamina, responsiveness, conformation, intelligence, and perhaps even some playfulness. His most important qualification is agility (far more important than speed). He should be able to turn rapidly, pivoting on his hindquarters and working with his

A cutting horse at work—in a contest, the rider cues his horse as little as possible. (Photo by June Fallaw)

head low. A cutting horse in action is beautiful to watch, attesting to an abundance of experience, training, and ability.

Team Penning

Team penning is relatively new to the show ring. It provides interest to the spectator as well as showing the riders' skill at cutting and handling cattle.

Within a two-minute time limit, a team of three riders cuts out three head of cattle from the herd and then pens them, using a designated course design. Unnecessary roughness is penalized, and the fastest team wins.

Part 5 · The Open Door

Though finished, this book can never be complete. We hope it has served as a guide through the corridors of understanding to the threshold of achievement. The door is open wide. The goal of harmonious horsemanship is attainable. Find the masters who most appeal to you. Study their books. Try their methods.

As you cross the threshold into more advanced concepts and deeper fulfillment, we know you are singing, with Browning and us, "Riding's a joy! For me, I ride."

GROOMING TOOLS

Grooming Tools

Currycombs

rubber and plastic

circular steel

Army
with hoof pick

cloth

Brushes

kinds:
mud (stiff)
plastic
soft white fiber
stiff whalebone type
stiff black nylon
body brushes

soft white
sturdy bristle

Combs

aluminum mane comb

aluminum pulling comb

The Horse and Equipment

GROOMING TOOLS

Sweat scrapers

Hoof picks

aluminum
wood
or
brass

folding hoof pick

shed 'n' blade
and
sweat scraper

colored handled
hoof pick

folding hammer head
hoof pick

hoof rasp

Fig. 27

GROOMING TOOLS
TEST SHEET

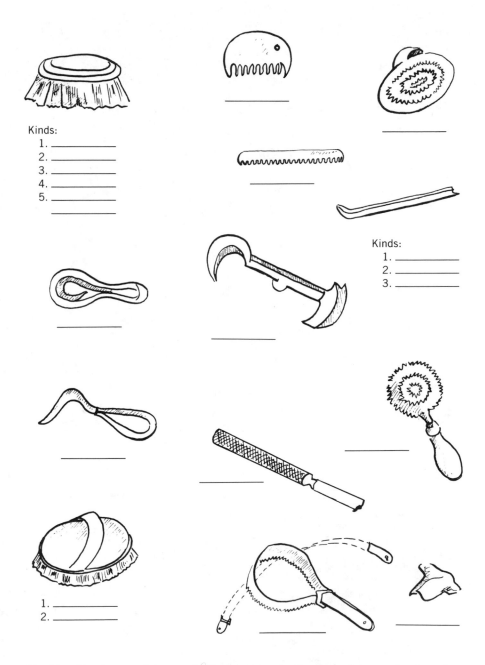

Kinds:
1. _____
2. _____
3. _____
4. _____
5. _____

Kinds:
1. _____
2. _____
3. _____

1. _____
2. _____

Fig. 28   Give the uses of these tools. Explain the order that the tools are used and on what part of the anatomy.

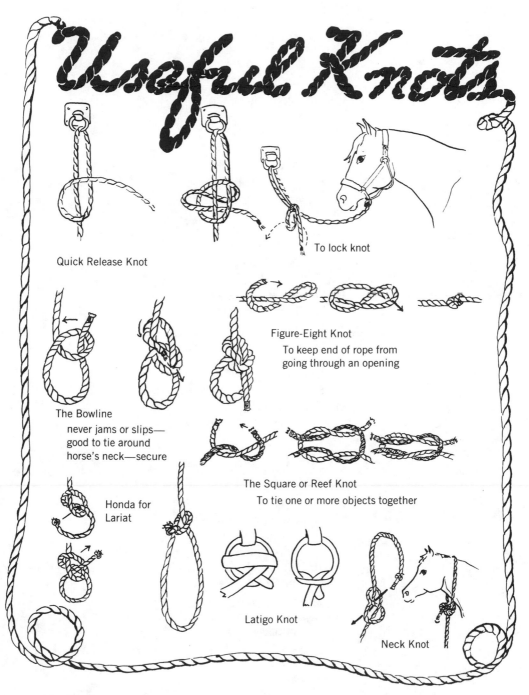

Useful Knots

Quick Release Knot

To lock knot

Figure-Eight Knot
To keep end of rope from
going through an opening

The Bowline
never jams or slips—
good to tie around
horse's neck—secure

The Square or Reef Knot
To tie one or more objects together

Honda for
Lariat

Latigo Knot

Neck Knot

Fig. 29

English Tack

A and B   English bridles
(A, snaffle; B, double)

   1. Crown piece or headstall
   2. Brow band
   3. Throatlatch
   4. Cheek piece
   5. Noseband or cavesson
   6. Snaffle bit
   7. Reins
   8. Bight of reins
   9. Weymouth (curb) bit
  10. Curb chain
  11. Lip strap

C   Pelham half-moon bit
D   Snaffle with full cheek bars
E   Low port curb
F   High port curb
G   Running martingale
H   Irish martingale
I   Standing martingale
J   English saddle

   1. Pommel
   2. Skirt
   3. Seat
   4. Cantle
   5. Panel
   6. Flap
   7. Stirrup bar (safety)
   8. Tread or stirrup iron
   9. Stirrup leather
  10. Knee pad or knee roll

K   Underside of English saddle

   1. Gullet
   2. Lining (part of panel)
   3. Buckle guard
   4. Girth strap or tabs
   5. Panel
   6. Saddle flap

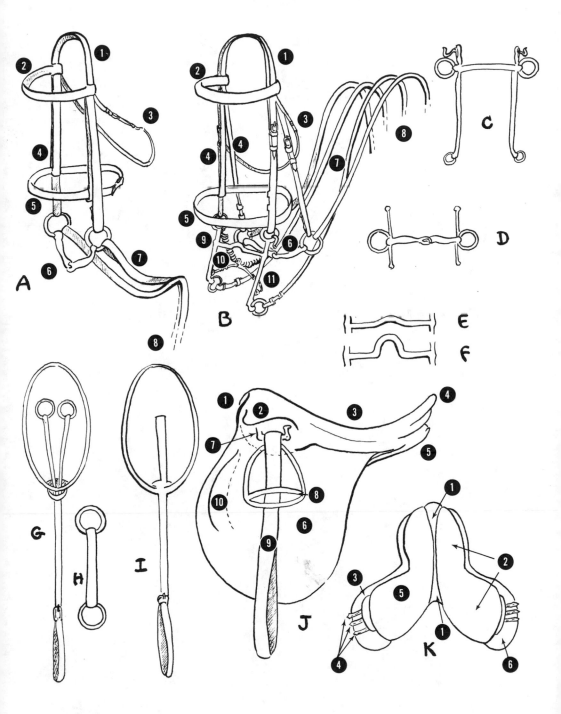

Fig. 31   English tack.

Kinds of English Saddles

Dressage saddle

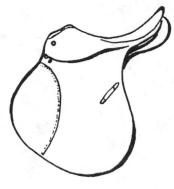

Jumping saddle

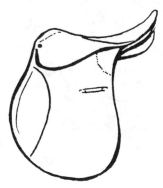

All-purpose saddle

Cut-back show saddle

Fig. 30   Kinds of English saddles.

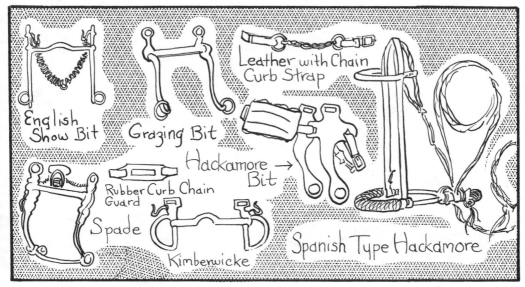

Fig. 33   Some curb bits and hackamores with accessories.

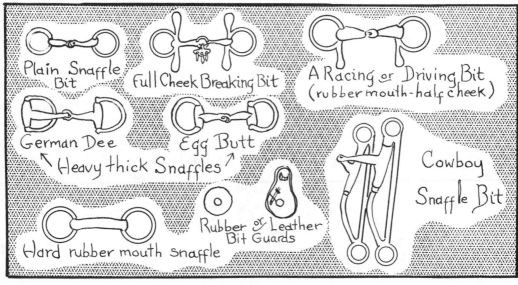

Fig. 33A   Some snaffle bits and accessories.

Western Tack

A   ¾ standard rig
B   Full double rig
C   ¾ double rig
D   Leather breast collar
E   Easy stop hackamore
F   Port (low) bit
G   Halfbreed bit ⎫ A spade bit
              ⎪ may be used
              ⎬ with a half-
              ⎪ breed roller.
H   Spade bit   ⎭
I   Standard bosal
   1.   Nose button
   2.   Side button
   3.   Noseband
   4.   Heel knot
J   Split ear bridle
   1.   Crown piece
   2.   Cheek piece
   3.   Curb bit
   4.   Curb strap
   5.   Reins
K   Tapaderos
L   Western saddle

   1.   Horn
   2.   Fork
   3.   Seat
   4.   Cantle
   5.   Skirt
   6.   Rear housing or jockey seat
   7.   Saddle strings
   8.   Rigging dees or dee rings
   9.   Rear cinch billet
   10. Fender
   11. Stirrup with tread cover
   12. Stirrup leather
   13. Long latigo, cinch strap, or front tie strap
   14. Seat jockey
   15. Wool lining
   16. Rope strap
   17. Gullet
   18. Swells
   19. Pommel

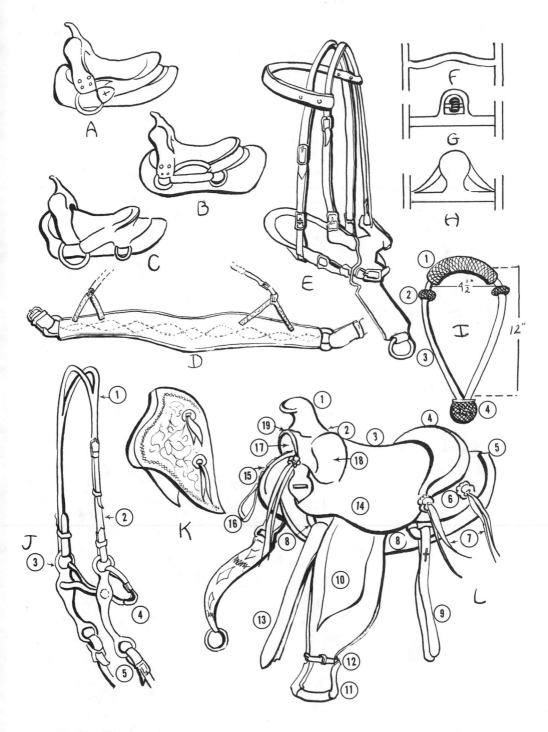

Fig. 32   Western tack.

Points of the Horse

1. Muzzle
2. Nostril
3. Jaw
4. Cheek
5. Face
6. Eye
7. Forehead and forelock
8. Poll
9. Ear
10. Mane
11. Crest
12. Neck
13. Throatlatch or throttle
14. Withers

15. Back
16. Loin
17. Croup
18. Hip
19. Coupling
20. Tail
21. Point of buttocks
22. Thigh
23. Quarter
24. Stifle
25. Flank
26. Sheath
27. Underline
28. Gaskin
29. Point of hock
30. Hock

31. Hoof or foot
32. Coronet
33. Pastern
34. Fetlock
35. Cannon
36. Knee
37. Forearm
38. Point of elbow
39. Arm
40. Point of shoulder
41. Ribs
42. Heart girth
43. Shoulder
44. Chestnuts
45. Dock

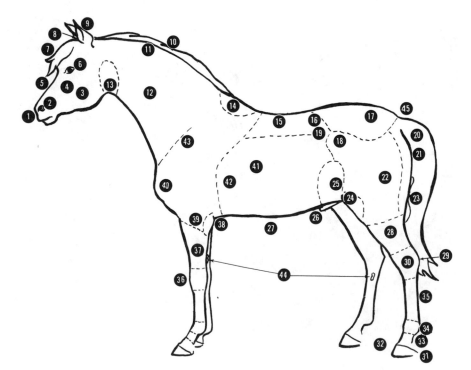

Fig. 34

Leg and Hoof Conformation

A   Good—normal
B   Buck-kneed
C   Calf-kneed
D   Tied in at the knee (or hock)
E   Too long cannon (either fore or hind)
F   Coon-footed (either fore or hind)
G   Short straight pastern (either fore or hind)
H   Camped (usually found fore and hind)
I   Good—normal
J   Base narrow (either fore or hind, can toe in or toe out)
K   Base wide (either fore or hind, can toe in or toe out)

L   Good—normal
M   Sickle hocks
N   Camped behind
O   Contracted foot
P   Foundered foot
Q   Normal front foot (pastern and hoof angle approximately forty-seven degrees)
R   Broken angle (toe too long; heel too low)
S   Broken angle (toe too short; heel too high)
T   Coon-footed
U   Paddling (accompanies toe-in)
V   Winging (accompanies toe-out)

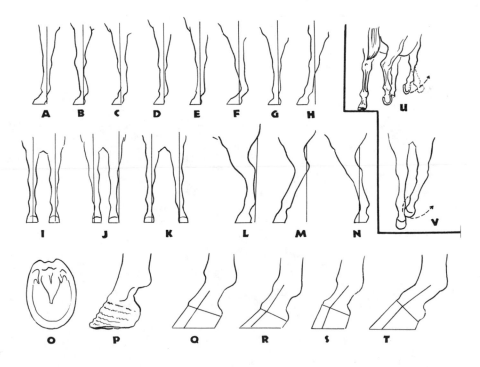

Fig. 35

Location of Common Lamenesses, Unsoundnesses, and Blemishes

1. Poll evil
2. Moon blindness or blindness
3. Parrot mouth
4. Monkey mouth
5. Distemper (strangles) swelling
6. Sweeny (shoulder)
7. Shoe boil
8. Splint
9. Bowed tendon
10. Wind puffs
11. Ring bone
12. Quittor
13. Navicular disease
14. Fistula (withers)
15. Stifled
16. Thoroughpin
17. Bone spavin
18. Bog spavin
19. Capped hock
20. Curb
21. Side bone
22. Feet—contracted feet (commonly shown in heels); corns; founder; thrush; quarter or sand crack; scratches or grease heel
23. Saddle galls
24. Hernia
25. Broken down hip

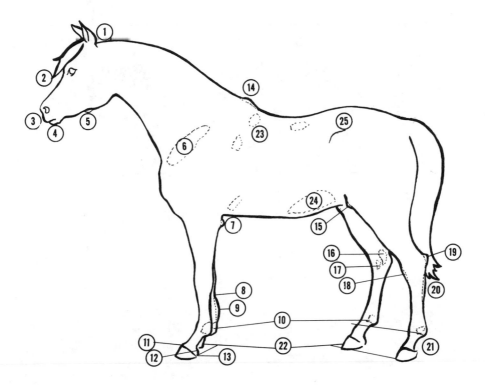

Fig. 36

The Hoof and Horseshoe

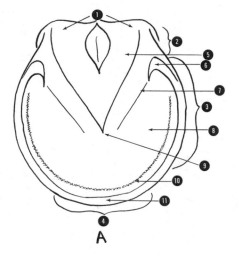
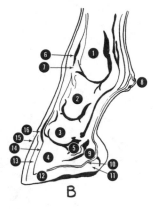

A   The hoof
1. Bulbs of the frog
2. Heel
3. Quarter
4. Toe
5. Frog
6. Buttress
7. Bar
8. Horny sole
9. Point of frog
10. White line
11. Bearing surface of the wall

B   The foot
1. Distal end of the third metacarpal bone
2. First phalanx, or long pastern
3. Second phalanx or short pastern
4. Third phalanx or coffin bone
5. Distal sesamoid or navicular bone
6. Bursa
7. Cavity of the fetlock joint
8. Ergot
9. Digital cushion
10. Corium of the frog
11. Frog of the hoof
12. Sole of the hoof
13. Wall of the hoof
14. Laminar corium
15. Periople of the hoof
16. Coronary border of the hoof

Fig. 37

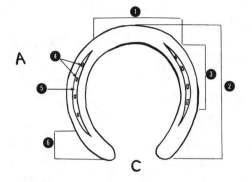

C

B

D

C The horseshoe
1. Toe
2. Branch
3. Quarter
4. Nail holes
5. Crease
6. Heel

D Horseshoe nail
1. Head
2. Neck
3. Shank
4. Bevel
5. Point
6. Inner face
7. Outer face

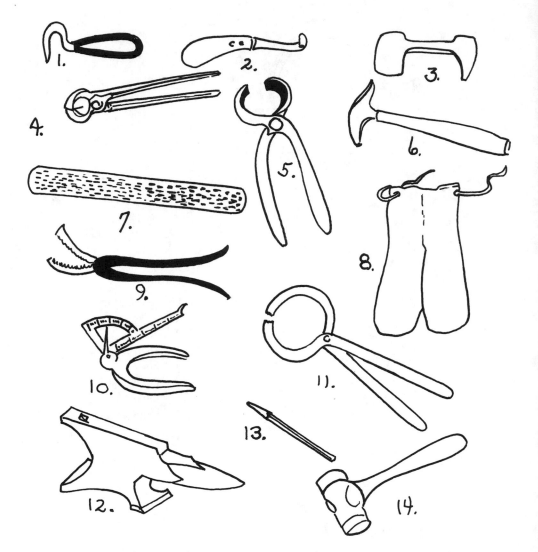

Fig. 38   Horseshoeing tools.

1.   Colored handled hoof pick
2.   Hoof knife
3.   Clinch cutter or buffer
4.   Cutting nippers
5.   Pincers
6.   Driving hammer
7.   Rasp (16″)

8.   Blacksmith's apron
9.   Clincher or "duckbill"
10. Hoof leveler
11. Hoof tester
12. Anvil
13. Pritchel
14. Rounding hammer

Skeletal System

1. Skull
2. Mandible
3. Scapula
4. Sternum
5. Humerus
6. Ulna
7. Radius
8. Carpus
9. Metacarpus
10. Phalanges
11. Ribs
12. Xiphoid cartilage

13. Accessory carpal bone
14. Patella
15. Tibia
16. Tarsus
17. Phalanges
18. Sacrum
19. Pelvis
20. Femur
21. Fibula
22. Tuber calcis
23. Metatarsus

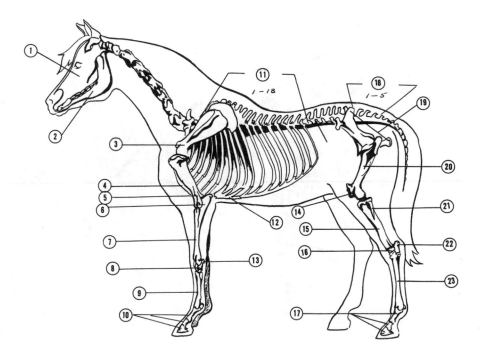

Fig. 39

Muscular System

1. Sterno cephalicus
2. Brachiocephalicus
3. Deltoideus
4. Pectoralis
5. Triceps brachii
6. Extensor carpi radialis
7. Extensor digitorum
8. Trapezius
9. Latissimus dorsi
10. Obliquus abdominis ext.
11. Glutaeus
12. Quadriceps femoris
13. Tibialis anterior
14. Extensor digitorum
15. Semitendinosus
16. Biceps femoris
17. Flexor digitorum

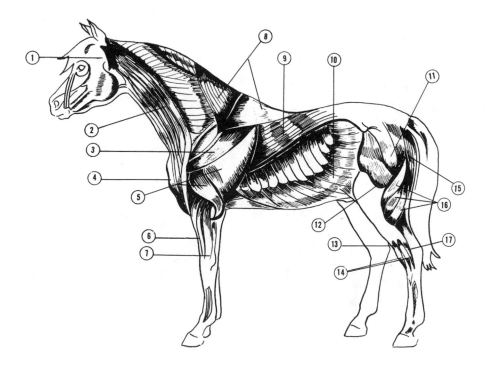

Fig. 40

Digestive System

1. Tongue
2. Epiglottis
3. Esophagus
4. Pharynx
5. Stomach
6. Spleen
7. Liver
8. Duodenum
9. Colon
10. Rectum
11. Bladder
12. Cecum

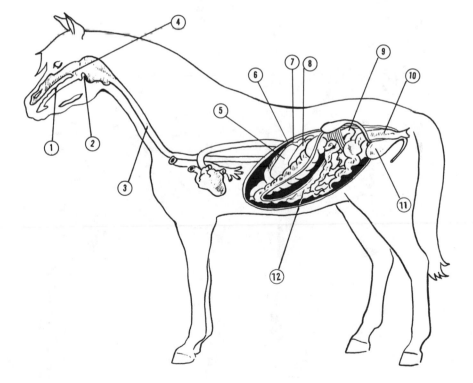

Fig. 41

Circulatory System

1. Common carotid artery
2. Jugular vein
3. Subclavian artery
4. Cephalic vein
5. Median artery
6. Thoracic artery (internal)
7. Pulmonary artery
8. Mesenteric artery
9. Femoral artery
10. Aorta
11. Hepatic vein
12. Portal vein
13. Renal artery

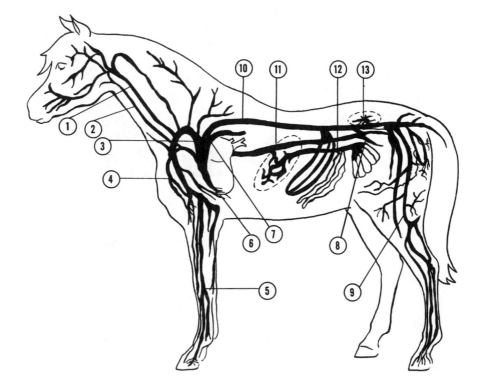

Fig. 42

Nervous System

1. Cerebrum
2. Cerebellum
3. Cranial nerves
4. Sympathetic
5. Stellate ganglion
6. Vagus (parasympathetic)
7. Cervical ganglion
8. Spinal cord
9. Mesenteric (solar) plexus

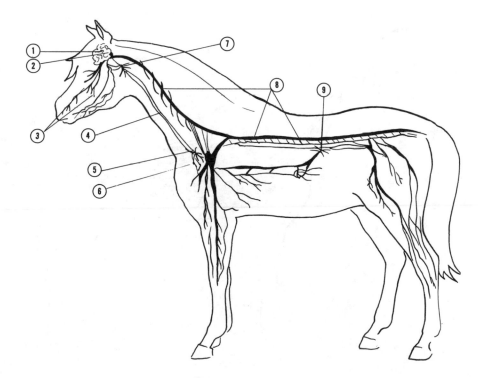

Fig. 43

Respiratory System

1. Nasal passages
2. Pharynx
3. Larynx
4. Epiglottis
5. Trachea
6. Bronchi
7. Diaphragm
8. Lungs

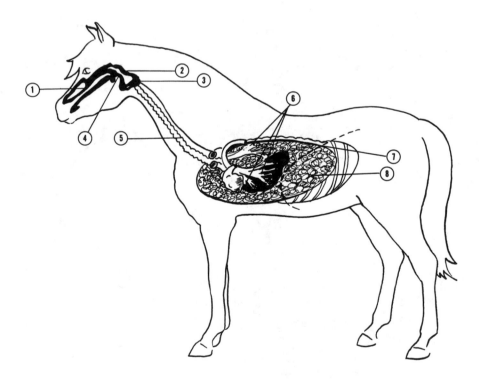

Fig. 44

Urinary Excretory System

1. Aorta
2. Renal arteries
3. Kidneys
4. Venae cavae
5. Adrenal glands
6. Renal veins
7. Ureters
8. Urinary bladder

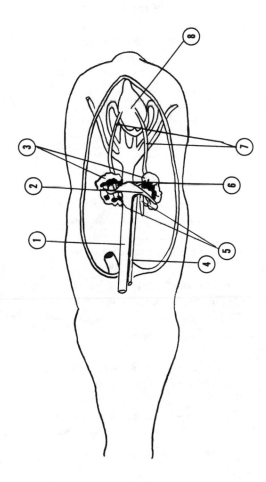

Fig. 45

The Age of a Horse

To tell the age of any horse,
Inspect the lower jaw, of course;
The six front teeth the tale will tell,
And every doubt and fear dispel.

Two middle nippers you behold
Before the colt is two weeks old;
Before eight weeks, two more will come.
Eight months the corners cut the gum.

The outside grooves will disappear
From middle two in just one year;
In two years from the second pair—
In three years "corners" too are bare.

At two the middle "nippers" drop;
At three the second pair can't stop;
When four years old the third pair goes,
At five a full new set he shows.

The deep black spots will pass from view
At six years, from the middle two;
The second pair at seven years,
At eight the spot each corner clears.

From middle "nippers" upper jaw,
At nine the black spots will withdraw;
The second pair at ten are bright,
Eleven finds the corners light.

As time goes on the horsemen know
The oval teeth three-sided grow;
They longer get, project before,
Till twenty—when we know no more.

Anonymous

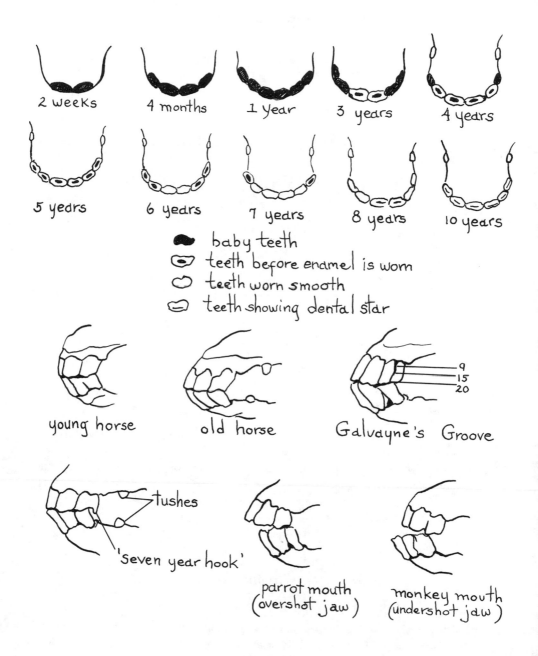

2 weeks   4 months   1 year   3 years   4 years

5 years   6 years   7 years   8 years   10 years

baby teeth
teeth before enamel is worn
teeth worn smooth
teeth showing dental star

young horse   old horse   Galvayne's Groove
9
15
20

tushes
'seven year hook'
parrot mouth (overshot jaw)   monkey mouth (undershot jaw)

Fig. 46   The age of a horse.

Suggested Topics for Home Study or Assignments

Breeds

1. Origin of common breeds in the United States (illustrate with map).
2. Brief report on five uncommon U.S. breeds, or ten breeds around the world (illustrate with map).
3. Pony breeds, including extent of use, past and present.
4. Draft and coach breeds.
5. Detailed reports on specific breeds, including history, size, use, type, special ability.
6. Purebred registries, including purpose, worth, value of registered horse vs. value of unregistered animal.
7. Learn how to read a pedigree; tell where studbooks are available; trace pedigrees of three horses; fill out a pedigree blank for your horse (or another).
8. Which breeds are more suitable for Western riding, jumping, dressage; why?

Hippology

1. Using six horses as examples, give color, markings, height, age, and sex.
2. Conformation—using three horses, note good and bad points.
3. Write out conformation standards for three breeds of horses.
4. Give comparative anatomy of horse and man.
5. Report on the evolution and origin of the horse.
6. Wild equidae.
7. Close relations of the horse—domestic and wild.

8. How do heredity, climate, soils, and work affect the development of a horse?
9. Discuss intelligence of the horse—consider memory, psychology, etc.
10. Compare likely basic reactions and psychology of a range-raised horse and a "back yard" horse (one raised with frequent contact with people).

Training

1. Steps in training a horse—groundwork.
2. Steps in training a horse to saddle.
3. Steps in training a foal—halter breaking, longeing, etc.
4. Discuss defenses of the horse and suggest ways of correction.
5. Discuss uses, benefits, and possible detrimental effects of:

Cavalletti	Gag bridles
Longeing	Long lines
Running W	Sacking out
Running martingale	Bitting exercise
Hackamore	Hitchcock pen
Dropped noseband	Anticribbing devices
Rattles	Tail sets
Spurs and whips	Blinkers
Longeing cavessons	Mouthing bits

Stable Care, Management, and Feeding

1. Care of stallion—feeding, stabling, exercise, special care for stud.
2. Care of mare—feeding, stabling, exercise, special care when in foal, care of brood mares.
3. Care of foal—handling, exercise, stabling, feeding, weaning.
4. Stable care—include farm hygiene.
5. Hoof care—proper trimming, when and why shoe, how often, corrective shoeing, hoof dressing, problems and diseases of hoof and foot.
6. Diseases of the horse.
7. Stable vices—what they are, how to prevent, how to correct.
8. Horse first aid—basic veterinary skills, medicines or equipment, know when to call the vet, what to do in the meantime.
9. Study stable plans and design an efficient stable that could be used on your farm, ranch, or in back yard—can remodel present facilities, may include stalls, tack room, grain room (or combination), small paddock.
10. Safety—in pasture, paddock, when handling.
11. Types of feed available in your area—grains, types of hay, pelleted or cubed feed, etc.
12. Types of hay and their nutritional value, types of grain and their nutritional value, grain substitutes.

13. Feed supplements and additives.
14. Prepare a ration (complete feed for a day, including roughage, concentrate, and supplement) for a roping horse in training, working cowhorse, stabled horse (occasionally ridden), or other. Give the approximate weight of the horse.
15. Horse parasites—draw and explain their cycles, how to prevent, how to worm.
16. Draw the different systems of the horse, such as respiratory, digestive, etc.

Breeding

1. Prepare an alphabetical listing of breeding terms, with definitions of each.
2. Artificial insemination—explain term; is this method of breeding accepted with all breed registries? Why?
3. Care and handling of stallion.
4. Procedure and care of mare and stallion before, during and after breeding.
5. Brood mares—diet, exercise, pasture vs. barn.
6. Tell how to keep a breeding chart, what to include.
7. Explain how to read a pedigree—explain terms such as top line, percentages in pedigrees, inbreeding, line breeding, crossbreeding, etc.
8. Pasture breeding—include size of herd for stallion, normal percentages of conception, under what circumstances this method is preferable to hand breeding.

Riding Theory

1. Early development of equitation.
2. Evolution and development of military equitation.
3. Compare Museler and Romazskan—or take two dressage books by different authors and compare.
4. Give brief biography and main theory or thoughts on riding of the following:

Xenophon	Newcastle	Caprilli
Grisone	La Gueriniere	Podhajsky
Pluvinel	Baucher	Romazskan

5. Compare riding schools (that is, theories of riding) of two different countries, such as Germany and France, or Russia and England. Choose dressage or show jumping to illustrate points.
6. Compare Western and English riding. Discuss similarities and differences.

Western and Trail Riding

1. Make up a trail horse course.
2. Plan a trail ride using maps—where to go, what permissions would be needed,

what type of obstacle would be encountered (gates, streams, etc.), what to take along, how long likely to be gone, etc.

3. Pack horses—kinds of hitches, how to pack, problems likely to encounter on a pack trip, overnight care of horses.
4. Famous trail rides in history.
5. Compare time and performance of different well-known breeds of horses on such rides as the Green Mountain Trail Ride or the Tevis Cup Ride.
6. Discuss ideal endurance horse conformation, age, breed, personality.
7. Conditioning the endurance horse and rider.
8. Rules, regulations, and methods of running an endurance ride or competitive trail ride—give specific rules from some well-known rides.
9. How would you ride an endurance contest? Consider length, terrain, weather, rating time, condition of horse, etc.

Jumping

1. Prepare a list of terms used in jumping, with definitions.
2. History of show jumping.
3. History or evolution of the jumping seat.
4. Exercises to prepare rider for jumping—invent two original exercises and tell how they will help prepare the rider.
5. Use of longe line and cavalletti in training horse to jump.
6. Tell story of famous jumping team (horse and rider).
7. Give ideal conformation of working hunter and reason for opinion.
8. Contrast qualities, conformation, etc., of working hunter and show jumper.
9. Draw some well-known types of jumps and label each.
10. Lay out a jump course, using at least eight different jumps:
    a. For beginners
    b. For intermediates
    c. For advanced jumpers
    Give heights of each jump.

Tack and Equipment

1. What are the tests for fitting the following equipment:
   stirrup length
   curb tightness
   length of running and standing martingales
   girth (cinch and second cinch on Western saddle)
2. Proper care of tack when using or storing, or moving (such as when taking to a show).
3. Uses of various types of bits.
4. Uses of different types of saddles, including advantages and disadvantages of each for different purposes.
5. Story of the sidesaddle—include development and use today.

6. Equipment used in longeing a horse.
7. Equipment used in driving and in training to drive.
8. Use of various restraining devices, such as Scotch hobble, running W, etc.

Horse Shows

1. Make out a premium list for a horse show.
2. Correct dress for English show classes.
3. Correct dress for Western show classes.
4. Grooming for a halter show class, both handler and horse.
5. Story of the American Horse Shows Association.
6. Story of the Federation Equestre Internationale.
7. Stories of three great American horse shows.
8. Tell about your experiences at a small horse show, a large horse show.
9. Tell about your greatest triumph—and your greatest disappointment—at a horse show. Give reasons for each.
10. Select a specific class, either halter or performance, and look at it from the judge's point of view. What is he looking for, where will he count off?

Recreation, Competition, and Games

1. Invent three exercises or games to be performed on horseback—explain how they will help to develop balance, position, suppleness, muscle tone, etc.
2. Make up a drill and teach the class to perform it.
3. Rodeo—include history, contests, RCA, famous annual rodeos.
4. Horse racing (Thoroughbred, Quarter Horse, Standardbred): history, state income, parimutuel system, training of race horses, race horse prices, purses, types of races.
5. Famous endurance contests and rides—conditioning horse and rider, types of terrain, purpose of contest, etc.
6. Circus—history, types of performance, horses' training.
7. Hunting—brief history, common terms, famous hunting areas of the United States, famous people and horses in hunting, etc.
8. Polo—brief history, common terms, types of horses, training.
9. Horse games around the world.
10. Make up a freestyle dressage test or "kur" and perform to music.

Selling and Buying

1. Report on various ways to advertise a horse.
2. Make out an advertisement on the sale of a horse or to advertise stallions at stud.
3. Horse auctions.
4. Go to a horse sale—report on sale, terms used, length of time in the ring, how

shown, average price compared to U.S. average prices, quality of stock offered, was sale favorable to both buyer and seller?—give reasons.

5. Points to consider when buying a horse.
6. Discuss advantages and disadvantages when buying a horse from a horse dealer and from a breeding farm.
7. Terms used by auctioneer, tricks sometimes used to sell horses (cover up unsoundness).

Specific Uses of Horses

1. Police horses—special training, uses where horses are better than mechanized vehicles, shoeing, specifications.
2. Army horses—remount stallions, specifications, development over the years in the United States, other countries with cavalry today.
3. Cutting horses.
4. Roping horses.
5. Dude horses, trail horses, pack ponies.
6. Pit ponies.
7. Polo ponies.
8. Draft horses and mules today (their place, if any).
9. Endurance horses.
10. School horses, dressage—mention specific schools, care and training.

History, Art, and Literature

1. Famous paintings—artist, horse or horses, medium, etc.
2. Famous sculptures and statues—artist, horse, rider.
3. History of the Spanish Riding School in Vienna.
4. History of other European riding schools, such as Saumur, Hanover.
5. History of Equestrian Olympic Games.
6. The horse and chivalry—tournaments, Crusades, etc.
7. The medieval great horse.
8. Wild horses in the West, around the world.
9. The Indian and his horse.
10. The Civil War soldier and his horse, or, the part played by the horse in the Civil War.
11. The Arab and the horse.
12. Famous horse stories—individual book reviews, or an overall view of horse heroes in literature.
13. History of veterinary medicine.
14. History of bits and bridles—or saddles, harness, horse brasses and other decorations, etc.
15. Story of horse-drawn vehicles.
16. Horses in Greek and Roman times (illustrate with famous art work).
17. Use of horses B.C.

Famous Individuals

1. Report on three famous horses—known for different things such as racing, cutting performance, in war, as sires, etc.
2. Report on three famous horsemen in history.
3. Report on three famous Western riders, ropers, barrel racers, etc.
4. Lives of three famous dressage riders, English show riders, or show jumpers.
5. Lives of three famous trainers.
6. Women in the saddle.
7. The King Ranch.
8. Kellogg Arabians.
9. Famous horses of famous people—Traveler, Bucephalus, Marengo, Copenhagen, Nelson.
10. Horses in Greek mythology.

Research and Information about Horses

1. Write out list of free or small-fee literature and videos and where to get them (include addresses).
2. Report on reference books.
3. Prepare catalogue of horse books—include author, titles, publisher, date, brief résumé (or subject area). Rate each title with stars to denote interest or worth to you. A three-star book would be tops, one you'd like to have.)
4. Make book report of fiction or nonfiction horse book.
5. Horse book clubs.
6. What colleges give courses in horseshoeing, horsemanship, horse husbandry? Correspondence courses?
7. List riding schools in the United States and the particular forte of that school. Also England, Europe.

Exercises for the Rider, Sample Requirements for Levels of Horsemanship, Sample Dressage Tests and Reining Patterns, Sample Release Agreements

Exercises for the Rider

Most of these exercises can be done on your own, in a class situation in the arena, or on the longe.

INSTRUCTOR: *Longeing the rider is one of the best possible ways to develop his seat. It improves balance, suppleness, coordination, and muscle development as well as preparing for jumping. Because the rider does not have to control the horse or worry about pulling on the horse's mouth, he can concentrate on position and balance. Exercises, either on the longe or when riding independently, also make a lesson more interesting for both the student and the horse by giving variety to the instruction. All mounts used by students should be thoroughly checked out and used often for exercises. Steadiness and quiet disposition are important for the safety and confidence of the student.*

Most exercises are performed without stirrups to encourage the lower leg to stay in the correct position for maximum support. Riding without stirrups also encourages students to rely on their own body control, balance, and coordination.

Being able to move all over the horse while doing exercises will give the rider confidence. The rider will not panic on losing a stirrup when used to working often without them.

Along with their other benefits, some of the following exercises will help the student relieve tension in the body (especially the back and shoulders) after extensive arena work. The exercises done at the walk or halt give arena horses a break between the more strenuous gaits and figures of ring work.

1. **Forward/back.**
   a. *The lower legs* (from knee down) swing forward and back in rhythm, while the upper body stays in position. Heels should be down.
   b. *Trunk of body.* Lean forward from the hips (back should be as straight as possible, not rounded) and touch the side of the forehead to the top of horse's neck. The legs should stay in position (with heels low) and not move back.
   c. You can vary the exercises by folding the arms, placing hands behind neck, or putting hands on waist. Exercises can be executed at the halt or walk.
2. **Flexibility** (for suppleness and coordination).
   Rotate wrists and ankles simultaneously (left counterclockwise, right clockwise) so that the hand or toe makes a circle. Legs, arms, and body stay in position.
3. **1–2 alternate leg:**
   Perform exercise 1a above, except that legs move alternately forward and back.
4. **Forward/back/rotate—legs and arms coordinating.**
   Use both arms and legs together or alternately. Hold arms(s) stretched forward, palm up, then rotate arm up and around vertically, and down by side. The leg on the same side moves forward when the arm is up, back as the arm comes down—fingertips should touch heel. The exercise should be performed rhythmically. It is excellent for coordination, encouraging the student to use the whole body.
5. **Touch on command.**
   As the horse stands, walks, or trots, ask the student to touch specified parts of the horse, the tack, or himself. This helps with coordination and reinforces general horse knowledge.
6. **Ankle-hold.**
   Take reins in the left hand and hold the right ankle with the right hand. Switch hands: Hold the reins in the right hand, grasp the left ankle with the left hand. Benefits coordination and balance.
7. **Around-the-world.**
   This exercise should be performed at the halt with the instructor or other competent person holding the horse and standing ready to steady the student. Without stirrups, begin in normal position. Swing the left leg over the horse's neck to sit sideways; then swing the right leg over the horse's hindquarters to sit facing backward; swing the left leg over the hindquarters to sit sideways on the other side; and finally swing the right leg over the horse's neck, to return to normal position. Repeat the exercise in the opposite direction. As the rider perfects balance and confidence (and for variation), he can fold arms or put hands on waist and move "around-the-world."
8. **Stand in stirrups.**
   Stand in the stirrups at the walk, with knees bent, upper body inclined forward, and seat bones off the saddle (as in the forward seat position). This exercise develops the ability to stay in balance over the horse's center of

gravity while the horse is in motion. As the rider progresses, the arms can be raised, placed at the waist, or held horizontally out to the side at shoulder height. With more experience, the student can progress to the trot and canter.

9. **Arms-up-and-out-pivot-pivot.**
Hold arms up vertically overhead, then straight out horizontally, and pivot torso first to the left, then to the right. Be sure the arms are vertical when held overhead, elbows straight but not stiff; arms in horizontal position should be held at shoulder level. This exercise benefits muscle development and coordination.

10. **Hand to poll to base of tail.**
Reach forward with one hand and touch the poll; then turn and reach back with the same hand to touch the base of the tail. Repeat with the other hand. The student must coordinate the movement of the upper body while holding the legs stationary in the correct position. This exercise also helps flexibility, coordination, and balance.

11. **The bicycle.**
While holding the upper body in position, raise and lower alternate legs in cadence, as in pedaling a bicycle. The knees are bent and should rise higher than the horse's withers, and heels should stay lower than toes during the exercise. The "bicycle" helps develop balance.

12. **Leg lift.**
Lift the right leg (held fairly straight, but not stiff) so that the right heel goes over to the left side of horse's neck. Return to normal position. Lift the left leg so that the left heel goes over to right side of neck. This exercise helps balance and muscle development.

13. **Cadence-count.**
   a. Count aloud in time with the horse's stride: walk, 1-2-3-4; trot, 1-2, 1-2; canter, 1-2-3, 1-2-3 (the canter would not be used until student is competent to ride this gait). The student will learn the feel and cadence of the horse's gaits.
   b. Hold arms in front of the body (elbows straight), post, and raise arms up and down in cadence with gait.
   c. Hold arms out to the side, rotate arms in forward circles in rhythm. A more advanced variation: Toss a rubber ball up and down in one hand in rhythm to the gait. Timing and coordination enter into this exercise.

14. **Heels in the stirrups.**
Ride with heels in the irons rather than the ball of the foot. This can also be a corrective exercise for students who tend to ride with their heels higher than their toes.

15. **Knees over the withers.**
With upper body in position, lift the knees higher than the horse's withers and return to normal position in rhythm. Coordination, flexibility, and muscle development are benefited. For more advanced students, the heels may be raised and touched together over the horse's neck in rhythm.

16. **Touch alternate hands to alternate toes.**
While the horse is at the halt, hold the right arm straight, swing it up

vertically and over so that the right hand touches the left toe. Repeat the exercise with the left hand to the right toe. Make sure the lower legs stay in place during this exercise, which develops flexibility, balance, and coordination.

17. **Poll to withers in rhythm.**
    We use this exercise to calm the horse and encourage him to relax after arena work. Extend both arms forward (with reins) and lean forward to touch the poll, then stroke back toward the withers along the top of the neck. When done in slow rhythm, the horse relaxes, lowering his head and neck.

18. **Sit normal—sit loose.**
    This exercise will relax and relieve tension in the rider after a strenuous workout. Assume normal position and, on direction, "sit loose": Completely relax the whole body (shoulders can slump, legs hang loose like spaghetti, hands quiet). Alternate normal and loose position several times.

19. **Punching forward with fists.**
    This exercise relieves tension in the neck and shoulders. At the halt, take the reins in one hand, make a fist with the other, and punch forward vigorously. Punching forward should be done up and over and forward, not straight underhand from the shoulder. After several punches with one arm, change hands on the reins and punch with the other.

20. **Rotating the whole leg.**
    This exercise, performed without stirrups and with the horse at the halt, helps toward total body control. However, too much repetition can induce a "charley-horse" and may be difficult for the beginner. Sit in normal position and begin with the left leg: Rotate the whole leg including the thigh in a counterclockwise motion, taking the thigh away from the saddle. Repeat with the right leg and rotate clockwise; then try with both legs.

More Advanced Exercises

21. **Sitting the active trot.**
    Begin by sitting the normal trot, taking the reins in one hand. With the other hand, grip the pommel of the saddle and pull yourself deep down into the seat. Encourage the horse to trot actively. This exercise helps the student sit deeply in the saddle and flex the muscles of the lower back. Use discretion in performing this exercise, gradually building up time. Too much repetition may also be uncomfortable for the horse, especially his back.

22. **Learning-to-post.**
    At the walk, rise and sit (with correct forward seat position) on the count of 1 to 10: (1) up-down, (2) up-down, (3) up-down, and so on. As the student progresses, the instructor will count faster until the count has the rhythm and timing of the normal trot. Explain that the horse will push the rider up at the trot and regulate the rhythm. (The student should be able to perform exercise 8 above before attempting this exercise.) Explain that the rider's post has the same cadence as the footfalls of the horse's forelegs: You post

slower at the slow trot, faster for the fast trot. Until the rider is balanced and stable at the posting trot, diagonals should not be taught. This method of teaching the posting trot is especially good for students that seem to have difficulty. The instructor should encourage the student to rise using thighs and knees, with lower legs quiet, and just enough weight in the stirrups to hold them.

23. **Learning diagonals.**

    Again, for students who have difficulty understanding diagonals, the instructor may use the following method. Begin at the *walk*. Tell the student to watch the horse's outside shoulder (when in an arena) and *start* rising from the saddle as the outside shoulder and foreleg *start* forward. When the horse's foreleg is at its farthest extension, the rider is at the highest point of the post. If the student starts to rise when the horse's shoulder is completely forward, he will be too late for the correct diagonal. The student should practice this exercise at the walk and then at the trot. He must first recognize the correct diagonal. The instructor or another rider can also test the student by posting correctly and incorrectly to the diagonal and ask the student to distinguish between them.

24. **Exercises at the trot** (one arm at a time off longe, both arms together if on longe).

    a. At the sitting trot, hold arms horizontal (elbow straight but not stiff), and make little circles with wrists and hands to the cadence of the trot.

    b. At the posting trot, move the outside arm up and forward when out of saddle; move the arm back and down when at lower point of the post.

    c. Fold arms across the chest and stand (or post) in stirrups for ten strides; sit ten strides; repeat several times. Work with and without stirrups. Variation: Student can stand one-two, sit one-two, and so on.

25. **Exercise on the longe** (do not use reins).

    Keep correct position at all gaits with hands held as though holding reins (quietly). If the student has problems keeping the hands quiet, have him touch little fingers to the horse's neck or withers while attempting to keep hands in position and quiet. This is a good exercise to test the student's coordination and independence of seat.

26. **On or off longe.**

    Hold the jumping position (seat bones off saddle; hands holding reins or in normal position without reins). While holding position, drop the stirrups for a few strides; pick up the stirrups again without altering position. This is an excellent exercise for intermediate and/or advanced riders to develop thigh and calf muscles as well as to aid balance. Posting several strides without stirrups and picking them up again, without losing the post or diagonal, is a variation of this exercise. The sitting trot can be used as a rest for the rider, when extending the time on the above exercises.

Sample Requirements for Elementary, Intermediate, Intermediate/Advanced, and Advanced Levels of Horsemanship

The habits learned in the elementary levels are reflected in mastering more advanced levels. Instructors should help their students understand horses and how they think. Basic knowledge (feeding, equine terms, care of horse and tack, and so on) and on-the-ground techniques such as learning how to longe a horse should be coordinated with the practical riding lesson. Lesson plans are invaluable for the instructor and necessary for adequate instruction.

Elementary-level Requirements

In this beginner level, the student should practice and understand courtesy and safety rules, gain confidence, and work toward adequately controlling his horse. In group lessons, instructors should stress the safety of distance between horses and how to pass other horses.

The student should be able to:

1. approach the horse safely, halter, lead, tie (with correct knot), groom, saddle, and bridle (with help).
2. mount correctly with and without the mounting block or assisted leg-up. Small riders may have assistance but should know how to proceed.
3. walk his horse with confidence, correct position, and adequate control.
4. halt the horse; start the sitting trot; start the posting trot; reverse at the walk.
5. ride bareback (with neck strap) at the walk, and perform easy exercises on the longe line.
6. dismount and prepare to lead his horse to the stable (that is, run up English stirrups, remove reins from horse's neck, etc.); untack with assistance, and care for his horse.

Intermediate-level Requirements

The intermediate student should be able to pass the above elementary requirements and also be able to:

1. adjust tack safely and correctly, including adjusting length of English leathers and Western fenders; adjust and tighten cinch or girth correctly, including leading the horse before mounting.
2. ride with good position at walk, sitting trot or jog trot, and posting trot both directions of arena; posting trot should be stabilized and performed on the correct diagonal.

3. stand balanced in stirrups at least twice around arena at walk and trot; make reasonably smooth transitions from halt to walk, halt to trot (sitting and posting), walk to trot, trot to walk, trot to halt.
4. initiate the canter/lope on correct lead (giving correct aids), and continue at least one full time around the arena.
5. perform selected school figures at walk, trot, and jog trot; change direction across the diagonal and down the center line.
6. perform selected more difficult exercises on or off longe.
7. ride uphill and downhill, step over poles or logs, ride through a shallow creek and over rough terrain; know major trail safety rules, keep correct distance from other horses in arena and on trail.
8. demonstrate jumping position (if jumping is included in the program) at walk and trot over practice poles and cavalletti (assuming position as defined by marker cones); take a one-foot or lower cross-rail fence with correct position, balance, and control; trot poles and cavalletti on the longe.

Intermediate- Advanced-level Requirements

The intermediate/advanced student should be able to ride all gaits in both directions, with and without stirrups. This includes posting without stirrups (optional for Western). He should also perform:

1. school figures (such as serpentine, change of rein, large and small circles, figure-eights), demonstrating the correct coordinated use of leg, hand, and seat aids.
2. the basic rein effects: leading (opening), neck rein (bearing, indirect), direct (English), and pulley rein.
3. smooth transitions from halt to walk, trot (jog trot), and canter (lope); and corresponding downward gait transitions; initiate and ride the extended trot.
4. more advanced distance riding; be able to tell when a horse is "hot" and how to cool a hot horse properly whatever the weather conditions.

When jumping is included in the program, the student should:

1. demonstrate competent jumping form while trotting or cantering over cross-rails or line of fences (not more that one-and-one-half feet high) and over a single fence not more than two feet high.
2. ride a simple course demonstrating the ability to turn the horse accurately and line up either a single jump or series.
3. ride more challenging horses, solving problems such as refusals, shying, runouts, and rushing.
4. jump cavalletti and low jumps at the trot on the longe, with and without stirrups or with and without reins.

Advanced-level Requirements

Advanced-level students should not only be able to control their mount but also be gentle, flexible, and sensitive but firm in training a horse in new disciplines. The advanced student should demonstrate:

1. extension and collection in all gaits:
   walk—on a long rein or with contact; show a normal and lengthened stride.
   trot—influence the cadence, energy, and rhythm as well as length of stride.
   canter/lope—lengthen and shorten canter stride on correct lead; execute simple and flying lead changes while performing a figure-eight.
2. lateral and diagonal aids while performing the counter-canter, turn (pivot) on the forehand and turn (pivot) on the haunches, and other two-track movements.
3. a competent dressage test, programmed ride, or Western reining pattern (including acceptable pivots, slides, roll-backs, and spins). Correctness should be emphasized before speed.

Advanced Jumping Requirements

Advanced jumping students should demonstrate good jumping form (with correct contact) over a variety of single, vertical jumps, spread jumps, and combinations, and should be able to start a young horse correctly.

The advanced student should jump:

1. cross-country fences and ditches at a trot, canter, and gallop.
2. a course of fences that can be scored as Open Jumpers or Working Hunters.

DRESSAGE TESTS

The following scoring system will be used for all AHSA tests:		
SCORING:		**PENALTIES:**
10 Excellent	5 Sufficient	ERRORS—First error, 2 points; second error, 4 points; third error, elimination; leaving the arena, elimination. (When test is part of a combined event, third error, 8 points; fourth error, elimination.)
9 Very Good	4 Insufficient	
8 Good	3 Fairly Bad	
7 Fairly Good	2 Bad	
6 Satisfactory	1 Very Bad	
0 Not Performed or Fall of Horse or Rider.		

Note: There are no longer any time penalties.

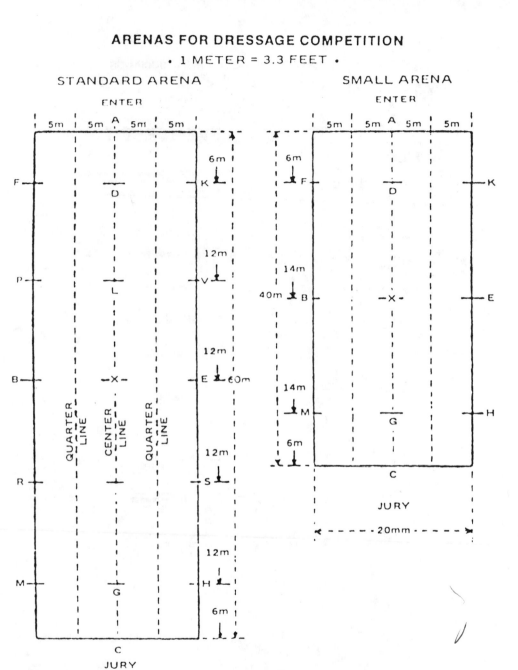

Fig. 47   Dressage Arenas. Reprinted with permission of AHSA. © 1991 American Horse Shows Association, Inc. All rights reserved. Reproduction without permission prohibited by law.

AMERICAN HORSE SHOWS ASSOCIATION
220 East 42nd Street
New York, NY 10017

1991
TRAINING LEVEL TEST 1

PURPOSE: To confirm that the horse has received proper dressage training as a result of which its muscles are supple and loose, it moves freely forward in clear and steady rhythm, accepting the bit. *(Drawing of arena shows movement #2.)*

CONDITIONS
Arena: Standard or small

Average Time:
- 5:00 standard arena
  4:00 small arena

MAXIMUM POSSIBLE POINTS:
210

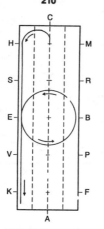

Name of Competition

Date of Competition

Number and Name of Horse

Name of Rider

FINAL SCORE

Points   Percent

Name of Judge

Signature of Judge

TRAINING LEVEL TEST 1

REQUIREMENTS:
20m circles in trot and canter

INSTRUCTIONS:
Transitions into and out of the halt
may be made through the walk

NO.

		TEST	DIRECTIVE IDEAS	POINTS	COEFFICIENT	TOTAL	REMARKS
1.	A X	Enter working trot sitting Halt, salute, proceed working trot sitting	Straightness on center line, transitions, quality of halt and trot				
2.	C H E K	Track left Working trot rising Circle left 20m Working trot sitting	Quality of turn at C, quality of trot, roundness of circle				
3.	Between K&A	Working canter left lead	Calmness and smoothness of depart				
4.	A	Circle left 20m	Quality of canter, roundness of circle				
5.	Between B&M	Working trot rising	Balance during transition				
6.	HXF	Working walk	Straightness, quality of walk		x2		
7.	F	Working trot rising	Smoothness of transition				
8.	E H	Circle right 20m Working trot sitting	Quality of trot, roundness of circle				
9.	Between H&C	Working canter right lead	Calmness and smoothness of depart				
10.	C	Circle right 20m	Quality of canter, roundness of circle				
11.	Between B&F	Working trot sitting	Balance during transition				
12.	A X	Down center line Halt, salute	Straightness on center line, quality of trot and halt				

Leave arena at free walk on long rein at A

COLLECTIVE MARKS:

Gaits (freedom and regularity)	2		
Impulsion (desire to move forward, elasticity of the steps, relaxation of the back)	2		
Submission (attention and confidence; harmony, lightness and ease of movements; acceptance of the bit)	2		
Rider's position and seat; correctness and effect of the aids	2		

FURTHER REMARKS:

SUBTOTAL   _____

ERRORS   (–_____)

TOTAL POINTS   _____

AMERICAN HORSE SHOWS ASSOCIATION
220 East 42nd Street
New York, NY 10017

1991
FIRST LEVEL TEST 2

PURPOSE: To confirm that the horse, having demonstrated that it has achieved the standard of the Training Level, has developed thrust (pushing power). *(Drawing of arena shows movement #2.)*

CONDITIONS
Arena: Standard or small
Average Time:
5:00 standard arena
4:00 small arena

MAXIMUM POSSIBLE POINTS:
280

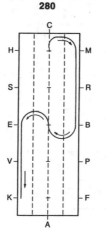

Name of Competition

Date of Competition

Number and Name of Horse

Name of Rider

FINAL SCORE

Points   Percent

Name of Judge

Signature of Judge

Fig. 49   First Level Dressage Test 2. Reprinted with permission of AHSA. © 1991 American Horse Shows Association, Inc. All rights reserved. Reproduction without permission prohibited by law.

NEW REQUIREMENTS:
10m circles in canter,
lengthen stride in canter.

INSTRUCTIONS:
All trot work is done sitting
unless otherwise specified

NO.

		TEST	DIRECTIVE IDEAS	POINTS	COEFFICIENT	TOTAL	REMARKS
1.	A X	Enter working trot sitting Halt, salute, proceed working trot sitting	Straightness on center line, transitions, quality of halt and trot				
2.	C B-X X-E	Track right Half circle right 10m Half circle left 10m	Quality of turn at C, execution and size of figures				
3.	K	Working canter left lead	Calmness and smoothness of depart				
4.	A	Circle left 10m	Quality of canter, roundness and size of circle				
5.	F-M M	Lengthen stride in canter Working canter	Straightness, quality of canters, transitions		x2		
6.	C	Working trot sitting	Balance during transition				
7.	HXF F	Lengthen stride in trot rising Working trot sitting	Straightness, quality of trots, transitions				
8.	A	Halt 5 seconds, proceed working walk	Quality of halt, transitions				
9.	KXM M	Free walk on long rein Working walk	Straightness, quality of walks, transitions		x2		
10.	C	Working trot sitting	Transition, quality of trot				
11.	E-X X-B	Half circle left 10m Half circle right 10m	Quality of trot, execution and size of figures				
12.	F	Working canter right lead	Calmness and smoothness of depart				
13.	A	Circle right 10m	Quality of canter, roundness and size of circle				
14.	K-H H	Lengthen stride in canter Working canter	Straightness, quality of canters, transitions		x2		
15.	C	Working trot	Balance during transition				
16.	MXK K	Lengthen stride in trot rising Working trot sitting	Straightness, quality of trots, transitions				
17.	A X	Down center line Halt, salute	Straightness on center line, quality of transitions, trot and halt				

Leave arena at free walk on long rein at A

COLLECTIVE MARKS:

Gaits (freedom and regularity)		2		
Impulsion (desire to move forward, elasticity of the steps, relaxation of the back)		2		
Submission (attention and confidence; harmony, lightness and ease of movements; acceptance of the bit)		2		
Rider's position and seat; correctness and effect of the aids		2		

FURTHER REMARKS:

SUBTOTAL   _____

ERRORS   (–_____)

TOTAL POINTS _____

AMERICAN HORSE SHOWS ASSOCIATION
220 East 42nd Street
New York, NY 10017

1991
SECOND LEVEL TEST 1

AMERICAN HORSE SHOWS ASSOCIATION, INC. ®

PURPOSE: To confirm that the horse, having demonstrated that it has achieved the thrust (pushing power) required in the First Level, now shows that through additional training it accepts more weight on the hind quarters (collection) and shows the thrust required at medium paces. A greater degree of straightness, bending and self-carriage is required than at First Level. *(Drawing of arena shows movements #3 and #4.)*

CONDITIONS
Arena: Standard or small
Average Time:
6:30 standard arena
5:30 small arena

MAXIMUM POSSIBLE POINTS:
280

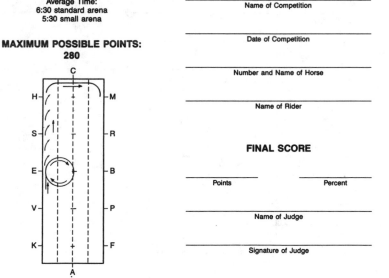

Name of Competition

Date of Competition

Number and Name of Horse

Name of Rider

FINAL SCORE

Points   Percent

Name of Judge

Signature of Judge

Fig. 50   Second Level Dressage Test 1. Reprinted with permission AHSA. © 1991 American Horse Shows Association, Inc. All rights reserved. Reproduction without permission prohibited by law.

SECOND LEVEL TEST 1

NEW REQUIREMENTS:
Shoulder-in in trot, rein back

INSTRUCTIONS:
All trot work is done sitting

NO.

		TEST	DIRECTIVE IDEAS	POINTS	COEFFICIENT	TOTAL	REMARKS
1.	A X	Enter collected trot Halt, salute, proceed collected trot	Straightness on center line, transitions, quality of halt and trot				
2.	C HXF F	Track left Medium trot Collected trot	Quality of turn at C, straightness, quality of trots, transitions				
3.	E	Circle right 10m	Quality of trot, roundness and size of circle				
4.	E-H	Shoulder-in right	Quality of trot, execution of movement		x2		
5.	MXK K	Medium trot Collected trot	Straightness, quality of trots, transitions				
6.	B	Circle left 10m	Quality of trot, roundness and size of circle				
7.	B-M	Shoulder-in left	Quality of trot, execution of movement		x2		
8.	C	Halt, rein back 3-4 steps, proceed medium walk	Quality of halt and rein back, transitions				
9.	HXF F	Free walk on long rein Medium walk	Straightness, quality of walks, transitions		x2		
10.	A	Collected canter right lead	Calmness and smoothness of depart				
11.	E	Circle right 10m	Quality of canter, roundness and size of circle				
12.	M-F F	Medium canter Collected canter	Straightness, quality of canters, transitions				
13.	KXM	Change rein, at X change of lead through trot	Straightness, calmness and smoothness of transitions				
14.	E	Circle left 10m	Quality of canter, roundness and size of circle				
15.	F-M M	Medium canter Collected canter	Straightness, quality of canters, transitions				
16.	HXF	Change rein, at X collected trot	Straightness, balance during transition				
17.	A X	Down center line Halt, salute	Straightness on center line, quality of transition, trot and halt				

Leave arena at free walk on long rein at A

COLLECTIVE MARKS:

Gaits (freedom and regularity)		2	
Impulsion (desire to move forward, elasticity of the steps, suppleness of the back and engagement of the hind quarters)		2	
Submission (attention and confidence; harmony, lightness and ease of movements; acceptance of the bridle and lightness of the forehand)		2	
Rider's position and seat; correctness and effect of the aids		2	

FURTHER REMARKS:

SUBTOTAL _____

ERRORS (–_____)

TOTAL POINTS _____

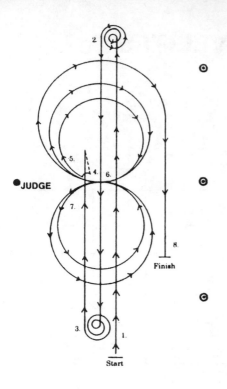

AQHA
REINING PATTERN
NUMBER 1

*MANDATORY MARKER ALONG FENCE OR WALL

The judge shall indicate with markers on arena fence or wall the length of the pattern. Markers within the area of the pattern will not be used.

Ride pattern as follows:

1. Run to the far end of the arena, stop and do 2½ spins to the left.
2. Run to the opposite end of the arena, stop and do 2½ spins to the right.
3. Run past center marker, do sliding stop, no hesitation, back over slide tracks to center, hesitate.
4. Make a ¼ pivot to the left to face left wall—hesitate.
5. Begin on right lead and make two circles to the right, the first small and slow, the second large and fast. Change leads at center of arena.
6. Make two circles to the left, first small and slow, the second large and fast. Change leads at the center of arena.
7. Begin a large fast circle to the right. Do not close this circle, but run straight down the side past the center, do a sliding stop. (Stop to be at least 20 feet from wall or fence.)
8. Hesitate to show completion of pattern.
9. Walk to judge and stop for inspection until dismissed.
10. The bridle may be dropped at the judge's discretion.

Fig. 51   Courtesy American Quarter Horse Association.

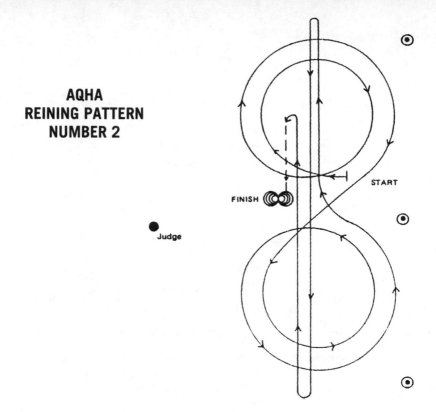

AQHA
REINING PATTERN
NUMBER 2

START

FINISH

Judge

*MANDATORY MARKER ALONG FENCE OR WALL

The judge shall indicate with markers on arena fence or wall the length of the pattern. Markers within the area of the pattern will not be used.

Ride pattern as follows:

1. Begin at center of the arena. Complete two circles to the right. The first circle small and slow, the second circle large and fast.
2. Change leads at the center of the arena.
3. Complete two circles to the left. The first circle small and slow, the second circle large and fast.
4. Change leads at the center of the arena.
5. Run to the far end of the arena, past end marker and do a left rollback, no hesitation.
6. Run to opposite end of arena, past end marker and do a right rollback, no hesitation.
7. Run past center of arena and do a sliding stop.
8. Back straight to center of the arena. Hesitate.
9. Complete four spins to the right.
10. Complete four spins to the left.
11. Hesitate to demonstrate the completion of the pattern.
12. The bridle may be dropped at the judges discretion.

Fig. 52   Courtesy American Quarter Horse Association.

Reining Pattern Check Sheet for Student, Teacher, or Judge

Run (at full speed)	too slow
	not a straight line
	not twenty feet from fence
Stop	not complete stop
	not smooth and square
	bouncing
	sideways
	not on haunches
	open-mouth
Back	not smooth and free
	not straight
Hesitate, settle	did not hesitate or settle horse
Circles, figure-eights	refusal to change leads
	no difference in size of circles
	no difference in speed of circles
	knocking over markers
	not smooth
Rollback over hocks	open mouth
	going straight up
	rushing rollback
	coming out of rollback on wrong lead
Spin	overspin
	underspin
	freezing up
Pivot	rushing horse
	awkward
	hind legs pivot
	crosses forelegs
Overall:	Neatness, calmness, speed, smoothness
	Completion of pattern in proper order.

FAULTS AGAINST RIDER: losing stirrup, spurring in front of cinch, any unnecessary aid (talking, petting, spurring, quirting, jerking reins).

FAULTS AGAINST HORSE: anticipating signals, stumbling, falling, wringing tail, breaking gaits, opening mouth excessively.

FAULTS IN TACK: wire curb, chin strap narrower than one-half inch, noseband or tie-down in bit reining.

DISQUALIFICATION: breaking pattern, use of illegal equipment, more than one finger between reins, changing hands on reins, two hands on reins.

Fig. 53a   Sample release form.

AGREEMENT

THIS AGREEMENT, made and entered into this _____ day of
_____, 19__, by and between (person's name) and (person's name),
doing business as (stable name) _____,
First Parties, and _____, parents of
_____, a minor, Second Parties, WITNESSETH:

THAT WHEREAS Second Parties' minor child is being enrolled in First Parties'
horsemanship school, and Second Parties recognize that there are certain dangers
normal and incident to the riding and handling of horses and the instruction in riding,
handling and care of horses, and desiring to relieve First Parties and hold them
harmless from any injuries or damages that said minor child might receive as a result
of enrollment and participation in the horsemanship school;

NOW, THEREFORE, be it understood and agreed between the parties
heretofore mentioned that for and in consideration of One Dollar and other valuable
considerations, each paid to the other, the receipt of which is hereby acknowledged,
Second Parties agree that if First Parties will accept their minor child as an enrollee
and participant in the _____ that they will assume the risk
and hold First Parties harmless from any injury, damage, or expense that might be
incurred as a result of the child's participation in the instruction and activity
embodied in the program of the horsemanship school; and do covenant and agree to
refrain from suit or any other action for injuries or damages growing out of injuries to
the child while an enrollee of the First Parties' school.

_____

_____

d/b/a _____ (stable name) _____

_____

WARNING, AGREEMENT TO OBEY INSTRUCTION, RELEASE ASSUMPTION OF RISK, AND AGREEMENT TO HOLD HARMLESS

Physical Education Sports: Gymnastics including trampolines, mountain climbing, scuba diving, horsemanship, rodeo, and skiing.

<u>Both the applicant student and a parent or guardian
must read carefully and sign if the student is a minor.</u>

STUDENT

I am aware that participating in any sport can be a dangerous activity involving MANY RISKS OF INJURY. I understand that the dangers and risks of participating in any of the above sports include, but are not limited to, death, serious neck and spinal injuries which may result in complete or partial paralysis, brain damage, serious injury or impairment to other aspects of my body, general health and well-being. I understand that the dangers and risks of participating in any of the above sports may result not only in serious injury, but in a serious impairment of my future abilities to earn a living, to engage in other business, social and recreational activities, and generally to enjoy life.

Because of the dangers of participating in the above sports, I recognize the importance of following instructions regarding techniques, training and other rules, etc., and agree to obey such instructions.

In consideration of the __(school)__ permitting me to participate in the above-mentioned sports. I hereby assume all the risks associated with participation and agree to hold the __(school)__ , its employees, agents, representatives, instructors, and volunteers harmless from any and all liability, actions, causes of action, debts, claims, or demands of any kind and nature whatsoever which may arise, including simple negligence, by or in connection with my participation in any of the aforementioned sports. The terms hereof shall serve as a release and assumption of risk for my heirs, estate, executor, administrator, assignees, and for all members of my family.

I also agree to have accident insurance coverage while participating in these sports. This may be purchased through the __(school)__ Student Health Insurance program or through a private carrier.

Date: _____   _____
                     Signature of Student

Date: _____   _____
                     Signature of Parent/Guardian

Fig. 53b   Sample release form.

> APPENDIX D <

Resources

Books, Videos, Associations

Books

General

Bits: Their History, Use and Misuse by Louis Taylor (Wilshire Book Co.)
The Body Language of Horses by Tom Ainslie and Bonnie Ledbetter (William Morrow & Co.)
The Color of Horses by Dr. Ben K. Green (Northland Press)
Great Horses of Our Time by M. A. Stoneridge (Doubleday)
Grooming to Win by Susan Harris (Charles Scribner's Sons)
A History of Horsemanship by Charles Chenevix Trench (Doubleday)
The Horse by D. J. Kays (Barnes)
A Horse of Your Own by M. A. Stoneridge (Doubleday)
Horse Safety Handbook by Peggy Bradbury (Cordovan Corporation)
Horsemastership by Margaret Cabell Self (Barnes)
The Mind of the Horse by R. H. Smythe (Stephen Greene Press)

Riding and Training

A.H.S.A. Rule Book (American Horse Shows Associations, Inc.)
Aids and Their Application by the British Horse Society & Pony Club (Barron)
The Art of Dressage by Alois Podhajsky (Doubleday)
The Art of Horsemanship by Xenophon (J. A. Allen)
The Art of Long Reining by Sylvia Stanier (J. A. Allen)

Basic Training for Horses by Eleanor F. Prince and Gaydell M. Collier (Doubleday)
Basic Training for Young Horses & Ponies by the British Horse Society & Pony Club (Barron)
Cavalletti by Reiner Klimke (J. A. Allen)
Centered Riding by Sally Swift (St. Martin's/Marek)
The Complete Training of Horse and Rider by Alois Podhajsky (Doubleday)
Creative Horsemanship by Charles de Kunffy (A. S. Barnes)
The De Némethy Method by Bertalan de Némethy (Doubleday)
Dressage by H. Wynmalen (Barnes)
Endurance and Competitive Trail Riding by Wentworth Tellington and Linda Tellington Jones (Doubleday)
The Event Horse by Sheila Wilcox (J. B. Lippincott)
Fundamentals of Riding by Gregor DeRomaszkhan (Doubleday, Stephen Greene)
Fundamentals of Riding: Theory and Practice by Charles Harris (J. A. Allen)
Give Your Horse a Chance by Lt. Col. A. L. d'Endrody (J. A. Allen)
Horsemanship by Waldemar Seunig (Doubleday)
Hunter Seat Equitation by George H. Morris (Doubleday)
The Instructors Handbook by the British Horse Society & Pony Club (Barron)
The Manual of Horsemanship by the British Horse Society & Pony Club (Barron)
My Horses, My Teachers by Alois Podhajsky (Doubleday)
Olympic Dressage Test in Pictures by Gregor DeRomaszkhan (Doubleday, Stephen Greene)
Practical Horseman's Book of Riding, Training, and Showing Hunters and Jumpers by M. A. Stoneridge, Editor (Doubleday)
Riding and Jumping by William Steinkraus (Doubleday)
Riding Logic by W. Museler (Methuen)
Riding Problems by Gregor DeRomaszkhan (Doubleday, Stephen Greene)
The Riding Teacher by Alois Podhajsky (Doubleday)
Saddle Seat Equitation by Helen K. Crabtree (Doubleday)
Sidesaddle by Doreen Houblon (J. A. Allen)
Teaching Riding by Diane S. Solomon (University of Oklahoma Press)
Training the Young Horse & Pony by the British Horse Society & Pony Club (Barron)
Training Your Own Horse by Mary Rose (David McKay)

Western

The Dave Jones Book of Western Horsemanship by Dave Jones (Cordovan)
Horses, Hitches and Rocky Trails by Joe Back (Sage Books/Swallow)
Lyons on Horses by John Lyons (Doubleday)
Official Handbook of the American Quarter Horse Association (AQHA)
Practical Western Training by Dave Jones (Van Nostrand)
The Western Horse: Its Types and Training by John A. Gorman (Interstate)
Western Horse Behavior and Training by Robert W. Miller (Doubleday)

Western Horseman Series (The Western Horseman)
Western Horsemanship by Richard Shrake *(The Western Horseman)*

Veterinary and Stable Management

Basic Horse Care by Eleanor F. Prince and Gaydell M. Collier (Doubleday)
Complete Horseshoeing Guide by Robert F. Wiseman (University of Oklahoma
    Press)
How to Be Your Own Veterinarian (Sometimes) by Ruth B. James, DVM (Alpine
    Press)
The Illustrated Veterinary Encyclopedia for Horsemen (Equine Research
    Publications)
Lameness in Horses by O. R. Adams, D.V.M., M.S. (Lea and Febiger)
Practical Horseman's Book of Horsekeeping by M. A. Stoneridge, Editor
    (Doubleday)
Veterinary Notes for Horse Owners by Captain N. Horace Hayes, F.R.C.N.S.
    (Arco)
Veterinary Treatments and Medications for Horsemen (Equine Research
    Publications)

Videos

Dressage; English; Jumping

The Official USDF Introduction to Dressage (United States Dressage Federation)	60 MINUTES
Spanish Riding School of Vienna	60 MINUTES
Centered Riding, Part 1, Part 2 (Sally Swift)	55/60 MINUTES
Selecting Your Dressage Horse (Hilda Gurney)	80 MINUTES
Saddle Seat Equitation (Helen Crabtree)	65 MINUTES
The Science of Riding with George Morris	90 MINUTES
Hunter Seat Equitation (Frank Madden and Bill Cooney)	60 MINUTES
Riding and Jumping: Basic Techniques (William Steinkraus)	60 MINUTES
Captain Mark Phillips Series	

Western; Trail

Horsemanship (Richard Shrake)	40 MINUTES
Showmanship and Halter (Richard Shrake)	75 MINUTES
Western Equitation: As the Judge Sees It (Don Burt)	40 MINUTES
Basic Horsemanship From the Ground Up (Don Burt)	60 MINUTES
Long Distance Riding (Farnam Series)	90 MINUTES

General Interest

Resistance Free Training 1 & 2 (and other videos by Richard Shrake)
Imprint Training the Foal (Robert Miller DVM)   60 MINUTES
Ballad of the Irish Horse (National Geographic Video)   60 MINUTES
Video Series (Linda Tellington-Jones, T.E.A.M. Method)

Associations

AMERICAN BUCKSKIN REGISTRY ASSN.
Box 3850
Redding, Ca 96049-3850

AMERICAN CONNEMARA PONY SOCIETY
Box 513
HoshieKon Farm
Goshen, CT 06756

AMERICAN HANOVERIAN SOCIETY
14615 N.E. 190th St., #108
Woodinville, WA 98072

AMERICAN HORSE SHOWS ASSN., INC.
220 E. 42nd St.
New York, NY 10017

AMERICAN INDIAN HORSE REGISTRY
Route 3, Box 64
Lockhart, TX 78644

AMERICAN MINIATURE HORSE ASSN.
2908 S.E. Loop 820
Fort Worth, TX 76140

AMERICAN MORGAN HORSE ASSN.
Box 960
Shelburne, VT 05482-0960

AMERICAN MULE ASSN.
Box 3545
Visalia, Ca 93278

AMERICAN PAINT HORSE ASSN.
Box 961023
Fort Worth, TX 76161-0023

AMERICAN QUARTER HORSE ASSN.
Box 200
Amarillo, TX 79168

AMERICAN SADDLEBRED HORSE
ASSN., INC.
Kentucky Horse Park
4093 Iron Works Pike
Lexington, KY 40511

AMERICAN SHETLAND PONY CLUB
Box 3415
Peoria, IL 61614-3415

AMERICAN TRAKEHNER ASSN., INC.
1520 W. Church St.
Newark, OH 43055

AMERICAN WARMBLOOD REGISTRY
Box 395
Hastings, NY 10706

APPALOOSA HORSE CLUB
Box 8403
Moscow, ID 83843-0903

ARABIAN HORSE REGISTRY OF
     AMERICA, INC.
     12000 Zuni St.
     Westminster, CO 80233-0696

FRIESIAN HORSE ASSN. OF AMERICA
     4127 Kentridge Drive S.E.
     Grand Rapids, MI 49508-3705

HAFLINGER REGISTRY OF NORTH
     AMERICA
     14640 State Route 83
     Coshocton, OH 43812-2119

INTERNATIONAL ANDALUSIAN
     HORSE ASSN.
     1201 S. Main, D-7
     Boerne, TX 78006

INTERNATIONAL ARABIAN HORSE ASSN.
     Half-Arab & Anglo-Arab Registry
     Box 33696
     Denver, CO 80233-0696

THE JOCKEY CLUB (Thoroughbreds)
     821 Corporate Drive
     Lexington, KY 40503

MISSOURI FOX TROTTING HORSE
     BREED ASSN.
     Box 1027
     Ava, MO 65608-1027

NATIONAL CUTTING HORSE ASSN.
     4704 Hwy. 377 S.
     Ft. Worth, TX 76116

NATIONAL REINING HORSE ASSN.
     28881 S.R.83
     Coshocton, OH 43812

NORTH AMERICAN TRAIL RIDE
     CONFERENCE, INC.
     Box 20315
     El Cajon, CA 92021

PALOMINO HORSE ASSN.
     Box 324
     Jefferson City, MO 65102-0324

PASO FINO HORSE ASSN., INC.
     Box 600
     Bowling Green, FL 33834-0600

PERUVIAN PASO HORSE REGISTRY OF
     NORTH AMERICA
     1038 4th St. Suite 4
     Santa Rosa, CA 95404-4319

PONY OF THE AMERICAS CLUB, INC.
     5240 Elmwood Ave.
     Indianapolis, IN 46203-5990

SPANISH MUSTANG REGISTRY, INC.
     8328 Stevenson Ave.
     Sacramento, CA 95828

TENNESSEE WALKING HORSE BREEDERS'
     & EXHIBITORS' ASSN.
     Box 286
     Lewisburg, TN 37091-0286

TRAIL RIDERS OF THE WILDERNESS
     American Forestry Association
     1516 P St. NW
     Washington, DC 20005

UNITED STATES DRESSAGE FEDERATION,
     INC.
     P.O. Box 80668
     Lincoln, NE 68501

UNITED STATES LIPIZZAN REGISTRY
     Route 4, Box 89Y
     Amelia, VA 23002

UNITED STATES TROTTING ASSN.
     (Standardbreds)
     750 Michigan Ave.
     Columbus, OH 43215-1191

Glossary

ACTION. The way a horse moves his feet and legs; the "play" of the bit that causes the horse to flex his jaw.

AGED. A mature animal, usually over eight years.

AGORAPHOBIA. Fear of the outside; usually the horse is afraid to leave the barn after being stalled for long periods.

AIDS. Signals by which the rider communicates with and controls his horse.

NATURAL AIDS: weight, voice, legs, and hands.

ARTIFICIAL AIDS support the natural aids. The whip or crop may be thought of as an extension or reinforcement of the arm; spurs as a reinforcement of the leg. Others are checkreins, martingales, dropped nosebands, and similar appliances.

AIRS ABOVE THE GROUND. Levade, croupade, ballotade, capriole, courbette; as perfected by the classical school of horsemanship.

ALTER. To castrate or geld a stallion.

ANTHRAX. An infectious, often fatal, disease caused by a bacillus. Symptoms include fever, abnormal swelling of the throat and mammary gland or sheath, pain, and muscular weakness. Treatment is rarely effective, but the disease can be prevented by immunization.

APPALOOSA. An American breed or type of horse developed by the Nez Percé Indians of Idaho and Washington. Appaloosas are noted for their distinctive spotted color patterns.

APPOINTMENTS. A general term including uniform or livery, equipment, and tack.

ARABIAN. The Arabian breed (originating in the Arabian desert) is known to be the oldest pure breed of horses. Most of today's light horse breeds and the French Percheron draft breed developed from the Arabian. Arabians are endowed with exceptional beauty, especially in their refined heads. They are close-coupled, with flat croup and high tail carriage. They have great weight-carrying ability despite their small size, and they are known for their endurance as well as for being easy keepers. The Arabian is both an English and Western riding horse, excelling in endurance competition.

AZOTURIA. Monday-morning sickness—caused by enforced idleness and overfeeding, usually recurring under similar conditions.

BALANCE. Impulsion combined with suppleness and flexibility; correct weight distribution for the movement the horse is performing. It is necessary for obedience. When referring to conformation, "a well-balanced horse" would be one in good proportion with substance and depth.

BALD FACED. A horse with a wide blaze blanketing most of the face.

BALK. To be stubborn, refusing to respond to the aids.

BALLING. Method of administering a physic by use of a "balling gun." Also, horses' hoofs "ball up," meaning that wet snowballs form in the shoes and make movement difficult. Greasing the soles helps to prevent balling up.

BALLOTADE. An air above the ground performed by a horse trained in the classical manner. The movement involves a half rear in which the horse lands on four feet in a collected stance.

BARN SOUR. Said of a horse that refuses to leave the stable area or a group of horses.

BARREN MARE. A mare incapable of breeding.

BARS. The lower portion of the jaw, devoid of teeth, where the bit rests.

BEHIND THE BIT. Said of a horse that evades the bit by bending the head toward the chest: The horse becomes overflexed and insensitive to the aids.

BITTING. Teaching the horse to be supple and willing in the bit.

BLAZE. A wide white stripe extending the entire length of the face.

BLEMISH. A scar left by disease or injury. It may count against a horse in the show ring, but will not limit his usefulness.

BLISTERING or BLISTER. Treatment used in chronic lameness; a counterirritant that produces severe inflammation for the purpose of drawing blood to the affected area and thereby helping healing.

BOLT. A desire to run uncontrollably; a serious vice. Also, to bolt food due to greed.

BOSAL, BOZAL. The noseband of the hackamore (old Spanish type).

BREAK. A Western term meaning to train or school, especially early training.

BRIDOON. Small snaffle bit used in conjunction with the curb on the double bridle.

BROKEN KNEES. Knees showing scars or broken skin due to an open injury caused by a fall.

BRUSHING (interfering). To strike the lower leg (in the fetlock area) with the inner side of the opposite hoof or shoe.

BUCKLING OVER. Knee appears bent over; seen often in old horses due to hard work and strain in younger years.

CADENCE. The rhythmical beat of a horse's gait (the length of stride may be varied); a dressage term.

TO CADENCE. A horse is cadenced when his gait is rhythmical, steady, elevated, and regular.

CAMP. Extending the forelegs out in front and the hind legs out behind—an indication of kidney disorder if done naturally. In some breeds, it is the accepted show stance.

CANTER. A natural three-beat gait (as opposed to a gallop, which is a four-beat gait). A horse at the canter takes either the right or left lead, usually depending on the direction of movement. The canter may be working, medium, collected, or extended in dressage terms.

CAPRIOLE. An air above the ground in which the horse leaps high into the air and kicks out with his hind legs.

CARRIAGE. The bearing of a horse, how he holds his head, neck, tail, and so on.

CAST. A horse is said to be cast when he has fallen or lain down and is unable to regain his feet; sometimes indicative of digestive disorder.

CAVESSON. A noseband that resembles a leather halter. It can be used as a dropped noseband to keep the horse's tongue from going over the bit and to keep the horse from opening his mouth and evading the bit. The dropped noseband is allowed in dressage test levels 1 and 2. A LONGEING CAVESSON has a metal ring at the top of the noseband and allows the handler full control of the horse's head while longeing.

CHANGE OF HAND or CHANGE OF REIN. Change of direction by crossing the long diagonal of the riding arena.

CHANGE OF LEAD or CHANGE OF LEG. SIMPLE change: The horse is brought down to a walk or trot and, after one or two well-defined walk steps, restarted into a canter on the opposite lead. FLYING change: The horse changes lead at the moment of suspension.

CHAPS. Outer garment, usually of leather, worn to protect the rider's legs from brush, cactus, and cold. There are two kinds: batwings (flared) and shotguns (fit close to the leg).

CHECKREIN. A restraining rein, either overhead or to the side, which sets (or limits the movement of) a horse's head to achieve a correct position. This may be used with harness horses or in a bitting rig as a training aid. Overuse may result in undesirable rigidity.

CINCH. Girth.

CLASSICAL ART OF RIDING. The method of riding promoted by schools such as the Spanish Riding School, in which the natural movements of the horse are controlled and perfected.

COLD-JAWED. Refers to a horse that has a hard (insensitive) mouth due to the rider's misuse of the bit.

COLLECTION. A dressage term meaning the shortening of the horse's body length by pushing him into the bit, thus flexing at the poll, raising the action, lowering the croup, and bringing the hindquarters under him. Collection may be light or heavy, depending on the extent of the horse's schooling. A "well-collected" horse responds instantly to the aids and performs any movement readily.

COLT. A male horse until the age of four.

COMBINATION HORSE. A horse that can be ridden or driven in harness.

CONFORMATION. The build of a horse.

CONTACT. The "feel" between the rider's hands and the bit (through the reins). Light contact is desirable because its sensitivity makes for a responsive horse.

CONTRACTED HEELS. The foot narrows at the heel, usually due to incorrect trimming or shoeing; can cause lameness.

COOLER. Light woolen blanket thrown over the horse after strenuous exercise.

CORN. A bruise to the sensitive sole of the foot in the heel region, either due to improper shoeing or to leaving the shoes on for too long a period.

COUNTER-CANTER (FALSE CANTER). A suppling exercise used in third-level dressage movements where the horse leads with the outside leg while remaining bent to the leading leg. It should not be confused with the disunited canter.

COURBETTE. Dressage term for an air above the ground wherein the horse executes little leaps from the levade position without allowing the forefeet to touch the ground.

COVER. A breeding term referring to the stallion "covering" (breeding) the mare.

COW-HOCKED. The hocks turn inward toward each other, resembling the conformation of a cow—not desirable.

COW KICK. A quick forward kick with a hind leg.

CROUPADE. A dressage term for an air above the ground wherein the horse springs from the levade position and keeps his legs under him.

DAM. The mother of a horse.

DIAGONAL. When the horse is trotting in a circle, the rider is said to be on the correct diagonal when he rises to the outside (forward) foreleg; i.e., going to the left, the rider would post to the right diagonal. To change diagonals, the rider sits one bounce.

DIAGONAL AIDS. Refers to the rider's aids (opposite hand and leg, i.e., right hand and left leg).

DISHING. Throwing the feet sideways in an outward arc, also called paddling.

DISTEMPER. See Strangles.

DISUNITED CANTER (CROSS CANTER). In a disunited canter, a horse will be on one lead in front and on the other lead with his hind legs. This is undesirable and should not be confused with false canter (see Counter-canter).

DOG. Horse that is not worth much, usually one that is stubborn and of poor conformation.

DRESSAGE. A French term meaning "training" or "schooling." Through adherence to three basic concepts—forward, straight, and calm—the horse is taught to be supple, balanced, cadenced, and obedient. Dressage principles build logically on step-by-step progress from simple to increasingly complex movements, gradually requiring more and more from the horse, both mentally and physically.

DRESSED (English saddle). Stirrups are run up on the leathers.

DROPPED NOSEBAND. See Cavesson.

ENCEPHALITIS (sleeping sickness). There are several types of sleeping sickness. Those affecting the United States are Eastern encephalitis, Western encephalitis, and Venezuelan equine encephalitis (VEE). It is an infectious virus disease affecting the central nervous system, often resulting in death. Those surviving often have permanent brain damage. Some symptoms are weakness, drowsiness, staggering. The disease is transmitted by bloodsucking bugs (primarily mosquitoes) with birds seemingly the primary host. There are now excellent equine vaccines available against all three U.S. varieties.

EQUINE. Term relating to horses.

EQUITATION. Horsemanship; the art of riding in harmony with the horse.

ERGOT. Small callus at the back of the fetlock joint.

EWE-NECKED. The crest of the neck is concave instead of convex—not desirable.

EXTENSION. The lengthening of the horse's body by causing the horse to reach forward with his head and neck while forelegs and hind legs also extend forward—as opposed to collection.

FALSE CANTER. See Counter-canter.

FARCY (glanders). A dangerous, highly contagious disease caused by bacteria. Prevention and treatment are ineffective.

FARRIER. Horseshoer.

FAVOR. To show pain by limping or shortening stride in the affected leg.

FEATHER. Long hair running up legs from the fetlock joint, usually found in horses with draft breeding.

FEDERATION EQUESTRE INTERNATIONALE (F.E.I.). The International Riding Association, the international governing body of horse shows.

FIADOR. A hackamore knot made of cord which fastens the bottom of the bosal to the headstall, used in the old Spanish type of hackamore.

FILLY. A female of four and under.

FISTULA OF THE WITHERS. An inflammatory disorder of the bursal sac, with pain, fluctuating swelling, and discharge.

FLAT BONE. Good, hard, clean appearance; desirable.

FLEXION. The relaxation of the lower jaw, with head correctly bent at the poll, in response to the bit. As a verb, to flex, to bend.

FLOATING A HORSE'S TEETH. Filing those teeth that have sharp points: produces a better grinding surface so that a horse can better utilize his feed; often necessary on older horses.

FOAL. A horse of either sex, under one year old; sex is designated by filly foal or colt.

FOAL HEAT. The first heat of the mare after foaling, usually about nine days (thus the expression "nine-day heat").

FORGING. Horse hits foreshoe with rear when traveling at a trot or pace; this makes a clicking sound, is undesirable, and can usually be helped by correct shoeing.

FRESH. Spirited, excitable due to lack of exercise.

FULL PASS. Same as half-pass except horse moves sideways only, not forward.

GAITED HORSE. A horse schooled to artificial as well as natural gaits.

GALLS. Sores caused by the rubbing of saddle or harness; untreated galls may result in white hair spots.

GELDING. A castrated male horse.

GESTATION. Period during which a mare is carrying her foal (approximately eleven months).

GET. All the progeny of a sire.

GIRTH. A band or strap that goes underneath the horse to hold the saddle in place.

GLANDERS. See Farcy.

GRADE HORSE. A grade horse is not a purebred. He has a mixed origin and neither possesses nor passes on distinctive characteristics. He cannot be registered (unless under a color breed such as a Palomino or Buckskin). Although he is usually not so refined or high spirited as a purebred, he may have characteristics of the purebred registered animal. Some grade horses have draft blood. His use depends on his breed type.

GREEN. A horse that has started his training, usually one that is young and inexperienced.

HACKAMORE. A type of headgear used instead of a bridle; there is no bit: Control is achieved through pressure on the nose and chin. Sometimes called a bitless bridle.

HALF-PASS. A dressage term: a two-track exercise in which the horse moves forward and sideways at the same time. Can be performed at the walk, trot, and canter, the head being flexed toward the direction of movement.

HALTER SHANK. Lead rope that attaches by means of a snap to the halter ring.

HAND. Four inches: a unit of measurement for determining the height of a horse (from the withers to the ground). A horse that is sixty inches tall is said to be 15 hands, a common saddle horse height.

HAUNCHES, TO ENGAGE THE. Bringing the haunches well under the horse (through collection), thus causing him to use them actively.

HAUNCHES-IN. Suppling exercise wherein the horse carries his haunches toward the center of the circle he is describing (travers).

HAUNCHES-OUT. Suppling exercise wherein the horse carries his haunches toward the outside of the circle he is describing (renvers).

HEAVES. Broken wind; noticeable double exhalation in the flank movement of the horse.

HEAVY HANDS. Said of a rider who has no sensibility in his hands; one who rides by force.

HIGH. Spirited.

HIPPOPHILE (HIPPOPHIL). A horse lover.

HOGGED MANE. Mane clipped entirely off; roached mane.

HONDA. A loop, tied in the rope or made from metal, in the end of a lariat.

HORSE. A mature male, either a stallion or gelding. May also refer to the whole species (*Equus caballus*).

IMPULSION. The urge, thrust, or inner drive to move forward; a controlled forward impulse.

INSIDE LEG. Refers to the leg toward the center of the circle being described. (See also p. 244 under "Circular Figures and Work on One Track.")

JOG (JOG TROT). Western term for a slow trot.

LATERAL AIDS. Refers to the rider's aids (hand and leg used on the same side, i.e., left rein, left leg).

LATIGO. The long leather on the near side or short leather on the off side of the Western saddle, used to fasten the cinch.

LEAD, or LEADING LEG. At the canter, the horse leads either with the left foreleg or the right foreleg. When cantering to the left on a circle, the horse should be on the left lead, his left foreleg advancing beyond the right.

LEG, ACTIVE. Leg (of the rider) giving the stronger aids to the horse.

LEG, ASSISTING or STABILIZING. The leg that reinforces (or assists) the active leg; the assisting leg steadies the horse and keeps him from reacting too strongly to the active leg.

LEUCODERMA. White patches that appear on hairless parts of the horse.

LEVADE. A dressage movement wherein the horse balances on his haunches (tucking his forelegs inward) while maintaining an immobile position.

LIBERTY HORSES. Horses that perform without personal contact from a rider or handler, as in circus acts.

LOCKJAW. See Tetanus.

LONG. Relates to the latter part of the year from birth; a long yearling is close to his second year; term used only with young horses.

LONGE (LUNGE). Refers to a long line attached to the longeing cavesson or halter. The trainer stands in the center and directs the horse to walk, trot, canter, and reverse around him, using a whip and voice as directional aids. This method of training can be used as a preliminary to saddle training and is also useful as exercise.

LOPE. Canter.

LUGGER. A horse that leans on the bit and tries to go faster than the rider wishes.

MANEGE. Riding hall used to school a horse and rider.

MARE. A mature female horse, usually at least four years old. MAIDEN MARE, a mare that has never been bred.

MARTINGALE, RUNNING. A training aid used in conjunction with a snaffle bit, generally to prevent the horse from carrying his head too high. The reins are passed through the rings at each branch of the martingale. Whenever the rider softens his hands, the martingale releases pressure, thus can be used or not as desired.

MARTINGALE, STANDING. A leather strap attached to the girth and the rear of the noseband. This prevents the horse from raising his head out of a natural position.

MCCLELLAN SADDLE. Saddle tree used by the United States Cavalry.

MECATE. A Western term indicating reins made of horse hair.

MEGRIMS or STAGGERS. Similar to fainting in humans; loss of balance; can be due to defective circulation, worms, digestion, or brain problems.

MORGAN. The Morgan Horse descended from one prepotent sire, Justin Morgan, who was raised in Vermont. Justin Morgan is thought to have Thoroughbred and Arabian blood. The modern Morgan is sturdy, with a short, broad back and deep chest. Morgans are spirited yet easily managed and good natured. They are unexcelled roadsters, capable of light farm work, and are popular all over the United States, ridden both English and Western.

MUD FEVER. Scratches occurring on the pastern (similar to chapped hands in humans) due to mud and wet. It usually occurs in the spring when horses stand on wet land and graze. Horses with white hair on the legs (thus pink skin) are especially susceptible to mud fever.

MULE. The progeny of a jack and a mare.

MUSTANG. The wild horse found on the western plains of North America.

NEAR (SIDE). The horse's left side.

OBEDIENCE. The desire of the horse to please; to perform and respond willingly.

OFF (SIDE). The horse's right side.

OPHTHALMIA. Serious disease of the eye; inflammation of the eyeball due to infection or to a blow.

OVERREACH. Indicates injury to the lower forelegs caused by the horse striking himself with his hind legs. The condition can be relieved by leveling the toes of the hind feet or by use of overreach boots.

PADDLING. See Dishing.

PALOMINO. A color breed or type of horse in which the coat color is yellow to golden and the mane and tail are white to cream.

PASSAGE. A dressage movement in which the horse trots in a very cadenced, floating manner with a marked period of suspension.

PAUNCHY. An undesirable ballooning shape of the paunch (stomach) area, usually due to unthrifty condition (infestation of worms, disease, lack of essential mineral, etc.).

PIAFFE (PIAFFER). A high, collected trot in place, with a prolonged period of suspension.

PIEBALD. A black and white pinto with large distinct patches.

PIROUETTE. A two-track movement performed at the canter. The forehand moves around the haunches in a small circle with a radius equal to the length of the horse.

PLEASURE HORSE. A well-mannered, obedient horse, having easy gaits and no serious vices.

PLEURISY. Inflammation of the membranous covering of the lungs, usually caused by bacterial infection. The symptoms are sweating, fever, and signs of pain.

POINTING. Horse stands on three feet and touches the tip of one forefoot without resting weight on it, a symptom of navicular disease, lameness, or damage to foot or leg.

PONY. A small horse 14.2 hands or under.

POPPING. A horse's undesirable, abrupt takeoff and landing while jumping.

POST ENTRY. A horse entered after the official entries have closed; double or triple fee is usually charged.

POSTING. Rising to the trot; the rider should change diagonals often; in ring, post to the outside diagonal.

PREPOTENCY. Ability to pass outstanding characteristics to get or produce; e.g., Justin Morgan was a prepotent sire.

PRODUCE. Progeny of a dam.

PROUD FLESH. Unhealthy tissue that sometimes forms around a wound.

PULSE. Heartbeat, normally thirty-six to forty-two beats per minute. The pulse is taken where the submaxillary artery passes under the jaw, or at a radial artery inside foreleg.

PUREBRED. See Registry.

QUALITY. A nobility of character and spirit; an attitude of majesty and fineness in appearance.

QUARTER HORSE. In the middle 1600s, quarter-mile races were popular in the southeastern states. Today's Quarter Horse is a descendant of these early racers (from which he gained his name) as well as of Thoroughbred and other stock. The imported Janus (1700s) was an important foundation sire of the breed, although the association was not actually founded until 1940. The typical Quarter Horse is about 15 hands, with small head, short back, muscular hindquarters, and an easily managed, equitable disposition. He is versatile, and is especially valued for ranch work, rodeo work, and racing for short distances.

QUITTOR. A fistulous sore on the coronet caused by an inury; lameness and discharge are symptoms.

RACK. One of the gaits of the five-gaited saddler; a fast, four-beat gait in which each foot comes down separately and in turn.

RATE. To establish a horse's gait and speed in order to arrive at a destination at a preselected time.

REGISTRY. Pedigree record kept by association of recognized breeds of horses.

PUREBRED. Horse whose parents are both recorded in the same registry.

HALF-BRED. Horse with one parent registered (usually the sire); the other parent may be grade or unregistered.

COLOR REGISTRY. Registry that has certain color requirements for registration, such as a palomino or pinto. A horse may be double registered, e.g., a palomino Quarter Horse.

REIN-BACK. The horse moves backward with the diagonal legs raised and put down simultaneously.

RENVERS. See Haunches-out.

RISLING (RIDGELING). A horse whose reproductive organs are only partially developed, making it difficult to geld him.

ROMAL. Braided leather attached to the end of the reins.

RUNNING WALK. One of the slow gaits of the five-gaited saddler.

SACKING OUT. Rubbing the horse with burlap sacks (or saddle blanket), letting it flap against him, to gentle the horse and teach him that such treatment is harmless and that he should stand quietly.

SAND CRACK. Perpendicular crack in the wall of the hoof due to injury to coronary band. Remove the pressure with quarter clips on the shoes or by isolating the crack to prevent it from spreading.

SCHOOL. A place used for training and schooling horses and riders; also for exercising horses; may be open, fenced, or covered.

SCHOOLING. To train the horse to the aids; beginning, intermediate, and advanced training; also, training for specialized tasks such as cutting, roping, jumping, etc.

SCOURING. A type of diarrhea, usually occurring in newborn foals.

SEASON. A mare is said to be in season when she is ready to be bred by a stallion. A mare is normally in season every twenty-one days and remains in from three to seven days.

SEAT. Refers to the rider's position in the saddle. Also, the low part of the saddle between the pommel and the cantle.

SHOULDER-IN. A schooling exercise to help a horse become supple, balanced, and obedient.

SICKLE-HOCKED. A conformation fault in which the hocks are too bent, thus weak; this fault is usually found in conjunction with cow hocks.

SIRE. Father of a horse.

SKEWBALD. A horse with pinto markings of white and any color other than black (usually brown).

SLEEPING SICKNESS. See Encephalitis.

SLOW TROT. A slower than normal trot. Riders usually sit (rather than post) the slow trot.

SNIP. A single, small white marking in the area of the nose.

SOUND. Said of a horse that is in good condition with no conformation problems or unsoundnesses to interfere with his performance.

SPEED OF HORSES. Approximate speed of normal gaits: walk, four m.p.h.; trot, nine m.p.h.; gallop, twelve m.p.h.

SPOOKY. Nervous and prone to shy; some horses shy at an unfamiliar movement or object.

STALLION. A mature male horse usually at least five years old.

STAR. A white mark of varied size on the forehead.

STARGAZER. A horse that holds his head too high and thrusts his nose out and upward.

STRANGLES (DISTEMPER). A contagious disease, especially common to young animals. Symptoms are depression, loss of appetite, high fever, and discharge from the nose. By the third or fourth day, the glands under the neck swell, break open, and discharge pus.

STRIKING. A form of brushing in which the horse strikes one leg with the toe or side of another leg. Also, a dangerous vice in which the horse strikes out with his forelegs.

STRIPE. A narrow white mark running from a horse's eyes to his nose.

STUD. Head stallion, or stallion and mares together, on a breeding farm; the farm itself.

STUDBOOKS. The records in which the horses of the various breeds are registered.

STUD FEES. Fees that the owner of the stallion collects from the owner of the mare when she is serviced.

STUD HORSE. A stallion kept for breeding.

STYLE. Usually relates to way of going; distinct personal flair of an individual horse; involves presence and personal magnetism.

STYLISH. Said of a horse that is endowed with individual style.

SUBSTANCE. Said of a horse whose conformation gives the impression of stamina and hardiness.

SURCINGLE. A strap (usually of webbing) that goes around the horse's girth area and holds a blanket or saddle pad in place.

TACK. A shortened form of "tackle," meaning saddlery, harness, etc. To tack up a horse is to put on the saddle and bridle.

TACK ROOM. Where saddles, bridles, and harness are kept.

TAPADERAS. Leather coverings on some Western stirrups that protect the rider's feet from thick brush, thorns, and cold weather. Tapederas are also useful on children's saddles to keep the rider's foot from becoming caught in the stirrup.

TETANUS (LOCKJAW). Disease due to a germ in the soil that gains access through a wound. After an incubation period of about ten days, the horse becomes stiff, chews weakly, and shoots the third eyelid across the forward surface of the eyeball. Prevention consists of injection of lockjaw serum whenever there is a wound, or protection can be secured through inoculation of tentanus toxoid.

THOROUGHBRED. The Thoroughbred is the product of at least two hundred years of breeding. The Darley Arabian, the Byerly Turk, and the Godolphin Arabian are the progenitors of the breed. Today's Thoroughbreds are usually between 16 and 17 hands, and are fine in conformation with long, straight, well-muscled legs. Their fame lies in racing, but they are also used as saddle horses, polo mounts, and hunters. The term "Thoroughbred" refers strictly to the breed and should not be used as a synonym for purebred.

THRUSH. A degenerative condition of the frog, characterized by offensive odor and black discharge, caused by keeping a horse in a filthy, wet stall or area or by lack of frog pressure due to poor shoeing or trimming.

TRAVERS. See Haunches-in.

TREE (SADDLETREE). The basic framework of a saddle (made of wood, metal, or fiberglass), which determines its shape and size.

TROT. A two-beat gait in which the horse moves from one diagonal pair of legs to the other.

TWO-TRACK. The horse moves forward and to the side at the same time. The outside legs pass and cross in front of the inside legs. Some lateral movements involving the two-track are: shoulder-in, half-pass, renvers, travers, counterchange of rein.

UNSOUNDNESS. Structural weakness that affects the normal use of a horse.

VEE (VENEZUELAN EQUINE ENCEPHALITIS). See Encephalitis.

WALK. A four-beat gait wherein each foot hits the ground separately. The walk should be free-moving, even, and flat-footed.

WALK-TROT HORSE. Show term meaning a saddle horse that only walks, trots, and canters, as distinguished from the five-gaited horse.

WALLEYE. A bluish eye surrounded by white, indicating a lack of pigment; it is not considered to be a blemish.

WEANING. Removing the foal from the dam. The foal generally stays with the dam until six months of age. Six weeks of separation from the dam will usually successfully wean the foal.

WEANLING. A young horse during the period from weaning until he becomes a yearling.

WOLF TEETH appear in front of molars on a horse. When they interfere with the action of the bit, they are said to impair the optic nerve, and should be removed.

YEARLING. A young horse from a year old to his second birthday.

>INDEX<